History

for the IB Diploma

Peacemaking, Peacekeeping: International Relations 1918–36

Nick Fellows
Series editor: Allan Todd

Cambridge University Press's mission is to advance learning, knowledge and research worldwide.

Our IB Diploma resources aim to:
- encourage learners to explore concepts, ideas and topics that have local and global significance
- help students develop a positive attitude to learning in preparation for higher education
- assist students in approaching complex questions, applying critical-thinking skills and forming reasoned answers.

CAMBRIDGE
UNIVERSITY PRESS

University Printing House, Cambridge CB2 8BS, United Kingdom

Cambridge University Press is part of the University of Cambridge.

It furthers the University's mission by disseminating knowledge in the pursuit of education, learning and research at the highest international levels of excellence.

www.cambridge.org
Information on this title: www.cambridge.org/9781107613911

© Cambridge University Press 2012

First published 2012
4th printing 2014

Printed in the United Kingdom by Cambrian Printers Ltd

A catalogue record for this publication is available from the British Library

ISBN 978-1-107-61391-1 Paperback

Contents

1 Introduction

This book is designed to prepare students taking the Paper 1 topic *International Relations 1919–39* (Prescribed Subject 1) in the IB History examination. It discusses the various aspects of the attempts to create a lasting peace after the First World War. It then examines the increasing problems associated with this process, culminating in the failure of the League of Nations in dealing with the major challenges it faced from Japan in 1931 and Italy in 1935.

A British soldier shares his water bottle with German prisoners of war, 1918

Themes

To help you prepare for your IB History exams, this book will cover the main themes and aspects relating to *International Relations 1919–39*, as set out in the IB *History Guide*. It will examine the major themes in the order below:

- the aims of the peacemakers
- the terms of the peace treaties
- the impact of the peace treaties on Europe
- the enforcement of the terms of the peace treaties
- the role and work of the League of Nations
- international order and conflicts in the 1920s
- the impact of the Great Depression and the challenges of Japan and Italy.

Each chapter will help you focus on the main issues that arose after the First World War, the roles of individuals and states, and the main developments affecting international relations during this period.

Theory of knowledge

In addition to the broad key themes, the chapters contain Theory of knowledge (ToK) links to get you thinking about aspects of Theory of knowledge that relate to history, which is a Group 3 subject in the IB Diploma. The *International Relations* topic has several clear links to ideas about knowledge and history. The struggle to re-establish international order after the First World War, and its ultimate failure, was highly political. Diplomatic manoeuvrings were important both for the key powers and for the historians writing about them at the time and since. Thus, questions relating to the selection of sources, and to differing interpretations of these sources by historians, are extremely relevant to the IB Theory of knowledge course.

For example, when trying to explain aspects of the motives of individuals (such as Woodrow Wilson or Benito Mussolini) or states (such as Britain or Germany), historians must decide which evidence to select and use to make their case, and which evidence to leave out. But to what extent do the historians' personal political views influence them when choosing what they consider to be the most important or relevant sources, and when they make judgements about the value and limitations of specific sources or sets of sources? Is there such a thing as objective 'historical truth'? Or is there just a range of subjective historical opinions and interpretations about the past, which vary according to the political interests of individual historians?

You are therefore encouraged to read a range of books offering different interpretations of the course of international relations and the origins of the Second World War. This will help you gain a clear understanding of the historiography of the period.

IB History and Paper 1 questions
Paper 1 and sources

Unlike Papers 2 and 3, which require you to write essays using just your own knowledge, Paper 1 questions are source-based. Whether you are taking Standard or Higher Level, the sources, the questions and the markschemes applied by your examiners are the same.

To answer these questions successfully, you need to be able to combine your own knowledge with the ability to assess and *use* a range of sources in a variety of ways. Each Paper 1 examination question is based on five sources – usually four written and one visual. The visual source might be a photograph, a cartoon, a poster, a painting or a table of statistics.

Captions and attributions

Before looking at the types of sources you will need to assess, it is important to establish one principle from the beginning. This is the issue of *captions and attributions* – the pieces of information about each source that are provided by the Chief Examiner.

Captions and attributions are there for a very good reason, as they give you vital information about the source. For example, they tell you who wrote it and when, or what it was intended to do. Chief Examiners spend a lot of time deciding what information to give you about each source, because they know it will help you give a full answer, so they expect you to make good use of it! Yet, every year, candidates throw away easy marks because they do not read – or do not use – this valuable information.

Essentially, you are being asked to approach the various sources in the same way as a historian. This means not just looking carefully at what a source says or shows, but also asking yourself questions about how reliable, useful and/or typical it may be. Many of the answers to these questions will come from the information provided in the captions and attributions.

Types of source

Most of the sources you will have to assess are written ones, and these are sometimes referred to as 'textual' sources. They might be extracts from books, official documents, speeches, newspapers, diaries or letters. Whatever type of source you are reading, the general questions you need to ask are the same. These questions concern the content (the information the source provides), its origin (who wrote or produced the source, when and why), and its possible limitations and relative value as a result of the answers to those questions.

Although visual (or non-textual) sources are clearly different from written sources in some respects, the same questions and considerations are relevant when looking at them.

> As an example of the relative value of a source, if you want to find out about a particular event, ask yourself if a recent history book is *more* valuable than a speech for finding out about a particular event or period.

Approaching sources as a set

As well as developing the ability to analyse individual sources, it is important to look at the five sources provided *as a set*. This means looking at them *all* and asking yourself to what extent they agree or disagree with each other.

This ability to look at the five sources together is particularly important when it comes to the last question in the exam paper. This is the question where you need to use the sources *and* your own knowledge to assess the validity of a statement or assertion, or to analyse the significance of a particular factor. Here you need to build an answer (a 'mini-essay') that combines precise knowledge with specific comments about the sources. Try to avoid falling into the trap of dealing with all the sources first and then giving some own knowledge (as an afterthought) that is not linked to the sources.

> **Fact**
> The new state of Germany had been created following France's defeat in the Franco–Prussian War of 1870–71. Prussia was the most powerful of the German states, and after its victory over France, all German states united under Prussia's leadership. At the end of the Franco–Prussian War, France was forced to make reparations, giving up the provinces of Alsace and Lorraine to the new Germany. This caused much bitterness among the French.

> **Wilhelm II (1859–1941)**
> Wilhelm II was the last German emperor (kaiser), ruling from 1888 to 1918. In 1890, he dismissed his more cautious chancellor Otto von Bismarck, and began what he called a 'New Course' in German foreign policy. This aimed to establish a German empire abroad, and to build and maintain a large army and navy that could rival those of other European powers. Bismarck had tried to keep France diplomatically isolated by allying Germany with Russia. However, Wilhelm II allowed this treaty to lapse, and Russia formed an alliance with France in 1892. Towards the end of the First World War, Wilhelm II abdicated and fled to the Netherlands.

Exam skills

If all this sounds a bit daunting, don't worry! Throughout the main chapters of this book, there are activities and questions to help you develop the understanding and the exam skills necessary for success. Before attempting the specific exam practice questions at the end of each main chapter, you might find it useful to refer *first* to Chapter 11, the final exam practice chapter. This suggestion is based on the idea that if you know where you are supposed to be going (in this instance, gaining a good grade), and how to get there, you stand a better chance of reaching your destination!

Questions and markschemes

To ensure that you develop the necessary understanding and skills, each chapter contains questions in the margins. In addition, Chapter 11 is devoted to exam practice. It provides help and advice for all Paper 1 questions and for Paper 2 essay questions, and sets out worked examples for Paper 1 judgement questions and for Paper 2 essays. Worked examples for the remaining three Paper 1-type questions (comprehension, value/limitations and cross-referencing) can be found at the end of Chapters 2 to 9.

In addition, simplified markschemes have been provided to make it easier for you to understand what examiners are looking for in your answers. The actual IB History markschemes can be found on the IB website.

Finally, you will find activities, along with examiners' tips and comments, to help you focus on the important aspects of questions. These examples will also make sure you avoid simple mistakes and oversights that, every year, result in some otherwise good students failing to gain the highest marks.

Background to the period

In order to put developments after 1918 into context, it is necessary to have a general understanding of the events leading up to this period. These include the main causes of the First World War (including developments in international relations and diplomacy), the states and leaders involved, the nature and impact of the war, and the events that occurred immediately before the Paris Peace Conferences began in 1919.

Rivalry and alliances 1890–1914

The First World War, which took place between 1914 and 1918, was a struggle that, at one time or another, involved many different countries across the various regions of the world. It stretched well beyond the boundaries of Europe, to include Asia, Africa and the Americas.

The war began after more than 40 years of tensions in Europe. Its causes included economic and colonial rivalries between the established European states of Britain, France and Russia and the relatively new state of Germany.

Britain, France and Germany

Britain and France had a long history of strained relations. In the later part of the 19th century, rivalry over land claims in parts of Asia and Africa – particularly Egypt – threatened to develop into open conflict. However, from 1890, when the German kaiser **Wilhelm II** took a greater control of foreign policy in his country, Britain and France began to resolve their differences and joined forces against the rising threat from Germany.

The rivaly between these nations sparked off arms races involving both armies and navies. There was also economic tension between Britain and Germany as the pace of German industrialisation increased and, in some areas, overtook Britain's production levels. German coal, iron and steel production soared, but it was in the new technological industries that Germany really outperformed Britain. These tensions led to the creation of two main rival alliances. By 1890, Germany had formed the Triple Alliance with **Austria-Hungary** and Italy; by 1907, Britain, France and Russia had united to form the Triple Entente.

Meanwhile, other new powers were also emerging. The two most significant were the United States and Japan. Like Germany, the USA witnessed a period of rapid industrialisation, with steel production rising from 5 million tonnes in 1890 to nearly 30 million tonnes by 1910. The USA's Gross National Product (GNP) also rose from just over $10 billion in 1890 to $35 billion by 1910.

The USA

Even before the First World War, the USA had begun extending its political influence. Although no territorial claims were made in Latin America, US leaders wanted to ensure stability in the region. To achieve this, they resolved the debts of the Dominican Republic, dominated Cuba, took over land in Panama to build the Panama Canal, opposed Mexican revolutionaries and supported trade and business ventures in Latin America.

However, it was the USA's involvement in the Far East that had the most significant consequences in the years immediately before and after the First World War. The markets of the Far East offered great opportunities for the United States. It therefore supported an 'open door' policy in the Far East, by which trade was open to all nations. In particular, the US government poured financial investment into China in an attempt to halt the growing influence of Japan in the region. The USA was determined to preserve Chinese independence (although not to the point where it would support armed intervention).

Japan

Japan was determined to increase its influence in the Far East and the Pacific. It was rapidly industrialising, and its 1905 victory against Russia in the Russo–Japanese War marked Japan's emergence as a major power. As a result of the war, Japan took over the Korean Peninsula and gained mineral rights in the Chinese province of Manchuria. The gradual collapse of China allowed Japan to exert greater control over Far Eastern trade policies, in direct conflict with the USA's 'open door' approach.

In the years leading up to the First World War, therefore, the USA and Japan were already coming into conflict over economic growth and the desire for new markets and raw materials.

The rise of nationalism

The 19th century saw a significant rise in nationalist movements in many parts of Europe. Both Italy and Germany were new states resulting from this development in the second half of the century. Nationalism was a particular problem for the long-established states of Austria-Hungary and Russia, as both of their European empires were made up of various ethnic groups. Many of these groups – some of them very small – were struggling for independence and national self-determination (see page 15). Nationalist feeling was particularly strong in the **Balkans**, where the Serbs and other groups fought for independence from the Austro-Hungarian and the Turkish (Ottoman) empires.

Austria-Hungary Sometimes known as the Habsburg or Austro-Hungarian Empire, Austria-Hungary was created in 1867 by the Austrian emperor, Franz Josef. The old kingdoms of Austria and Hungary were brought under a single ruler, but remained as self-governing entities.

Fact
The USA did not enter the First World War until 1917, so its economic progress continued unchecked. At the end of the war it emerged as the strongest economic power in the world. In the period from 1914 to 1916, US trade with Britain and France rose from $753 million to $2.75 billion. This economic power gave the USA significant political influence on the world stage.

Balkans This geographic area covers present-day states including Serbia, Bulgaria and Romania. Much of this region had been part of the Turkish Empire for centuries but, by 1900, Greece, Bulgaria, Romania and Serbia had won their independence. As Turkish power in the Balkans declined, other states – such as Britain and Germany, but especially Austria-Hungary and Russia – competed with each other to extend their influence there. Russia, for example, saw its role as defending the Slavic peoples of the area, and so supported the Serbs against the Austro-Hungarian Empire.

Nationalism was also strong in parts of Eastern and Central Europe – particularly amongst Polish people, whose country had been divided between Prussia, Austria and Russia at the end of the 18th century. Tensions increased in 1908, when Austria-Hungary annexed (seized without authority) the province of Bosnia-Herzegovina. This province had been part of the Turkish Empire, and its mainly Serbian population wanted to unite with Serbia.

Two Balkan Wars occurred, in 1912–13 and 1913, which resulted in Serbia emerging as the strongest Balkan state. This increased Austrian concerns about stability in the rest of its empire. Significantly, it was the assassination of Archduke Franz Ferdinand, heir to the Austrian throne, in the Bosnian capital of Sarajevo in June 1914 that triggered the First World War. Furthermore, nationalism – and the desire for self-determination – continued in Serbia after the end of the war.

New methods of warfare

At first, the assassination of the Austrian heir did not seem likely to lead to a European-wide conflict. However, the system of alliances that had built up over the past four decades meant that all the major powers were committed to supporting their allies, and soon war plans were put into operation.

When the First World War began on 4 August 1914, no one – including military leaders – expected it to be an extended conflict. However, a stalemate quickly emerged and, by November 1914, a line of trenches stretched across Western Europe from the North Sea to Switzerland. It was clear that the war would not be 'over by Christmas', as many had initially believed.

By 1916, the situation had descended into a **war of attrition**, resulting in casualties on an unprecedented scale. The horrors of trench warfare, along with new weapons and tactics such as poison gas and heavy artillery barrages, created a determination that this should be 'the war to end all wars'.

war of attrition A form of warfare in which each side attempts to wear down the enemy by a process of steady killing. It was a tactic used particularly by the Allied commanders during the offensives of 1916–17. At the time, many people felt that this tactic was a costly failure. However, several historians now believe that these offensives – which inflicted heavy losses on the Germans and weakened their morale – were just as important in the final Allied victory as the arrival of US troops (the USA joined the Allies in 1917).

A soldier without a mask falls victim to a gas attack; the use of gas in the First World War marked a new development in the weapons and tactics of warfare

This was also the first war to involve large numbers of civilians. People contributed to the war effort by working in armaments factories, for example, or by working the land to produce food for the state. In addition, there were high numbers of civilian casualties, as navy and air force bombardments increased in the later years of the war. The First World War was thus the first *total* war – one that required all the resources of the states involved, from their economic power to the people on the home front.

Eventually, after more than four years of human and material destruction on a scale never witnessed before, an armistice (a temporary ceasefire or truce) was signed between the Entente nations and the **Central Powers** in November 1918.

Post-war expectations

By the time the fighting ceased, the political and economic situation in Europe was vastly different from that of 1914. The Russian monarchy had been overthrown, and a communist-led revolution in November 1917 resulted in Russia's withdrawal from the war four months later. The Austro-Hungarian Empire had virtually collapsed. The German kaiser had abdicated. He had been replaced by a democratic provisional government (a temporary government established until elections can be held), which fully expected a moderate peace treaty.

In large part, this expectation was based on the Fourteen Points, issued by US president **Woodrow Wilson** some months before the end of the war. The Fourteen Points will be covered in more detail in Chapter 2, but in essence they suggested that the USA would insist on a 'just' peace to end the war.

The hopes of the new German government, and those of the other defeated powers (Austria-Hungary, Bulgaria and Turkey), were dashed by Britain and France. These countries felt great bitterness at the huge human and financial cost of the war. French and British leaders were under great pressure to punish Germany and to ensure that it would never again be a threat. Both countries also wanted German land and colonies.

Nations such as Italy and Japan, which had fought for the Allies, also sought German territory as a reward for their support. Wilson's plans for a 'just' peace proved to be idealistic, as the 'Big Three' Allies – Britain, France and the USA – could not agree on the shape of Europe after the war.

The situation in Europe in 1918

By the time the guns fell silent, large parts of Europe – including Germany – were suffering from economic collapse. The Allied naval blockade on Germany set up during the war remained in place, and the German people were near starvation. The situation was made worse by the outbreak of a flu epidemic that eventually claimed millions of lives.

Partly as a result of these issues, political upheaval and even revolution spread through several parts of the Austro-Hungarian Empire (especially Hungary). There was also the growing problem of the demands for self-determination and independence by many small national and ethnic groups in Central and Eastern Europe. The Arabs in the Middle East also expected the promises of independence made to them by Britain and France to be honoured.

Central Powers The three main states in the Central Powers were Germany, Austria-Hungary and Turkey (which had signed an alliance with Germany in 1914). Bulgaria also supported the Central Powers. Although Italy had been a member of the Triple Alliance, it did not fight on Germany's side in the First World War and, by the Treaty of London in 1915, Italy joined the Entente powers instead. To weaken the Turkish war effort, Britain and France encouraged rebellion among the Arabs in the Middle East (still part of the Turkish Empire at that time), in return for promises to support their independence after the war.

Woodrow Wilson (1856–1924) Wilson worked as a university professor and entered politics in 1910. Within two years he was elected president, and he was re-elected in 1916. At first Wilson tried to keep the USA out of the First World War, but he favoured the Allies and was drawn into the conflict when Germany launched an unrestricted U-boat (submarine) campaign that resulted in the loss of US shipping. After suffering a stroke in 1919 Wilson's political influence waned, although he remained president until 1921.

11

reparations This term means compensation paid by a defeated nation for war damage. Germany was eventually forced to pay reparations for having 'caused' the First World War. Georges Clemenceau had at first asked the USA to cancel France's war debts, so that there would be no need for Germany to pay France heavy compensation. However, the USA refused so Clemenceau was forced to take a harder line against Germany.

David Lloyd George (1863–1945) Lloyd George entered British politics in 1890. He served as chancellor in the Liberal government of 1906, and helped to push through a number of welfare reforms. He became prime minister of a coalition government in 1916, at the height of the First World War. However, there were already splits within the Liberal Party, and by the time of the Paris Peace Conferences of 1919 Lloyd George was in sole charge, largely due to Conservative support.

Britain and France were economically weak in 1918. They had lost international trade to the USA and Japan, and were in debt to the US after borrowing heavily to finance the war effort. In addition, most of the fighting had taken place on French soil, causing widespread destruction of farmland, factories, railway lines, roads, bridges and homes. Therefore, Britain and especially France desperately needed Germany to make heavy **reparations**.

The armistice and the Paris Peace Conferences

The First World War officially ended on 11 November 1918, when Germany signed the armistice agreement. By the terms of this agreement, the Germans handed over their naval fleet and war materials. They also evacuated all German-occupied land in France and Belgium, and allowed Allied occupation of the left bank of the River Rhine. Armistices had already been reached with Turkey (30 October) and Austria-Hungary (3 November).

The terms of the armistices guaranteed an end to immediate hostilities, but Allied leaders still faced the problem of ensuring a lasting peace – not only in Europe, but across the world. Eventually it was agreed that a series of conferences would be held in Paris to discuss how this could be achieved. The peace talks would be attended by the leaders of the victorious powers, including British prime minister **David Lloyd George**. French premier **Georges Clemenceau** (see page 13) acted as chairman. Woodrow Wilson decided to attend the conferences in person, so they were scheduled for January 1919 to allow him to deliver his State of the Union address in early December, and also to allow for a general election to take place in Britain.

Almost as soon as the peace talks began, it became clear that the participants had conflicting demands and problems. In theory, the main decisions were to be made by the Council of Four (Britain, France, the USA and Italy). In practice, however, Italy was largely ignored and it was the 'Big Three' who took the most important decisions. The virtual exclusion of Italy – and Japan – from the decision-making process, and from the 'division of the spoils', caused problems in the following decades.

In addition, it was decided that the main discussions would not include representatives from the defeated powers, in case this slowed negotiations. Instead, Germany and its supporters would be presented with the final terms and if they rejected these, the war would continue. This also caused a resentment that took on a new significance as events unfolded in the 1920s and 1930s.

Terminology and definitions

In order to understand this topic, including the motives and propaganda produced by the main countries involved (the USA, Britain, France, Germany, Italy and Japan), and the various historical arguments and interpretations of the period, you will need to understand the meaning of several terms. These include 'democracy', 'authoritarianism' and 'totalitarianism', 'left' and 'right', and 'communist' and 'capitalist'.

Left wing and right wing

These terms describe the two ends of the political spectrum. The left wing refers to socialist groups, often those on the extreme left (such as communists). The right wing refers to conservative groups, but often those with extreme views (such as fascists).

Street fighting in Berlin during the Spartacist uprising of January 1919, in which members of the extreme left-wing Spartacist movement attempted to overthrow the new unelected provisional government of Germany

Democracy

Democracy literally means 'rule by the people'. In practice this has come to mean that there is political equality – an equal distribution of political power and influence. The people in a democracy have the opportunity to participate in government, usually through elections in which they can vote for the person who best represents their interests or political beliefs. A democratically elected government also rules in the interests of all the people rather than any particular group. This system ensures that individual rights are protected and that the powers of the government are restrained. Before the First World War, the USA, Britain and France were seen as the upholders of democracy, but in fact women were not allowed to vote in Britain and the USA at that time, and many working men were also not eligible to vote.

Authoritarianism

When referring to authoritarianism, historians mean a political system in which rulers have virtually unlimited powers and the people have few or no individual rights or freedoms. Today, democracy has replaced authoritarianism as the most common form of government, particularly in the West. Before the First World War, however, the governments of Germany, Russia and Austria-Hungary in particular had authoritarian rulers. In these nations, government was imposed upon the people without their consent, opposition was often repressed and political liberty was limited. These regimes protected those who had traditionally held power, such as landowners, and prevented the middle and working classes from achieving influence and bringing about change.

Georges Clemenceau (1841–1929) Clemenceau served two terms as prime minister of France (1906–09 and 1917–20). He led France through the final year of the First World War, and was very critical of the army leadership. Clemenceau was 77 years old by the time of the Paris Peace Conferences, and he could remember the German invasion of France in 1870. His determination that this should never happen again influenced his uncompromising attitude.

Totalitarianism

Totalitarianism differs from authoritarianism in that it attempts to establish total or complete power. In a totalitarian system, the state controls and influences all aspects of public and private life. The system originated after the First World War in fascist Italy, where everything the people did was supposed to be for the benefit of the state. However, the term later became more closely associated with the rule of Hitler in Germany and Stalin in the Soviet Union. Totalitarianism can therefore be used to describe both fascist and communist regimes. These regimes were characterised by the existence of only one political party, an official ideology or set of beliefs that everyone was expected to follow, the use of terror to maintain control of the population, and state control of the media and economic affairs.

Fascism

This term is derived from the Italian word *fascio* (plural *fasci*), meaning a group, band, league or union. In 1919, Mussolini applied it to his Fascio di Combattimento ('Fighting' or 'Battle Group'), which was set up to fight socialists and communists. Mussolini later formed the far-right ultra-nationalist Fascist Party. After October 1922, he began to turn Italy into a one-party fascist dictatorship. Other far-right nationalist politicians in interwar Europe tried to follow his lead, although often with significant differences or additions. Hitler and the Nazi Party in Germany is one example of this. The term fascist was then used to describe this political ideology, and all groups holding such views.

Capitalism

This is an economic system based on the idea of private ownership and control of industry and banking, as opposed to state or social ownership. In a capitalist system, wealth is in the hands of individuals and they invest that wealth in areas where they expect to make the greatest profit.

Many critics of capitalism, including Karl Marx, have argued that it leads to the exploitation of workers, as investors try to keep wages low in order to maximise their profits. However, there are no purely capitalist systems, as governments also shape economic policy, provide welfare benefits and protect workers (although this was much more limited in the period after the First World War than it is now). In many capitalist states today the government also controls key industries, but this was not the case after the First World War. Governments may also intervene to protect industries, which means that the demands of the market alone do not determine economic developments. An example of this can be seen in the 1920s, when governments introduced tariffs to protect their nations' industries from competition as the demand for goods began to shrink.

Communism

Communism refers to the far-left political ideology associated with Karl Marx and Friedrich Engels, which aimed to overthrow capitalism and replace it with a classless society. The first attempt to apply these theories was made by the Bolsheviks in Russia. Under the leadership of Vladimir Ilyich Lenin, the Bolsheviks encouraged workers' uprisings in other parts of Europe and, in 1919, established the Communist International (Comintern) to help spread revolution.

The Bolshevik regime was widely feared in the West and, in order to prevent the spread of revolution, other major European states tried to overthrow the Bolsheviks. When this failed, the European powers applied economic and trade embargos (bans) in order to isolate and weaken the Bolsheviks. For many European politicians, the communist Soviet Union posed the most serious threat to stability in Europe, even after the Nazis came to power in Germany in 1933.

Self-determination

This refers to the idea – defended in particular by US president Woodrow Wilson at the 1919–20 peace negotiations – that national groups should be able to live in independent countries. However, although self-determination was applied to some ethnic and national groups from the former Austro-Hungarian and Russian empires, the claims of others were ignored. In particular, German speakers in Austria and some of the newly created states were not allowed to be united with Weimar Germany. In some areas, the decision about where such populations should be placed was decided by **plebiscites** organised by the new League of Nations.

plebiscites Direct votes, or referendums, open to the people of an entire country or region to approve or oppose a specific issue.

Collective security

Collective security is the attempt by a group of nations to prevent military aggression as a means of solving problems. The League of Nations tried to do this through negotiation and, if this failed, by applying **sanctions**. Another aspect of collective security was the attempt to uphold the peace treaties of 1919–20. In particular, France was determined to enforce the demilitarisation of the Rhineland, the German territory west of the River Rhine, as outlined in the Treaty of Versailles. However, attempts by the League to uphold collective security were undermined by several key countries, who regarded it as a 'club of victors' whose main role was to enforce the 'unfair' terms of the treaty.

sanctions These are actions taken to put pressure on a country (or individual) to force them to do, or to stop doing, something. For example, economic sanctions might include a trade ban or boycott, especially of vital products such as armaments or coal. As a last resort, military force might be applied.

15

Successor states

This term refers to the new states in Central and Eastern Europe that were created – or, in Poland's case, re-created – by the peace treaties of 1919–20. Poland had been divided between the pre-1914 German, Austro-Hungarian and Russian empires in the 18th century, and was re-formed after the war.

Two totally new states were established: Czechoslovakia (from land formerly part of the Austro-Hungarian Empire) and the Kingdom of Serbs, Croats and Slovenes – later called Yugoslavia. This was created by uniting parts of Austro-Hungarian land with the formerly independent Kingdom of Serbia. In addition, Austria and Hungary became two separate states, with reduced territory. Finland and the Baltic states (Estonia, Latvia and Lithuania) also gained their independence, having previously been part of Tsarist Russia.

Most of these new states were economically and militarily weak, and many had significant minority ethnic groups as part of their populations. These ethnic groups often wanted to be ruled by another country, or felt unfairly treated. Because of the general insecurity of the successor states, some of them formed alliances. For example, Czechoslovakia and Yugoslavia joined Romania to form the Little Entente (from the French for 'understanding' or 'agreement' and applied to diplomatic agreements between states) in 1920–21.

The Wall Street Crash and the Great Depression

Wall Street was, and still is, the location of the US Stock Exchange, where shares in companies are bought and sold. In October 1929, share prices plummeted and investors lost large amounts of money. This collapse – known as the Wall Street Crash – caused a severe economic depression in the US; factories closed and millions became unemployed. As a result, the US ended its loans to other countries. Germany was particularly affected, as it relied in part on US loans to pay the reparations imposed on it by the Treaty of Versailles.

As a result of the Wall Street Crash, most countries were soon plunged into what became known as the Great Depression. This was a global economic event, resulting in widespread distress (high unemployment, inflation, industrial decline in production and trade, poverty) in most capitalist countries in the 1930s. One of its impacts was to turn many of its victims towards supporting extremist parties.

Countries responded to this crisis in a number of ways. Some resorted to protectionism – imposing tariffs (import taxes) on goods coming from other countries in order to limit competition in the home market. However, other countries often retaliated by applying their own tariffs, so the overall effect was to reduce world trade even further. During the 1930s, some nations – notably those with fascist or militaristic regimes – increasingly resorted to an aggressive foreign policy to solve their economic problems.

Summary

By the time you have worked through this book, you should be able to:

- show a broad understanding of the nature of international relations, both within the major states involved and on a global scale
- understand and explain the various factors behind the breakdown of the attempts at peacemaking and peacekeeping, and be able to evaluate the different historical interpretations surrounding them
- show an awareness of the impact of the events of 1918–36 in various regions of the world, and in turn how developments in different parts of the world affected international relations elsewhere
- understand the complexities of international relations resulting from the absence of the USA from the major peacekeeping body, and the exclusion of Russia from the peacekeeping process following the communist seizure of power in 1917
- explain the key events and turning points in international relations in the years 1918–36, from the early attempts at international co-operation to the final stages
- understand and explain the various factors that contributed to the breakdown of international order in the 1930s.

2 The aims of the peacemakers

Key questions

- What problems faced the peacemakers?
- How did the aims and motives of the 'Big Three' differ?
- What did Germany expect from the Paris Peace Conferences?

Overview

- The First World War changed the political, economic and social landscape of Europe and the wider world. More than 8 million soldiers were killed, along with a further 8 million civilian casualties. The scale of the changes and the widespread damage the war caused placed huge expectations on the leaders when they met in Paris in 1919.
- The Bolshevik Revolution in Russia created further problems. There were fears that Central and Eastern Europe might fall to communism if stability was not restored quickly through clear and enforceable peace terms.
- Promises made during the war to win the support of countries such as Italy added to the difficulties facing the peacemakers, who now had to find ways of fulfilling those promises.
- Public opinion demanded that Germany be punished severely for the damage caused during the war. However, this conflicted with the need to rebuild Europe both physically and economically.
- The impact of the war on the USA was less extensive than it was on France or Britain. This meant that the three leading powers had different aims and motives at the peace conferences, because the war had affected them in different ways.
- President Woodrow Wilson's Fourteen Points were viewed as a new start in international relations and a move away from the old diplomacy of secret treaties, which was blamed for the global nature of the First World War.
- Although Germany had signed an armistice with the Allies, it had defeated Russia in the east and successfully defended its western borders. As a result, many Germans did not believe they had truly lost the war.
- The new German government was very unpopular and faced many internal threats, as well as the possibility of revolution. The situation in Germany was further complicated by the government's belief that any peace agreement would be based on Wilson's Fourteen Points – a belief that was not upheld by the final treaties.

Timeline

1915 Apr: Treaty of London between the Allies and Italy

1917 Mar: revolution in Russia; Tsar Nicholas II abdicates

Nov: Bolshevik Revolution

Dec: ceasefire between Russia and Germany

1918 Jan: President Wilson announces his Fourteen Points

Mar: Germany signs Treaty of Brest-Litovsk with Russia

Nov: Kaiser Wilhelm II abdicates; provisional government takes over in Germany; armistice signed between Allies and Central Powers; Wilson's Democrats lose US midterm elections

Dec: elections in Britain

1919 Jan: Paris Peace Conferences begin

Nov: elections in France (results announced January 1920)

What problems faced the peacemakers?

When the peacemakers met in Paris in the early months of 1919, they faced many problems. Much of Europe was gripped by economic chaos, and the war had caused widespread political instability, especially in parts of Central and Eastern Europe.

The impact of the First World War

Although the precise numbers of those killed in the First World War – either soldiers or civilians – are not known, there is no doubt that the conflict had a huge impact on the world. There had been four years of fighting, much of it on the **Western Front** but a significant amount also on the **Eastern Front** and in the Middle East. This had left large areas of farmland devastated, and factories and homes destroyed.

Western Front This is the name given to the land that ran from the Belgian coast through France, on which most of the heavy fighting took place during the First World War.

Eastern Front This is the name given to the land that ran through Eastern and parts of Central Europe, from the Baltic Sea in the north to the Black Sea in the south, which marked the battle lines in the east.

Questions

What does this photograph reveal about the scale of the damage suffered by towns on the front lines? How do you think such damage would have affected the demands made at the Paris Peace Conferences? How useful to historians are pictures like this?

The ruins of the Belgian town of Ypres, on the Western Front, in 1918

The economic impact

The war severely disrupted international trade. Many economies were damaged and nations were in debt. Even those European states that remained neutral in the war suffered economically, as a result of German U-boat attacks on their ships or due to the British naval blockade of the German coast.

During the war, Britain and France changed their economic focus to meet the demands of the fighting, which meant that they lost their overseas markets to non-European countries such as Japan and the USA. These non-European nations were free from fighting on their home soil, and faced little trade competition from those countries more directly involved in the conflict. As a result, the USA emerged as the strongest economic power in the world at the end of the First World War.

Unable to continue funding the fighting, the Allies had been forced to borrow from US bankers. At the end of the war, they needed to find a way of repaying these loans. This could only be done by demanding reparations for the cost of the war from the defeated powers. However, in order for full stability to be returned to Europe, the economies of all the nations involved – on both sides – needed to be rebuilt.

SOURCE A

Increase in national debt of the key European powers, 1914–22

Country	Increase in national debt (US$ million)
Great Britain	30,811
France	21,266
Italy	5,605
Germany	75
	(this figure is low because of the impact of inflation)

Adapted from Peaple, S. 2002. European Diplomacy 1870–1939. London, UK. Heinemann. p. 99.

The social impact

The human cost of the war was also significant, with huge numbers of casualties on all sides.

SOURCE B

Casualties of key nations in the First World War

Country	Estimated numbers killed
Germany	2,000,000
France	2,000,000
Russia	1,650,000
Austria-Hungary	1,100,000
Great Britain	750,000
British Empire	250,000
Romania	250,000

Adapted from Peaple, S. 2002. European Diplomacy 1870–1939. London, UK. Heinemann. p. 99.

The impact on the European population was heightened by an influenza (flu) epidemic that swept through Europe in the winter of 1918. The disease killed an estimated 40 million people – more than had died in the war itself. Many people were weakened by food rationing or poverty caused by the war.

autocratic This word is used to describe rule by one person who maintains absolute or total power over a country or group.

Fact

At the time of the first revolution, Russia was using a calendar that ran 13 days behind the calendar used in the rest of Europe. Thus, what is commonly referred to as the February Revolution actually took place in March 1917 according to the more widely used European calendar. The Bolshevik Revolution took place in October/November 1917. In 1918, Russia adopted the more modern calendar.

Treaty of Brest-Litovsk The treaty signed in March 1918 between Russia and Germany. Although it fulfilled the Bolsheviks' aim of withdrawing Russia from the war, the terms of the treaty were harsh, and resulted in the loss of vast amounts of Russian territory. These losses included the Baltic states, parts of what had been Poland, Finland, Ukraine, and land in the Caucasus.

world revolution This was the belief among some Russian communists that their main concern should be to export communist beliefs to other countries. This would not only help the spread of communism, but also help Russia to become socialist, as well as ensuring that it was not the only workers' state. This would increase the country's security.

The First World War involved large numbers of civilians, as whole nations were encouraged to help the war effort, creating for the first time the concept of total war (see page 11). This had political repercussions, particularly in Germany, where the British naval blockade had a serious impact. The British navy prevented war supplies, raw materials and food from reaching Germany. This caused food shortages and led to what many Germans called the 'Turnip Winter' (as that was all there was to eat). It also created a great deal of bitterness, leading to strikes and demonstrations in Germany throughout October 1918. The protestors were joined by soldiers and sailors who wanted an end to the war. By 9 November, the unrest had turned into a general strike in Berlin, causing widespread fears of a German revolution similar to the revolution that had taken place in Russia in 1917 (see below).

There was thus a high level of civilian involvement in events both during and immediately after the war. The public wanted those responsible for the war and its associated hardships to be punished, and the leaders who attended the Paris Peace Conferences had to respond to these public demands. In addition, the press had stirred up nationalist feelings during the war. This raised public expectations, which governments now also had to face.

Revolution and collapse

Politically, the war brought about dramatic changes. It resulted in the collapse of **autocratic** and monarchical rule in many areas of Central and Eastern Europe. Tsarist Russia was taken over by the Bolsheviks, and both the Austro-Hungarian Empire and the German Reich (empire) ceased to exist. The Turkish Empire was also on the verge of collapse, and did not survive the peace conferences.

The Russian Revolution

In Russia, the war placed increasing strain on the tsarist regime, and this eventually brought about revolution in February/March 1917. Tsar Nicholas II abdicated, leaving the country under the control of a provisional government.

In October/November 1917, the provisional government – which had kept Russia in the First World War – was overthrown by the Bolsheviks, who wanted to end Russia's involvement in the conflict. The Allies refused to consider peace terms at this point, so Russia concluded its own peace negotiations with the Central Powers in the **Treaty of Brest-Litovsk**.

The Bolshevik victory in Russia marked the emergence of the first communist state. Many people across Europe were sympathetic to the Bolsheviks' aim of ending the war, and European leaders became concerned that similar revolutions might break out in their own countries. Communists such as Leon Trotsky openly encouraged '**world revolution**', and in March 1919 the communist leader Béla Kun seized power in Hungary. It seemed to many that Europe was vulnerable to a communist takeover.

These fears were heightened because communism's opposition to private ownership and its aim to place all industry under state control were a threat to the capitalist system (see page 14), and especially to middle-class factory owners. The victorious powers were also worried about the communist ideal of 'no annexations and no indemnities'. This meant that land would not be taken away from defeated nations, nor would they have to pay for the cost of the war. There was therefore a risk of communism taking hold in the countries on the losing side.

In the face of these fears, the leaders at the peace conferences had to act quickly to prevent further chaos. Already there were clashes in western parts of Russia, such as Georgia, where minority groups sought to establish their own states.

Central and Eastern Europe and the Middle and Far East

Problems in Central and Eastern Europe and the Middle and Far East arose because Britain and France had made commitments during the war that they were now expected to honour. The longer the war lasted, the more willing nations became to make secret agreements based on future promises. The Allies tried desperately to secure the help and support of other countries in order to achieve a breakthrough in the war.

This was most evident in the promises made to Italy in the secret Treaty of London in 1915. At the start of the First World War, Italy was allied to the Central Powers of Germany and Austria-Hungary, but it did not declare war. To win Italy's support, Britain and France offered it a share in the partition of the Turkish Empire, further territory if France or Britain annexed any German colonies, sovereignty over the **Dodecanese Islands**, and gains in the north from Austro-Hungarian lands. Such promises conflicted with US president Woodrow Wilson's belief in self-determination (see page 15), as large numbers of non-Italians would find themselves under Italian rule. However, after the war the Italian government – eager to make its country a great power and to show its people that their sacrifices had not been in vain – was unwilling to release Britain and France from their promises.

A similar problem arose in the Middle East. Britain had promised support and recognition for Arab independence in most areas, in order to encourage rebellion against the Arabs' Turkish overlords. However, this conflicted with the post-war claims of France, Italy and Greece (which had joined the Allies in 1917). This agreement also contradicted Britain's Balfour Declaration of 1917 (see page 92), which promised the Jews a national homeland in Palestine. The various demands relating to all these promises needed to be resolved at the Paris Peace Conferences.

Britain had also made guarantees to Japan over its rights to former German possessions, in return for which Japan had agreed to support British claims to German lands south of the Equator. In 1915, Japan forced a weak and divided China to agree to Japanese political and economic privileges in the province of Manchuria and in Inner Mongolia. The British acknowledged their support of Japan's right to dispose of German **concessions** in Shantung. The USA had also agreed to recognise Japan's rights in Shantung, southern Manchuria and eastern Mongolia.

Public opinion

One of the greatest difficulties faced by the leaders of Britain and France in particular in their search for a lasting peace was the fact that they were operating under pressure from the public. People were elated by victory, but were also determined to make the defeated nations meet the cost of the war.

Dodecanese Islands A group of islands off the Greek coast, including the island of Rhodes. The Dodecanese had long been under Turkish rule. The islands had declared independence in 1912, but during the First World War they were occupied by Italy, which considered Rhodes in particular to be of strategic importance.

concessions These were regions in certain nations, such as China, in which other countries had used force, or the threat of force, to obtain sole or favourable trading rights.

21

SOURCE C

If I am elected, Germany is going to pay. I have personally no doubt we will get everything that you can squeeze out of a lemon, and a bit more. I propose that every bit of German-owned property; moveable and immovable, in Allied and neutral countries, whether State property or private property; should be surrendered by the Germans.

Sir Eric Geddes, a British government minister, speaking to a rally in the general election campaign, December 1918. Quoted in Mowatt, C. L. 1972. Britain Between the Wars 1918–1940. London, UK. Methuen. p. 4.

The influence of the press

The press had played a significant role in stirring up nationalist feeling during the war. The media now put forward the view that the peace settlement was the last fight of the campaign – an opportunity to exercise the rights that had been so hard-won on the battlefield. The popular press presented a simplistic view of the situation, and raised public expectations to a level that governments could not hope to satisfy. The press led a campaign to 'hang the kaiser' and firmly blamed Germany for the war.

Such sentiments were particularly strong in countries that had been invaded, such as France and Belgium. This made it harder for the leaders to adopt a lenient approach to the peace process. The presence of the press throughout the conferences ensured that daily discussions were reported and that any apparent weakening of attitude was attacked.

The public desire for a 'harsh peace' grew after details of the Treaty of Brest-Litovsk (see page 20) were published in March 1918. By the terms of this peace treaty between Russia and Germany, Russia lost 25% of its population as large amounts of land in Eastern Europe were redistributed among the Central Powers. People felt that if Germany could treat Russia so harshly, then Germany itself should expect similar treatment.

Elections and public pressure

Both Britain and France had general elections scheduled within a year of the war ending (Britain in December 1918 and France in November 1919). In their campaigns, the candidates were acutely aware that if they did not support public opinion they risked defeat in the election. Their fears were well-founded. In Britain, the candidates who supported the call to 'make Germany pay' were elected with large majorities, whilst those who supported Wilson's more moderate views were defeated. In France, the Chamber of Deputies became known as the 'one-legged Chamber' because of the number of injured soldiers who were elected to it. Their presence made it even more difficult for Clemenceau to be lenient in the later stages of the peace talks.

Questions

Look at the poster below. What is its message? What were the concerns of the British Empire Union? How useful is the poster as evidence of public opinion in Britain at the end of the First World War?

A poster issued by the British Empire Union (a strongly anti-German organisation established during the First World War), giving a clear indication of its views towards Germany

However, perhaps the greatest pressure from the public was felt in Italy. The war had drained Italian resources and weakened the economy. The growing social and political unrest put the government under pressure to achieve even more than had been promised in the Treaty of London. The public called for Italy to be granted the port of Fiume (in modern Croatia), which had a substantial Italian population, as well as former Austrian land occupied by Germans. Italian prime minister Vittorio Orlando had to ensure Italy made significant gains from the peace treaties.

Activities

1 Research the social, political and economic impact of the First World War on any country you have studied. How severely was your chosen country affected?

2 Woodrow Wilson had little knowledge of the conditions in Europe at the end of the First World War, particularly the situation in Central and Eastern Europe. Imagine you are one of Wilson's advisors, and write a brief summary of the situation for him to read before the Paris Peace Conferences.

3 Construct a spider diagram to show the social, political and economic problems caused by the First World War.

How did the aims and motives of the 'Big Three' differ?

The USA

The USA entered the war in 1917, following the unrestricted German U-boat campaign that resulted in attacks on US shipping. This had been a major source of tension between the US and Germany since Germany began attacking any ships carrying supplies to Britain. In the past, a warning had been issued before an attack so that crews could abandon ship; now the Germans attacked without warning. The most notable victim of this new policy was the *Lusitania*, which was sunk in May 1915 with the loss of 128 American lives. This caused a rise in tensions between Germany and the USA, even though the Germans temporarily abandoned the campaign.

However, what finally pushed the USA into the war was a telegram that was intercepted from the German foreign secretary, Arthur Zimmerman, to the German ambassador in Mexico. The Zimmerman telegram encouraged Mexico to attack the USA, and promised German support for such an action. The fact that Germany was encouraging an attack within the Americas turned public opinion in the USA, and encouraged pro-war feeling.

Wilson's ideals

In committing the USA to the war on the Allied side, President Wilson claimed he was fighting for the ideals of freedom and democracy, rather than territorial gain. He believed that this was a moral commitment, entrusted to the USA by its founders. Wilson was convinced that the war had been caused by an outdated form of international diplomacy, characterised by secret treaties and economic and military competition. He was now determined to remove these areas of conflict and establish a new political world order, or 'New Diplomacy'. This would involve open negotiations rather than secret agreements, global disarmament to end the arms races (see page 9), economic co-operation, and a League of Nations to resolve disputes between states. Wilson outlined his aims in a number of speeches throughout 1917 and 1918.

Fact
The aim of the U-boat campaign was to prevent vital supplies reaching Britain. At first the Germans attacked only Allied warships, and then Allied merchant ships. However, in February 1915 they began a campaign of unrestricted submarine warfare, which resulted in the sinking of the liner *Lusitania*. Fearing this would cause the US to join the war, Germany abandoned its unrestricted campaign soon after. However, in 1916 – as Germany became more desperate to gain an advantage – the campaign was launched again. Later, the US claimed that this was one of the reasons it entered the war in 1917.

Fact
Although Wilson is often seen as an idealist, he was also determined to protect US interests. For example, he used the USA's financial strength to try and force Britain and France to accept his own aims after 1918. He also sent US troops to Russia to help overthrow the new Bolshevik government, and imposed a blockade against Hungary to undermine the revolution there.

23

SOURCE D

It must be a peace without victory. Victory would mean peace forced upon the loser, a victor's terms imposed upon the vanquished. It would be accepted in humiliation, under duress, at an intolerable sacrifice, and would leave a sting, a resentment, a bitter memory upon which terms of peace would rest, not permanently, but only upon quicksand. Only a peace between equals can last.

Extract from a speech given by Woodrow Wilson in January 1917, outlining his aims for the peace process.

Questions

What is the message of Source D? What is there in the speech that would particularly appeal to the Germans? How useful is this source in explaining Wilson's attitude towards the Paris Peace Conferences?

The traditional view of Woodrow Wilson is that he was an unworldly idealist, and that he did not fully understand European politics or the concerns of nations such as France. Many contemporaries, particularly in France and Britain, believed that because the USA only joined the war in 1917 and endured less suffering and material damage than other countries, Wilson did not fully understand their concerns.

This attitude seemed to be reinforced in January 1918, when Wilson outlined his Fourteen Points. Although these shaped a new moral world order, they did not offer the protection and guarantees that many hoped for, and they distanced Wilson from his allies in Europe. Wilson had taken the USA into the war to uphold democracy. He now wanted to see democracy extended, and to establish a just and equal system through international law and the association of nations.

Wilson did not believe that Germany should escape completely unpunished; however, he did not want this punishment to be excessive. He was concerned that a harsh peace would simply result in a German desire for revenge, which would create further instability. Some contemporaries suggested that one of the main motivations for the USA seeking a fair peace and German reconstruction was that Germany was a major trading partner and potential market for American goods. Wilson may have been an idealist, but he also wanted to protect the USA's economic interests and those gains that had been made before and during the war. These concerns may explain the call for free trade that Wilson made in his speech outlining the Fourteen Points.

SOURCE E

[The treaty] seeks to punish one of the greatest wrongs ever done in history, the wrong which Germany sought to do to the world and to civilization, and there ought to be no weak purpose with regard to punishment. She attempted an intolerable thing and she must be made to pay for the attempt.

Extract from a speech given by Woodrow Wilson in Omaha, September 1919.

Activity

Compare Sources D and E. Are you surprised by the view Wilson expresses in Source E? Why?

SOURCE F

If America is not to have free enterprise then she can have freedom of no sort whatever … Our industries have expanded to such a point that they will burst their jackets if they cannot find a free outlet to the markets of the world … Our domestic markets no longer suffice. We need foreign markets.

From Wilson's speech to Congress, 8 January 1918. Quoted in Williams, W. A. 1972. The Tragedy of American Diplomacy. London, UK. Norton. p. 58.

The Fourteen Points

As the end of the war approached, Britain and France demonstrated a desire for revenge and the prevention of future German political and economic domination of Europe. Wilson, however, had assured the American people that they were fighting for the ideals of democracy and freedom, and played down the potential territorial and economic benefits. The clearest statement of his beliefs was made in his address to Congress on 8 January 1918, when he outlined what became known as the Fourteen Points. In these, Wilson actually widened the scope of the Allies' war aims.

autonomous This term means self-governing, rather than being under the control or rule of another state.

SOURCE G

1 Open covenants of peace, openly arrived at, after which there shall be no private understandings of any kind.

2 Absolute freedom of navigation upon the seas, both in peacetime and war.

3 The removal, so far as it is possible, of all economic barriers and the establishment of equality of trade conditions among all nations.

4 Adequate guarantees given and taken that national armaments will be reduced to the lowest point consistent with domestic safety.

5 A free, open-minded and impartial adjustment of all colonial claims, based upon a strict observance of the principle that the interests of the population concerned must have equal weight with the equitable claims of the government whose title is to be determined.

6 The evacuation of all Russian territory for the independent determination of her own political development and national policy and for a sincere welcome into the society of free nations under institutions of her own choosing.

7 Belgium must be evacuated and restored.

8 All French territory should be freed and the invaded portions restored, and the wrong done to France by Prussia in 1871 in the manner of Alsace-Lorraine should be righted.

9 A readjustment of the frontiers of Italy should be effected along clearly recognizable lines of nationality.

10 The peoples of Austria-Hungary should be accorded the freest opportunity of **autonomous** development.

11 Romania, Serbia and Montenegro should be evacuated; occupied territories restored; Serbia accorded free and secure access to the sea; international guarantees of the political and economic independence and territorial integrity of the several Balkan states should be entered into.

12 The Turkish portion of the present Ottoman [Turkish] Empire should be assured a secure sovereignty, but the other nationalities which are now under Turkish rule should be assured an undoubted security of life and an absolutely unmolested opportunity of autonomous development, and the Dardanelles should be permanently opened as a free passage to the ships and commerce of all nations under international guarantees.

13 An independent Polish state should be erected which should include the territories inhabited by indisputably Polish populations, which should be assured a free and secure access to the sea.

14 A general association of nations must be formed under specific covenants for the purposes of affording mutual guarantees of political independence and territorial integrity to great and small states alike.

Wilson's Fourteen Points, 8 January 1918.

Questions

What do you think the aims and motives were of Wilson's Fourteen Points? What do the Fourteen Points tell us about Wilson's view of the causes of the First World War?

25

Historical debate

Woodrow Wilson is usually portrayed as an idealist who took the USA into the First World War to make the world safe for democracy and to create a fair and just world order. However, more recent work by historians such as Frank McDonough has suggested that Wilson was actually more of a realist, and that a closer examination of his actions at the Paris Peace Conferences shows that he was not completely faithful to his principles. There was certainly little democracy about the decision-making process at the conferences, and Wilson was also concerned to protect US industry, hence his desire for free trade. This suggests that he was less idealistic than historians such as Ruth Henig have argued.

Activity

What is the message of this cartoon? Use the information given in the text and your own knowledge to explain your answer. Write a paragraph describing how accurate you think the view of Wilson is in the cartoon.

imperialism A policy of expanding a country's power and influence through maintaining or extending an overseas empire. Britain had the largest empire in the world at the start of the First World War, and was concerned that self-determination would give people living in distant parts of the British Empire the right to decide their own futures.

The reaction of the major powers to the Fourteen Points

Many people in the Allied nations disapproved of both the content of the Fourteen Points and the ideals behind them. They believed Wilson's plan to be impractical and idealistic, and felt that their countries would be better preparing for the eventuality of another war.

OVERWEIGHTED.

PRESIDENT WILSON. "HERE'S YOUR OLIVE BRANCH. NOW GET BUSY."
DOVE OF PEACE. "OF COURSE I WANT TO PLEASE EVERYBODY; BUT ISN'T THIS A BIT THICK?"

A cartoon published in the British magazine Punch, *1919*

The former British prime minister, Arthur Balfour, agreed with this point of view, stating that the Fourteen Points were 'admirable but very abstract'. The British newspaper the *Times* commented that the Fourteen Points 'did not take into account certain hard realities of the situation'. This was particularly true of Wilson's plan for the peoples of Eastern Europe to rule themselves. The different ethnic groups were scattered across a wide area, and it was therefore inevitable that some would be ruled by people from other races with different customs and traditions.

Britain and France were also concerned that the proposed League of Nations (Point 14) would not be compatible with the protection of national interests, particularly in the resolution of conflicts. Britain saw the Fourteen Points as an attack on **imperialism**, believing they would encourage parts of the British Empire to demand self-determination. France was concerned about the impact of the Fourteen Points on its land and influence in the Middle East and Africa.

There were also fears in Britain about the possibility of free access to the seas in wartime (Point 2). Moreover, the question of former German colonies caused concern as many of these had been promised to other countries – most notably Japan and South Africa – to win their support during the war. Self-determination also conflicted with the promises made to Italy in the Treaty of London about land up to the Brenner Pass (see page 55), which would place 200,000 Germans under Italian rule. Finally, both Britain and France were also keen to seize as much former German colonial territory as possible in order to expand their own empires.

When the Fourteen Points were first published in January 1918, Britain and France were too busy fighting the war to fully address the question of self-determination and the difficulties it might cause for their empires. Despite some reservations, both nations accepted the Fourteen Points, fearing that refusing to do so would encourage the USA to make a separate peace with Germany. When the German government indicated that it was willing to consider signing an armistice based on the Fourteen Points, the Allied governments issued their own statement (Source H).

Fact

During periods of war, Britain had often closed the seas to other nations. In the past it had prevented the Russian fleet from entering the Mediterranean. Britain wanted to maintain this position, as it allowed British domination of the seas and made it easier to impose blockades.

SOURCE H

The Allied Governments have given careful consideration to the correspondence which has passed between the President of the United States and the German Government. Subject to the qualifications which follow they declare their willingness to make peace with the Government of Germany on the terms of peace laid down in the President's address to Congress of January, 1918, and the principles of settlement enunciated in his subsequent addresses. In the conditions of peace laid down in his address to Congress of January 8, 1918, the President declared that invaded territories must be restored as well as evacuated and freed, the Allies feel that no doubt ought to be allowed to exist as to what this provision implies. By it they understand that compensation will be made by Germany for all damage done to the civilian population of the Allies and their property by the aggression of Germany by land, by sea and from the air.

Statement issued by the Allied governments, 5 November 1918.

Questions

Look at Source H. What is there in the statement from the Allies that would appeal to Germany? What is there in the statement that would displease Germany?

Although Wilson was determined that the Fourteen Points should provide the basis of the peace negotiations, implementing them fully would have created severe tensions between the USA and the other Allies. Although reparations were not included in the Fourteen Points, France and Belgium eventually gained US support for the principle of German compensation, but the final figure was not agreed until 1921 (see pages 46–48). Meanwhile, Britain won assurances that Point 2, which called for 'freedom of the seas', did not mean that the blockade against Germany had to be lifted immediately. However, these difficulties and the need for compromise were a clear indication that drawing up a peace treaty that would be acceptable to all sides was going to be a difficult process, as we shall see in Chapter 3.

Discussion point

In issuing his Fourteen Points, Wilson was accused of being far too idealistic. In what ways is idealism dangerous for a politician?

Fact

France and Prussia had gone to war in 1870 and Prussia had invaded and defeated France at Sedan, taking the provinces of Alsace and Lorraine and unifying the whole of Germany. The German Empire was proclaimed at the Palace of Versailles in 1871. The second invasion came in 1914, when German forces got close to Paris and were only halted by the Battle of the Marne in September of that year.

Questions

What did Clemenceau mean by 'America is very far from Germany, but France is very near'? What 'wrongs' did France feel needed to be righted?

balance of power This is an international situation in which the major powers or alliances have roughly equal power. It was believed that by achieving a balance of power, nations or alliances would not attack one another.

France

The main aim of French foreign policy in the period from 1870 to 1914 was security. France had been invaded by Germany twice in this time, and French leaders were determined that they would not suffer such humiliation again. Therefore, in 1918, security was still a priority for France.

SOURCE I

America is very far from Germany, but France is very near and I have preoccupations which do not affect President Wilson as they do a man who has seen the Germans for four years in his country. There are wrongs to be righted.

Georges Clemenceau, commenting on relations with the USA before the Paris Peace Conferences. Quoted in Mimmack, B., Senes, S. and Price, E. 2009. History: A Comprehensive Guide to Paper 1 for the IB Diploma. London, UK. Pearson. p. 25.

France's need for security

The French wanted Germany to pay for the suffering and humiliation it had inflicted during the Franco–Prussian War of 1870–71 and the First World War. Much of the fighting in the First World War had taken place in France, devastating French land and industry. The human cost was also high: two-thirds of the French army had been either killed or wounded. German land, industry and population had not suffered to the same extent, so France felt even more vulnerable to attack from Germany. As a result, prime minister Georges Clemenceau believed that restoring the **balance of power** in Europe was the best way of containing Germany in the future.

SOURCE J

There was an old system which seems condemned today and to which I do not hesitate to say that I remain to some extent faithful: nations organise their defence. It was very prosaic. They tried to have strong frontiers. This system seems condemned today by the very high authorities. Yet I believe that if this balance, which had been spontaneously produced during the war, had existed earlier: if, for example, England, America and Italy had agreed in saying that whoever attacked one of them had attacked the whole world, this war would never have taken place.

Statement by Georges Clemenceau to the French parliament, 1918. Quoted in Williamson, D. 1994. War and Peace: International Relations 1914–45. London, UK. Hodder. pp. 28–29.

Historians such as Anthony Adamthwaite have suggested that in fact Clemenceau wanted Germany broken up into a series of smaller states, and in particular the establishment of an independent Rhineland. This would crush Germany and ensure that it never threatened French security again. Such an interpretation makes Clemenceau seem cunning and cynical, living up to his nickname of 'the Tiger'. However, more recently, historians such as Margaret Macmillan have argued that Clemenceau himself did not want to punish Germany too severely, but that he was responding to public pressure for a 'harsh peace'. This inclination towards compromise can be seen in Clemenceau's response to David Lloyd George's **Fontainebleau Memorandum** (see Source K). Despite this, Clemenceau remained determined that France would never again have to defend itself from a German invasion.

Fontainebleau Memorandum
This was a document drawn up by British prime minister David Lloyd George in March 1919, near the town of Fontainebleau in France. In this document, he urged more lenient terms for Germany. Lloyd George did not want to see German-speaking peoples forced into other states, and argued that the financial terms imposed on Germany should not be so severe that they made reconstruction impossible.

SOURCE K

I said yesterday that I entirely agree with Mr. Lloyd George and President Wilson on how Germany should be treated; we cannot take unfair advantage of our victory; we must deal tolerantly with people for fear of provoking a surge of national feeling. But permit me to make a fundamental objection: Every effort must be made to be just toward the Germans; but when it comes to persuading them that we are just to them, that is another matter. Do not believe that these principles of justice that satisfy us will also satisfy the Germans.

Georges Clemenceau's response to David Lloyd George's Fontainebleau Memorandum. From http://tmh.floonet.net/articles/fontainebleaumemo.htm

Territorial issues

French aims at Versailles were thus geared towards preventing a German recovery. This was to be achieved by imposing reparations, redrawing the frontiers of Germany, limiting its armed forces and excluding it from the League of Nations. More specifically, France wanted the return of **Alsace-Lorraine** and the annexation of the Saarland (an area of Germany on the French border, which was rich in iron and coal deposits), as well as the left bank of the Rhine. These gains would help complete a natural French boundary and increase the country's security.

At the same time, Clemenceau supported the restoration of Belgian sovereignty. The French were also concerned about restraining Germany in Central Europe. In the past, France had looked to Russia to act as a buffer against German aggression, but with the Russian Revolution and the rise of communism, this was no longer realistic. France therefore wanted the creation of a strong and independent Poland and Czechoslovakia, both of which would be able to restrain German ambitions. In addition, the French wanted to preserve their wartime links with both the USA and Britain. This would provide a further guarantee of security, as well as helping rebuild France's damaged economy through continued Allied financial and economic co-operation.

Alsace-Lorraine An area of land on the border between France and Germany. It had been under French rule until seized by Germany in the Franco–Prussian War of 1870–71. The region was largely French-speaking, and was rich in raw materials.

Discussion point

Historian Margaret Macmillan has commented that French aims at the Paris Peace Conferences were 'punishment, payment, protection'. What evidence is there to support this view?

29

Britain

British prime minister David Lloyd George is often seen as occupying the middle ground between the USA and France – seeking a balance between Clemenceau's desire for revenge and Wilson's idealism.

SOURCE L

We want a peace which will be just, but not vindictive. We want a stern peace because the occasion demands it, but the severity must be designed, not for vengeance, but for justice. Above all, we want to protect the future against the horrors of this war.

David Lloyd George, in a speech to the House of Commons before the Paris Peace Conferences, 1919.

dominions These were former territories of the British Empire that had been granted self-government. Britain's dominions included Australia, Canada and South Africa.

However, this view of Lloyd George does not survive closer scrutiny, particularly over the issue of reparations. Lloyd George had just fought a general election in which he was forced to respond to public demands for a harsh peace, or face defeat. He was also under pressure from the **dominions**, which wanted a share of the reparations. At the peace talks, therefore, the British wanted to 'endeavour to secure from Germany the greatest possible indemnity she can pay consistently with the well being of the British Empire and the peace of the world without involving an army of occupation in Germany for its collection'.

The naval threat

Central to British interests at the peace conferences was concern over the German naval threat. By June 1917, the German U-boat campaign (see page 23) had resulted in the loss of 500,000 tonnes of British shipping, and London was believed to have only six weeks' worth of food left. At the same time, Britain did not want a single strong power controlling the whole of the Channel coast. It was thus necessary for Britain to help re-establish Belgian strength, to prevent either Germany or France dominating the area in the future.

Fact
Following its surrender at the end of the war, the German fleet had been taken to Scapa Flow – a stretch of water off the Orkney Islands in Scotland, where there was an important British naval base. Rather than hand the fleet over to the British, the Germans scuttled (deliberately sank) their own ships in June 1919, as a final act of defiance.

The German ship Hindenburg *sinks after being scuttled by its crew in Scapa Flow, June 1919*

The Fontainebleau Memorandum

Lloyd George's aims can be seen most clearly in the Fontainebleau Memorandum (see page 29), issued on 25 March 1919 during the peace conferences. In it, he called for reconciliation in Europe and, more importantly, argued that unless Germany regarded the treaty as fair, there was little hope of a lasting peace. It should be remembered that even at this early stage, Britain had already achieved some of its aims, which may explain Lloyd George's more lenient attitude. The threat from the German navy had disappeared after the German fleet was scuttled at Scapa Flow. The German Empire was dismantled and much of its former territory was in British hands. Germany was also no longer a major trade rival – at least in the short term.

Question

Why do you think David Lloyd George issued the Fontainebleau Memorandum?

SOURCE M

To achieve redress our terms may be severe, they may be stern and even ruthless, but at the same time they can be so just that the country on which they are imposed will feel in its heart that it has no right to complain. But injustice, arrogance, displayed in the hour of triumph, will never be forgotten or forgiven.

Extract from David Lloyd George's Fontainebleau Memorandum, 25 March 1919. From http://tmh.floonet.net/articles/fontainebleaumemo.htm

Activity

Compare and contrast Lloyd George's message about the treatment of Germany in his Fontainebleau Memorandum with Clemenceau's response in Source K (page 29). Why do you think they have such different views?

The communist threat

Lloyd George was also concerned about the threat of communism in the post-war world.

SOURCE N

The whole existing order in its political, social and economic aspects is questioned by the masses of the population from one end of Europe to the other. The greatest danger that I see in the present situation is that Germany may throw her lot in with Bolshevism and place her resources, her brains, her vast organising power at the disposal of the revolutionary fanatics whose dream is to conquer the world for Bolshevism by force of arms. The danger is no mere chimera [illusion].

Extract from David Lloyd George's Fontainebleau Memorandum, 25 March 1919. From http://tmh.floonet.net/articles/fontainebleaumemo.htm

Questions

What reasons does Lloyd George give in Source N for treating Germany fairly? How reliable is the source as evidence of Lloyd George's view of how Germany should be treated?

The British prime minister believed that if Germany was humiliated and stripped of its resources, this would create the ideal breeding ground for communism. A strong and united Germany, however, would provide a barrier to the spread of communism. Lloyd George believed that provoking a German desire for revenge would only lead to another war, so he was keen to ensure that Germany did not lose too much of its border lands.

Theory of knowledge

History, empathy and motives

The historian R. G. Collingwood (1889–1943) said: 'All history is the history of thought'. By this, he meant that we can only understand people's actions in the past by trying to discover what was in their minds and what their motives were. He thus stressed the importance of empathy in trying to see a situation in the same way people did at the time. The motives of the leaders of the Allied powers after the First World War are a matter of debate. Is it possible ever to discover their true motives?

Although Britain supported the idea of French security, it also wanted to avoid continental commitments and to ensure that no single country dominated mainland Europe. In practice, this meant that Lloyd George did not want France to become too powerful. He therefore encouraged the restoration of the traditional balance of power in Europe – a policy that had guided British attitudes to foreign affairs throughout the 19th century.

Lloyd George's attitude towards Germany may have masked an ulterior motive. Before the war, Germany had been Britain's second-largest trading partner, and if the British economy was to recover in the post-war years, it was essential that Germany was allowed to buy British goods.

The 'Big Three' and the expectations of Italy and Japan

In order to win the support of other nations in the war, Britain and France made promises to a variety of countries, most notably Italy and Japan, but also Romania and Greece. However, at the end of the war Britain and France faced the problem of balancing the promises made against the principles of the Fourteen Points. The 1915 Treaty of London, for example, promised Italy the northern coast of Dalmatia, Trieste and South Tyrol, and a protectorate over Albania, but much of this went against Wilson's concept of self-determination.

The situation was further complicated in April 1919, when the Italians presented the Council of Four (see page 12) with additional territorial demands that were not included in the Treaty of London. The war had put a huge strain on the Italian economy, and the country was experiencing a rise in social and political unrest. The government therefore hoped that if it could obtain significant rewards at the Paris Peace Conferences it would be able to strengthen its position with the Italian public.

However, the 'Big Three' nations had little sympathy for the Italians. At the outbreak of the war Italy had an agreement with Germany, and only joined the Allied war effort after April 1915. Italy was not treated as an equal at the peace conferences. It soon became clear that not only would the Big Three ignore Italy's additional demands, but they were also going to disregard some of the terms of the Treaty of London. Naturally this caused a great deal of discontent in Italy.

Activity

Find out what impact the First World War had on Japan. In what ways did the war improve Japan's international position?

The Allies' relationship with Japan in the immediate post-war period was similar to that of Italy. Japanese dissatisfaction soon developed at the peace talks, when it became clear that the Allies would not honour their promises of 1915 and 1917 (see page 21). Japan also felt that it was not being treated as an equal, but rather was being racially discriminated against.

The need for compromise

The conflicting aims of the major powers ensured that any peace would have to be a compromise. As Henig notes: 'The Treaty represented an uneasy compromise between Wilson's idealism, French security requirements and British pragmatism.' Wilson appeared to be too idealistic, particularly over the issue of self-determination, and this brought him into conflict with both Clemenceau and Lloyd George. Clemenceau in particular was angered by Wilson's attitude towards the future of the Saarland and the Rhineland regions.

However, there were also disagreements between Clemenceau and Lloyd George. The French prime minister believed that Britain's attitude towards Germany was inconsistent – encouraging leniency towards its position in Europe, but demanding harsher terms in regions where it threatened the British Empire.

These different views and the need to arrive at a settlement were complicated by the promises that had been made to other nations during the war. These promises particularly annoyed Wilson, as they were often in conflict with his principle of self-determination. The intense pressure to satisfy the public at home made the task even more difficult for all the politicians who attended the peace conferences.

The armistice that had been signed in November 1918 was only a temporary truce. The Allies continued to blockade Germany, causing more problems within the country and increasing the associated risk of public unrest or even the spread of communism. Meanwhile, the break-up of the Austro-Hungarian Empire resulted in the formation of new states, including Hungary, Czechoslovakia and Yugoslavia, which began to argue about their frontiers. The same was true in north-east Europe. The Treaty of Brest-Litovsk (see page 20) was annulled by Germany's defeat, but people in the areas taken from Russia in the treaty were determined to rule themselves, adding another potential threat of instability.

All these political circumstances made a quick resolution essential. However, as the following chapters will show, the conferences resulted in a compromise peace that satisfied no one, as the map of Europe was drawn and redrawn. The hopes and principles with which the leaders arrived in Paris were largely abandoned in the face of short-term political necessity.

Activities

1 Using the information in the section above, copy and complete the chart below to summarise the motives of the leaders of the 'Big Three' at the Paris Peace Conferences.

Country	Leader	Motives	Explanation
France			
USA			
Britain			

2 Make a list of the points of conflict between the different countries. How far does this help you to understand the difficulties facing the leaders at the Paris Peace Conferences?

3 Organise a class debate. Each of three groups should take the role of one of the Big Three powers at the Paris Peace Conferences and explain and justify its views as to the type of peace that should be reached. The rest of the class should then vote on which argument they find the most convincing.

4 'Why did the Allies disagree over the terms that should be offered to Germany at the peace conferences?'

Using the information in this section and any other sources available to you, plan an answer to this question.

33

Discussion point

US president Abraham Lincoln once called for those involved in war to 'do all which may achieve and cherish a just and lasting peace among ourselves, and with all nations'. To what extent is it possible to achieve a just and lasting peace?

What did Germany expect from the Paris Peace Conferences?

If there were disagreements among the Allies over what they hoped to achieve from the Paris Peace Conferences, there was far greater unity among the German people on what they expected. Germany had come close to winning the war in early 1918, and most of the population neither perceived themselves or expected to be treated as a defeated nation.

The military situation

In March 1918, the German army launched a massive attack, known as the Spring Offensive, against British and French troops. This initially came close to success, but exhaustion in the German army and the strength of the Allied forces – which had by now been reinforced by US troops – meant that the offensive ground to a halt.

The German command realised that this failure effectively sealed Germany's fate – the war was lost. They appealed first to the USA for an armistice, believing that the Americans would negotiate a more lenient peace than either the French or the British, especially if Germany removed the kaiser and introduced a new democratic regime.

On 4 October 1918, therefore, the German government asked President Wilson to bring about a ceasefire as a starting point for negotiations for a peace treaty that would be based on his Fourteen Points. Wilson agreed in principle, but warned the Germans that any suspension of hostilities would require the approval of Allied military commanders. The armistice was signed between Germany and the Allied commanders on 11 November 1918.

Revolution in Germany

The armistice was only possible because of a series of events that took place in Germany in the week leading up to 11 November. Unrest had started among the sailors at the naval base in Kiel in late October 1918. This was triggered by a call from naval commanders there for the fleet to put to sea in a last desperate bid to defeat the British. However, most of the sailors knew that the war was already lost. They refused to obey the order and took over the town of Kiel. Kaiser Wilhelm II failed to send troops to put down the mutiny, and this encouraged further strikes and demonstrations. Soon the German sailors were joined by war-weary soldiers.

The British naval blockade of Germany had caused severe food shortages – and even near-starvation in some areas – and this led increasing numbers of people to join the rebellion. By 6 November, soldiers and workers had taken control in many towns and cities across Germany, and had established a series of soviets, or workers' councils, to run the country. The aim of the rebellion was simply to bring about an end to the war, but many politicians regarded the action as the first step in a nationwide revolution, similar to the communist seizure of power in Russia in 1917.

The major political party in Germany, the Social Democrats, disapproved of the rebellion – and in particular the actions of the soldiers who had joined it. Nonetheless, members of the party warned Wilhelm II that unless he abdicated they would have little choice but to join the revolution. On 9 November, a general strike took place in Berlin and it appeared that events were spiralling out of control.

Fearing a wider revolution, the Social Democrats announced publicly that the kaiser had abdicated and proclaimed the establishment of a new German republic. This became known as the Weimar Republic, as the extent of the unrest meant that the new government was unable to meet in Berlin, and was instead forced to gather in the small city of Weimar, outside the capital. This republic would be run by a coalition of socialist parties. Two days later, Wilhelm II went into exile in the Netherlands.

The armistice

Faced with serious food shortages and public unrest, the new government of Germany was clearly in no position to continue the war. It immediately arranged an armistice, which stated that:

- German troops were to withdraw beyond the Rhine
- German territory on the left bank of the Rhine was to be occupied
- a 16-km (10-mile) zone on the right bank of the Rhine was to be fully demilitarised
- the Allies would garrison three points on the Rhine and establish 50-km (30-mile) **bridgeheads**
- the blockade of the German coast would continue
- Germany would be deprived of much war material, including submarines, surface fleet, transport and air force.

At the time, most Germans were unaware of the fact that their military leaders had informed the government that they could no longer maintain an offensive. Consequently, many Germans blamed the Weimar Republic for Germany's surrender, believing that Field Marshal **Paul von Hindenburg** was a hero who had been betrayed by a weak government. This 'stab-in-the-back' myth (*Dolchestosslegende*) later played an important part in the development of German anger towards the terms of the Treaty of Versailles and the Weimar Republic. Such attitudes also contributed to Hitler's rise to power in the 1930s and the eventual outbreak of the Second World War.

The problems facing the new provisional government

The new unelected provisional government faced several difficulties. Despite the Allies' insistence on a democratic form of government, Germans were not accustomed to democracy, so the Weimar Republic had to win the confidence of the people. This aim was almost immediately undermined by the signing of the armistice, which most Germans believed to be an act of cowardice. They called the government signatories to the armistice the 'November Criminals'.

The social and economic problems created by the war added to the difficulties of the new regime. German national income had dropped by two-thirds since 1913, and there was a huge gap between the living standards of rich and poor. Such problems were made worse by the food shortages resulting from the Allied naval blockade. Many people blamed the new government for the difficulties, rather than accepting that they were a consequence of the war. This further weakened the government's position.

bridgeheads This is a military term dating from the Middle Ages. It originally meant a fortification position to protect the end of a bridge. By the First World War, it had come to mean any large fortified area established by an invading force in enemy territory. These were sometimes (but not necessarily) created at strategic points along river banks.

Paul von Hindenburg (1847–1934) Hindenburg was a Prussian soldier who had fought in the German wars of unification. He was recalled from retirement at the start of the First World War and, alongside Erich von Ludendorff, took command of German forces in the east. His successes there resulted in his promotion to chief of general staff in 1916. Very popular in Germany, Hindenburg became president in 1925.

Freikorps These were groups of right-wing nationalist, anti-socialist and anti-communist soldiers. At the end of the First World War, they acted as armed vigilante squads against left-wingers. Members of the Freikorps also hated the democracy of the Weimar Republic.

Freikorps troops attack Spartacists besieged in a police building in Berlin, January 1919

Throughout December 1918 there were frequent clashes between the new government and its opponents. However, the first serious challenge came from the Spartacists in January 1919. This group of communist sympathisers captured the headquarters of the government newspaper and telegraph bureau, but they were unable to seize any other buildings. The rising did not win support from other left-wing groups and was easily crushed by the **Freikorps**, which the new president, **Friedrich Ebert**, used against the Spartacists. The leaders of the rising were executed. Communist unrest also erupted in other cities across Germany, where it was suppressed by the government with equal brutality.

After the armistice

Friedrich Ebert (1871–1925)
Ebert was a member of the German parliament (Reichstag) before the First World War. He was deputy leader, then leader, of the Social Democratic Party and became president of the Weimar Republic established at the end of the war. Although elected with 85% of the vote, Ebert's support began to decline after the devastating impact of the Treaty of Versailles on Germany in the 1920s. He remained president until his death in 1925.

The defeat in the war was a surprise for many Germans, particularly in light of press campaigns, the successes at the start of 1918 and the fact that Germany had not actually been invaded by the enemy. Most Germans also believed that responsibility for the war was not Germany's alone, and that all countries should share the blame – and the punishment, if one was to be imposed. They were encouraged by President Wilson's Fourteen Points, and trusted that his presence at the peace talks would ensure fair terms in the treaty that would formally end the war. After all, the kaiser had been overthrown and the new democratic government was not responsible for the war.

German leaders also believed that the Allies recognised the vulnerability of the new government. Ebert hoped that any demands would not undermine or further weaken this position, and felt that the threat of communist expansion – emphasised by the Spartacist uprising – would encourage the Allies to impose a just peace for the benefit of European-wide security.

36

Historical debates

Traditionally, historians such as David Williamson have taken the view that most Germans and, later, the provisional government, accepted Wilson's Fourteen Points as a basis for peace. However, more recent historical writing has argued that at first the Germans did not like the Fourteen Points. German newspapers denounced them as hypocritical, claiming they were part of the plan to achieve 'Anglo-Saxon world **hegemony**'. Henig argues that the German people only began to support the Fourteen Points when they realised that defeat was inevitable.

Historians such as Henig also challenge the claim that the Germans were expecting the peace treaty to be fully based on the Fourteen Points. Such commentators point out that the armistice was drawn up by military leaders, not the government, and was therefore unrelated to the Fourteen Points. These historians also claim that the Allies initially sought a 'just peace', as they feared firstly that German forces would resume fighting if the terms were too strict, and secondly that further conflict would weaken Germany to the point that it would be unable to resist the spread of communism.

hegemony The dominant influence of one region or country over others in political affairs. It can also refer to the power and influence of some social classes or groups over others.

An unstable peace

In view of the circumstances and military situation at the end of the war, many Germans expected to be treated mercifully at the peace talks. However, the terms of the armistice suggested that this was unlikely. More ominously, the defeated nations were not allowed representatives at the peace conferences. The Allies recognised that Germany had no alternative but to accept whatever terms were imposed, as it was in no position to keep fighting. They could therefore present the terms to Germany without negotiation.

In reality, whatever terms the Allies offered were likely to be regarded by the German people as a *diktat* – a dictated peace – because they had not been consulted in the process, nor did many of them believe that Germany had really lost the war. As a result, the eventual terms of the treaty created opposition to the new government and would, in the long term, weaken attempts at international co-operation.

Activities

1   In two groups, produce a front page each for a French and German newspaper on the eve of the opening of the Paris Peace Conferences. For each, explain the attitude of the public towards Germany's punishment.

2   Make a list of the problems facing the new German government at the end of the First World War. They should come under the following headings: Political, Social, Economic and Psychological. For each problem, explain how serious it was and give it a mark out of 5 – the higher the mark, the more serious the problem. Which problem was the most severe? Now write a paragraph to explain your choice.

3   Turn the above activity into a class debate. Each person should explain what they think was the most serious problem. After the explanations, take a vote to see if there is agreement.

4   'Was there a revolution in Germany at the end of the First World War?' Using the information in this section and any other available resources, draw up a chart to show evidence for both sides of this question. When you have completed the chart, decide on and explain your answer to the question.

End of chapter activities

Summary

You should now be aware of the difficulties that faced the peacemakers when they met in Paris in the early months of 1919, in terms of political, economic, financial and social problems. You should understand the political changes that took place in Europe as a result of the war, and how these affected international relations. In particular, you should recognise the significance of the emergence of communism in Russia, the fear that this generated in other European countries, and how it forced the peacemakers to speed up the process of reaching a settlement.

You should also be able to explain how these problems were heightened by the promises the Allies made to other countries to win their support during the war, and the expectations that those countries had going into the Paris Peace Conferences – particularly Italy and Japan. You should now be able to explain why public opinion was such an important factor at the peace conferences, and how far this limited the options available to the leaders. Finally, you should have an understanding of German hopes and expectations of the conferences, and how these were often in direct contrast to the aims of the 'Big Three'.

In light of all these issues, you should be able to explain the different aims and motives of the major powers at the conferences, as well as Germany, and assess the difficulties these would pose in reaching an agreement.

Summary activities

1 Copy the chart below, then complete it to show the attitudes of Clemenceau and Lloyd George towards the Fourteen Points.

Fourteen Points	Clemenceau	Lloyd George
1		
2		
3		
4		
5		
6		
7		
8		
9		
10		
11		
12		
13		
14		

2 Using the chart you drew up in the first activity, explain the attitudes of:
a Clemenceau towards Wilson
b Lloyd George towards Wilson
c Clemenceau towards Lloyd George

3 Consider the following possible aims of the Paris Peace Conferences:
- to establish a just and lasting peace
- to punish Germany
- to reward the victors
- to prevent Germany from starting another war.

Using the information in this chapter, which of the aims listed above do you think was the most important for the countries at the Paris Peace Conferences? What do you think *should* have been the order of priorities? Is there a difference?

Paper 1 exam practice

Question

What does Source A below suggest about British attitudes towards Germany at the end of the First World War?
[3 marks]

Skill

Comprehension of a source

Before you start

Comprehension questions are the most straightforward questions you will face in Paper 1. They simply require you to understand a source and extract two or three relevant points that relate to the question. Before you attempt this question, refer to page 212 for advice on how to tackle comprehension questions and a simplified markscheme.

39

SOURCE A

The prime minister and his principal colleagues were astonished by the passions they encountered in the constituencies. The brave people whom nothing had daunted had suffered much. Their feelings were lashed by the popular press into fury. The crippled and mutilated soldiers darkened the streets. Every cottage had its empty chair. Hatred of the beaten foe, thirst for his just punishment, rushed up from the heart of deeply injured millions. In my own constituency of Dundee, respectable, orthodox, life-long Liberals demanded the sternest punishment for the broken enemy. All over the country the most bitter were the women, of whom seven million were the first time to vote. In this turmoil, state policy and national dignity were speedily engulfed.

Winston Churchill, writing about the election campaign of 1918. Quoted in Siracusa, J. M. 2010. Diplomacy. Oxford, UK. Oxford University Press. p. 47.

Student answer

Churchill suggests that the attitudes of the British public towards Germany were far harsher than those of politicians. He puts forward the view that the public wanted the harshest possible punishment inflicted on Germany, even though he acknowledges that Germany was already broken. This desire is shown through the use of words such as 'hatred'. However, he also notes that the public believed that such a punishment was justifiable, perhaps because of the 'empty chairs' and 'crippled and mutilated soldiers' that he comments on. Churchill also believed that the attitude of women towards Germany was far harsher than that of men, possibly because many women had lost husbands.

Examiner comments

This is a very thorough answer, which identifies more than two points about public attitudes towards Germany. The student uses some brief quotations to support the views put forward; this is acceptable, as the answer does not rely on large amounts of text copied out without showing an understanding of the passage. The answer shows a clear comprehension of the views offered in the source, the difference in attitudes between politicians and the public, and the harsher attitudes of women. As a result of making at least three relevant points based on the source, this would be awarded the maximum 3 marks.

Paper 2 practice questions

1 Analyse the ways in which Europe was affected by the First World War.

2 Assess the view that Germany suffered more than France in the First World War.

3 Why was it so difficult for the Allied leaders to reach an agreement over the terms to be imposed on Germany at the end of the First World War?

4 Assess the reasons why the leaders of the Allied nations had different aims at the Paris Peace Conferences of 1919.

5 'Britain and France were concerned about their national interests, the USA by the ideals of peace and justice.' Explain the reasons for these views.

6 'Idealistic and impractical.' Analyse the arguments for and against this view of President Wilson's Fourteen Points.

7 Examine why German hopes of a fair and just peace were unrealistic.

8 Analyse the role of public opinion in affecting the aims of the Allied leaders at the Paris Peace Conferences of 1919.

3 The peace treaties of 1919–20

Key questions

- What were the main terms of the Treaty of Versailles?
- What was agreed in the other peace treaties?
- How did the various nations react to the peace treaties?

Overview

- The peace treaties that evolved throughout 1919 and 1920 were largely the work of the Big Three powers at the Paris Peace Conferences – the USA, Britain and France.
- The terms of the treaties were often compromises between these three nations. However, all treaties dealt with the issues of war guilt, land loss, military reductions, reparations and the establishment of the League of Nations.
- The 'War Guilt' clause was significant, as this justified enforcing reparations and other losses on the defeated powers. Germany was declared guilty of starting the war, reparations were imposed, large amounts of land – including its colonies – were taken away, and its armed forces were severely reduced.
- The treaties with Austria and Hungary created a series of new, weak states in central and south-eastern Europe, which experienced economic and political difficulties throughout the 1920s and 1930s.
- The initial treaty with Turkey caused a nationalist uprising. This ended with the overthrow of the government in Turkey, the establishment of a new republic, and a series of revisions being made to the treaty. These revisions resulted in the return of some of the land Turkey had lost by the original treaty.
- Turkey's successful challenge to the treaty showed the relative weakness of the Allies in enforcing their terms. This situation was made worse by the USA's failure to ratify (formally approve) the treaties.
- Whether the terms of the treaties were too harsh has been the subject of much historical debate. Soon after Versailles, many people in Britain expressed concern about the severity of the conditions imposed on Germany.
- The need for compromise among the Big Three powers meant that the Treaty of Versailles satisfied none of the main Allies.
- Germany believed that the terms of the Treaty of Versailles were too harsh. The German government objected to the War Guilt clause, the scale of reparations, the limits on its armed forces and the overall loss of status that resulted from the treaty.

Timeline

1919 **19 Jan:** Paris Peace Conferences begin

25 Mar: Fontainebleau Memorandum issued by Lloyd George

Apr: Treaty of Versailles completed

7 May: draft treaty handed to Germany

16 Jun: final treaty given to Germany

28 Jun: Germany signs Treaty of Versailles

20 Jul: Treaty of St Germain submitted to Austria

10 Sep: Austria signs Treaty of St Germain

27 Nov: Treaty of Neuilly signed with Bulgaria

1920 League of Nations established; US Senate votes against joining; British granted mandate for Palestine; French granted mandate for Syria

Jan: Clemenceau defeated in French elections

4 Jun: Treaty of Trianon signed with Hungary

10 Aug: Turkey signs Treaty of Sèvres, prompting nationalist uprising led by Mustafa Kemal

1921 **Mar:** Russian Civil War ends

Apr: Reparations Commission fixes German debt

1922 **Sep–Oct:** crisis in Turkey ends in nationalist victory

1923 **24 Jul:** Treaty of Lausanne signed with Turkey

The four main leaders gathering at the Paris Peace Conferences: (left to right) David Lloyd George, Vittorio Orlando, Georges Clemenceau and Woodrow Wilson

What were the main terms of the Treaty of Versailles?

State of the Union An annual speech given by the US president, in which he delivers an assessment of the state of the country and outlines his legislative agenda for the coming year.

The Paris Peace Conferences finally began on 19 January 1919, nine weeks after the signing of the armistice. The delay was partly due to the political situation in both the USA and Britain. In America, Woodrow Wilson had to deliver the **State of the Union** speech in December; in Britain, David Lloyd George and his coalition partners had a general election to win, in order to get parliamentary approval for any decisions made at the conference. At the same time, there were debates about where the conferences should be held. Initially, Geneva was suggested as a location, but in the end the Palace of Versailles in Paris was chosen. In some ways, this decision was controversial: it was in the Hall of Mirrors at Versailles that the German nation had been proclaimed in 1871 (see page 28), so issuing Germany's punishment for the First World War from the same venue might be thought of as revenge.

The Paris Peace Conferences and the Treaty of Versailles: an overview

The conference at Versailles was to be a showpiece. It had its own printing press and telephone lines, and there was even a direct daily air link from Paris to Croydon, near London, to improve communication between the two capital cities. Despite these arrangements, though, the conference lacked clear organisation or formal procedures.

Early discussions January–March

The opening was attended by delegates from 27 states (although 32 nations were ultimately represented). However, little progress was made in the first two months, partly due to organisational difficulties, but also because the representatives from each country were more concerned with resolving the immediate problems facing post-war Europe. Food supplies had to be found for people who were starving in Central and Eastern Europe. There were also financial and economic challenges, such as negotiating the surrender of the German fleet in return for easing the wartime blockade (see page 30). In order to deal with these issues, a Supreme Economic Council was established. Time was also spent discussing whether or not the Allies should intervene in the Russian Civil War.

Discussions about the terms were not attended by all 32 states. Instead, special commissions and committees were established (58 in total) to draft the clauses of the treaty. However, as there was no central co-ordinating body, the committees often came up with conflicting solutions. The most important group at the conferences was the Council of Ten, which was made up of the prime ministers and foreign ministers of France, Britain, the USA, Italy and Japan. Any state that hoped to gain something from the peace terms had to submit its request in writing to the Council of Ten, and then appear before the Council to argue its case. This slowed progress considerably.

Changes in process

Traditionally after a war, peace conferences took place in two stages. A preliminary peace was agreed as soon as possible, but this was followed later by an international congress to finalise the agreement. This method ensured that peace terms were not decided in the bitterness of the immediate post-war period, and defeated nations were allowed to participate in the international congress. However, several people – most notably the French general **Ferdinand Foch** – argued that if this process was adopted after the First World War, Germany would use it to gain more lenient terms. After the first few weeks of the peace talks, therefore, it was decided to drop the idea of a preliminary peace and move more quickly towards a final agreement so that Germany did not exploit the growing differences between the Allied powers.

It was only after Lloyd George issued his Fontainebleau Memorandum (see page 29) in March that the conference became more efficient. Fears that delays would drive Germany towards communism encouraged changes in procedures. The major powers held secret discussions about the need to offer Germany some concessions. The Council of Ten was replaced by the Council of Four (Britain, France, the USA and Italy), which would make the key decisions.

The terms of the treaty

Many of the decisions at Versailles were only agreed when the conference appeared to be on the brink of collapse as nations threatened to walk out. This meant that many of the terms were compromises, designed simply to keep the peace process alive. However, in June 1919, the Treaty of Versailles was finally signed. This was the first and most important of the post-First World War peace agreements, and the basis for all the other treaties that resulted from the peace talks.

Fact

Following the Bolshevik Revolution in October/November 1917, civil war broke out in Russia. The victorious Bolsheviks faced opposition from forces known as the 'Whites', who fought a bitter war against the rule of the communist 'Reds'. The war continued until 1921, when the Whites were defeated.

Questions

Why do you think only the main powers were involved in the decision-making at Versailles? What weaknesses can you identify in the organisation of the Paris Peace Conferences?

Ferdinand Foch (1851–1929)

Foch had been commander of the French military academy, but during the First World War he commanded troops in northern France. He was appointed chief of general staff in 1917, and finally commander of combined allied forces in 1918. Foch signed the armistice with Germany in November 1918.

43

The final version of the Treaty of Versailles was over 200 pages long and contained 440 clauses. Some of these were very detailed, particularly where the transfer of territory was concerned. Other clauses were surprising – for example, the treaty ordered the return of astronomical instruments to China and an African chieftain's skull to Britain. However, discussions in the first months of the peace talks focused on five main areas:

- the formation of the League of Nations
- responsibility for the outbreak of the war
- reparations for the cost of and damage caused by the war
- the redistribution of territories in Europe and colonies
- disarmament.

The League of Nations

Wilson had proposed the formation of the League of Nations in his Fourteen Points, and it was the first issue considered at the peace talks. This was a triumph for Wilson, who believed that it was key to all other negotiations. Eventually, the League's **covenant** became a feature of all the peace treaties after the First World War, forming the first 26 clauses in each. A commission drew up a draft constitution for the League, and agreement was reached by mid February 1919. This was largely the result of a series of meetings between US and British legal experts.

However, during the discussion process it became clear that each of the Big Three had different views about the structure and purpose of the League.

The USA's view

Wilson was driven by the ideals that had brought the USA into the war in the first place, stating that 'merely to win the war was not enough. It must be won in such a way as to ensure the future peace of the world.' He believed that this future peace could only be achieved through the League, which would allow nations to discuss their differences. Wilson suggested that if the European powers had 'dared to discuss their problems for a single fortnight in 1914 the First World War would never have happened. If they had been forced to discuss them for a whole year, war would have been inconceivable.' The US delegation therefore wanted the League to operate like a world parliament, where representatives of all nations reached decisions on matters that affected them.

The British and French views

Meanwhile, the British sought to avoid anything as formal as a world parliament. They preferred the idea of a loose organisation that met when there was an emergency. In contrast, the French imagined the League to be more of a military alliance – an organisation that would enforce the peace treaties, ensure France's future security, prevent Germany from recovery, and intervene in disputes as necessary.

The debate about the League was a clear indication of disagreement between the USA, Britain and France right from the start. The problems arising from the final agreement on the League of Nations' role and structure are discussed further in Chapter 5.

covenant This was the document that established the rules and regulations of the League of Nations. It explained how each institution would function, how decisions would be reached and the role of each body within the League.

44

Question

What were the advantages of discussing the establishment of the League of Nations at the start of the conferences?

Responsibility for the outbreak of the war

It was vital to establish responsibility for the outbreak of the war early on in the peace talks, as this was ultimately linked to who would pay for it. There was little doubt in the public mind that Germany was almost solely responsible, and this made it difficult for leaders at the conference to express any other opinion. A Commission on the Responsibility of the Authors of the War and on the Enforcement of Penalties was established and given the task of assigning responsibility for the outbreak of the war. This commission consisted of representatives from Britain, Belgium, Italy, France, Japan, Greece, Poland, Romania and Serbia. The commission's findings are summarised in Source A.

SOURCE A

Responsibility rests first on Germany and Austria, secondly on Turkey and Bulgaria. The responsibility is made all the graver by reason of the violation by Germany and Austria of the neutrality of Belgium and Luxemburg, which they themselves had guaranteed. It is increased, with regard to both France and Serbia, by the violation of their frontiers before the declaration of war.

Extract from the Commission on the Responsibility of the Authors of the War and on the Enforcement of Penalties report, 1919. Adapted from www.firstworldwar.com/source/commissionwarguilt.htm

This resulted in Clause 231 of the Treaty of Versailles, which became known as the 'War Guilt' clause.

SOURCE B

The Allied and Associated Governments affirm and Germany accepts the responsibility of Germany and her allies for causing all the loss and damage to which the Allied and Associated Governments and their nationals have been subjected as a consequence of the war imposed upon them by the aggression of Germany and her allies.

Clause 231 of the Treaty of Versailles, June 1919.

The War Guilt clause provided the legal argument for Germany to pay the costs of the war, and Clause 232 stated that Germany must compensate the Allies for 'all the damage done to the civilian population of the Allied and Associated powers'. This implied that in addition to reparations for physical damage, Germany was also accountable for **war pensions**. Germany was also required to pay compensation for the violation of the 1839 Treaty of London and for the destruction of neutral Belgium.

Question

Why was it important for the Allies to establish that Germany and its supporters were responsible for the outbreak of the war?

Question

On what grounds do you think the commission argued that Germany and Austria were more responsible for the outbreak of war than Turkey and Bulgaria?

45

war pensions Money given to those wounded during the war who were unable to work as a result of those wounds, or to the families of those whose husbands had been killed fighting in the war.

Fact

The 1839 Treaty of London was signed by Britain, Austria, France, Prussia, Russia and the Netherlands, and recognised the independence and neutrality of Belgium. In 1914, Germany overlooked this treaty and asked Britain to do the same, but Britain refused. When Germany invaded Belgium, therefore, Britain honoured its agreement to protect Belgium and declared war on Germany.

Reparations

At the time of the Paris Peace Conferences, no one yet knew how much damage the war had caused. This made it difficult to assess how much the cost of reconstruction would be. The major powers also had different views about the purpose of reparations.

France wanted to use reparations to prevent Germany's economic recovery and therefore limit any future threat to French security. Britain believed that German recovery was essential for the economic reconstruction of Europe as a whole, and British trading relationships in particular. However, British leaders had to balance this more moderate view against the strength of public opinion against Germany. They also needed reparations in order to reduce Britain's financial burden and repay its war loans from the USA. US leaders agreed more with Britain than France, but certainly did not believe that Germany should escape without any financial punishment.

Reparations were seen as a way of covering the costs of the war. Britain had covered one-third of its war expenditure by public taxation, and France had covered one-sixth in the same way. However, both countries needed reparations to meet the shortfall, and neither wanted to risk social unrest by either raising taxes or cutting public spending. The importance of reparations became even more apparent when the USA refused to cancel the Allied war debts. As a result, in March 1919 Britain withdrew the financial assistance it had been providing to France.

This placed France in even more desperate need of reparations, causing internal disagreement about which policy to follow. The finance minister and the Chamber of Deputies (as well as much of the French press) wanted Germany to pay the maximum possible, whilst the minister for reconstruction argued that France needed immediate cash and should therefore accept a moderate sum, which Germany could raise more quickly by selling bonds on the international market.

SOURCE C

Many paragraphs of the Treaty, and especially in the economic sections, were in fact inserted as 'maximum statements' such as would provide some area of concession to Germany at the eventual Congress. This Congress never materialised: the last weeks of the conference flew past us in a hysterical nightmare; and these 'maximum statements' remained unmodified and were eventually imposed by ultimatum.

Harold Nicholson, a member of the British delegation, writing in 1933. Nicholson, H. 1933. Peacemaking 1919. Safety Harbor, USA. Simon Publications. p. 100.

Questions

What does Nicholson mean by 'maximum statements'? Nicholson was present at the Paris Peace Conferences as a member of the British delegation. Does this make his evidence reliable?

The British also pursued a policy of seeking the maximum possible reparations. This was partly in response to public pressure, but there were also concerns that if the total figure was low there would be little money left once France and Belgium had taken what they needed to repair the physical damage in their countries. It was for this reason that Britain's Imperial War Council included the request that war pensions be added to the costs (see page 45). There was some disagreement about this, and Lloyd George got his way only by threatening to walk out of the conference.

These disputes resulted in the formation of the Reparations Commission, set up to investigate what Germany could afford to pay. Germany immediately made an interim payment of 20 billion gold marks. In December 1919, the Reparations Commission established a 25:55 ratio for payments between Britain and France. Belgium would receive full compensation for its damage, partly because it had been a neutral country, but also because the Belgian delegation threatened to leave the talks if these terms were not agreed.

A German cartoon from 1922 showing the French squeezing the Germans for reparations

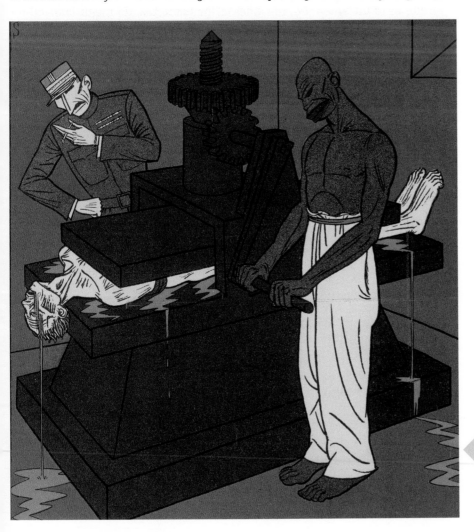

Activity

What is the message of this cartoon? Explain your answer by reference to both details from the cartoon and your own knowledge. Write a paragraph explaining why the issue of reparations was so important to leaders at the conferences.

Historical debate

The issue of reparations has been very controversial amongst historians. The debate about to how much Germany could afford to pay dates back to the 1920s, when John Maynard Keynes attacked what he saw as the folly of the reparations clauses and argued that they ignored 'the economic solidarity of Europe, and by aiming at the economic life of Germany, it threatens the health and prosperity of the allies themselves'. This view was successfully challenged by Etienne Mantoux, writing in 1944, who argued that the productivity of German industry in the 1930s showed that the country could meet the level of reparations demanded. More recently, Sally Marks argued that the only obstacle to Germany paying reparations was its attitude.

The final sum for reparations was not settled on by the commission until 1921. In fact, this worked to Germany's benefit, as if the final cost had been established at Versailles it would probably have been much higher than the sum eventually agreed on. The demands made in 1919 were excessive, as leaders tried to satisfy public expectations while memories of the war were still fresh. However, the lack of agreement at Versailles over a definite figure for reparations created problems in the future – it appeared that Germany had handed over a blank cheque to the Allies in 1919.

SOURCE D

If this round sum had been named in the Treaty, the settlement would have been placed on a more business-like basis. But this was impossible for two reasons. Two different kinds of false statements had been widely promulgated, one as to Germany's capacity to pay, the other as to the amount of the Allies' claims in respect of the devastated areas. The fixing of either of these figures presented a dilemma. A figure for Germany's prospective capacity to pay would have fallen hopelessly short of popular expectations both in England and in France. On the other hand, a definite figure for damage done which would not disastrously disappoint the expectations which had been raised in France and Belgium might have been open to damaging criticism on the part of the Germans.

Extract from economist John Maynard Keynes' book The Economic Consequences of the Peace, *published in 1919.*

Covering the cost

The issue of how Germany would cover the cost of reparations caused much controversy, both within the country at the time and amongst historians.

SOURCE E

It is evident that Germany could have paid a good deal more if she had chosen to do so, particularly since she paid little out of her own considerable resources. But Germany saw no reason to pay and from start to finish deemed reparations a gratuitous insult.

Sally Marks (1978). 'The Myths of Reparations'. Central European History, 11, pp. 231–255 doi:10.1017/S0008938900018707

Activity

Compare and contrast the views of John Maynard Keynes and Sally Marks in Sources D and E on this page about the level of reparations. Why do you think they have such different opinions?

SOURCE F

The Allies have made a stern and uncompromising reply to Rantzau's [the German foreign minister] pleas that German industry will be ruined and her population rendered destitute by the economic terms of the Peace Treaty. The reply points out that the terms have been determined by Germany's capacity to pay, not by her guilt; and the Huns are reminded that as they were responsible for the war they must suffer the consequences as well as other nations. The German delegation has left Spa [a town in Belgium where the German delegation was based] to consult with their Government, probably with the idea of arranging a means for 'saving their face', as it is now believed they will sign the Treaty.

Extract from the British newspaper The People, *25 May 1919. Quoted in Walsh, B. 2009.* Modern World History. *London, UK. Hodder. p. 11.*

Questions

What is the opinion of writer of this article in *The People* about the scale of reparations? Why do you think the newspaper would have such a view? How accurate do you think this view is?

There was disagreement among the Allies about how much Germany could afford to pay. Britain estimated that Germany could pay £24 billion, although the British economist John Maynard Keynes argued that £2 billion was the maximum. Wilson declared himself 'not much interested in the economic subjects'. In the end the sum agreed upon was £6.6 billion. If these terms had not been modified later, Germany would have continued making payments until 1984.

The form of payments

There was also the question of what form reparation payments would take. The gold reserves in the German Central Bank were not enough, so much of the payment would need to take the form of goods, including coal, cattle and even fishing boats.

The Germans were instructed to hand over all merchant ships of more than 1600 tonnes, half of those between 800 and 1600 tonnes, and a quarter of their fishing fleet. An additional 200,000 tonnes of shipping was to be built for the Allies each year for the next five years. Germany had to deliver coal and timber to France, Belgium and Italy. It was also ordered to meet the cost of the Allied occupation force.

The Germans considered the sum agreed on for reparations to be excessive, but recent work by historians suggests that the payments could have been met if Germany had the political will. Indeed, this view was expressed by some contemporaries as well.

Theory of knowledge

History, perception and reality
No two groups of people are likely to see things in the same way; their perceptions are usually shaped by differing interests, emotions and prejudices. Recent historical research has suggested that Germany could afford to pay the reparations, but Germany perceived the amount to be too great. How far do you agree with the view that what matters in history is not reality, but the perception of events?

49

Redistribution of territories

The situation in Europe

The collapse of empires in Central and Eastern Europe, with the disintegration of the German, Austro-Hungarian and Turkish empires, provided the opportunity for a redistribution of land along national lines. However, in practice this was not always possible, as new states needed economic resources in order to remain independent. As a result, a significant number of minorities found themselves within the boundaries of other nations once the new national borders were drawn. The most notable example of this was in the new state of Czechoslovakia, which contained large numbers of both Germans and Magyars (Hungarians).

Germany lost 10% of its land, 12.5% of its population and, as a result of land losses, 16% of its coalfields and nearly 50% of its iron and steel industry. Most of these territorial changes were in the east, but there were some losses in the west.

A map showing the loss of German land in Europe after the First World War

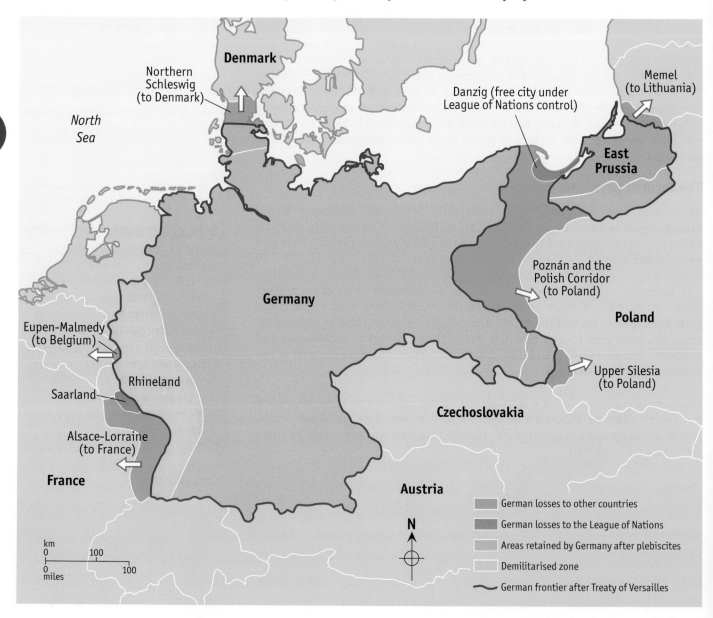

Western Europe

In the west, Alsace-Lorraine was returned to France. This area had been taken by Germany in the Franco–Prussian War (see page 8) and its return was universally expected at the peace conferences. The resources in this region would assist in France's economic recovery. Also in the west, Belgium won the regions of Eupen and Malmedy from Germany. The area of Schleswig was seized by Prussia in 1864, and parts of it were heavily Danish in population. A plebiscite (see page 15) was held to decide its future; the northern area was returned to Denmark, whilst the south remained with Germany.

The Saarland

The French initially hoped to gain the Saarland – an area rich in coal and iron ore – as it had historically been settled by French peoples and was only granted to Prussia in the Treaty of Vienna in 1814. France also requested that the Rhineland – which formed the frontier between France and Germany – be made into an independent state, giving France greater security. However, neither of these aims was satisfied.

Once it was apparent that France would not gain the Saarland, the French suggested that the industrial and mineral-rich north of the region should be detached from Germany and placed under an independent non-German administration. The French argued that they should have ownership of the coal mines as compensation for the damage done to their mines in the Nord and Pas de Calais regions, where much of the First World War was fought. However, Wilson opposed these proposals as they went against his strong belief in self-determination. Lloyd George negotiated a compromise, by which France would receive coal from the mines, but the Saarland itself would be placed under League of Nations control for 15 years. After this time, its inhabitants would decide their own future through a plebiscite.

The Rhineland

The future of the Rhineland created similar clashes. The creation of a separate Rhineland state would almost certainly fuel German bitterness. Britain was also afraid that it would drastically alter the balance of power in Europe in favour of the French. In the end, it was agreed that an army of occupation would be stationed west of the Rhine, with three bridgeheads at Cologne, Koblenz and Mainz. The area was divided into three zones, which would be evacuated at five-year intervals, with full demilitarisation to be complete after 15 years. In return, an Anglo–American treaty was drawn up which promised protection for France in the case of attack. Although this satisfied French concerns about security in the short term, the USA's later refusal to ratify the Treaty of Versailles rendered it meaningless. After the US pulled out, Britain also refused to honour its part in the protection agreement.

Poland

Territorial issues in the east were no easier to solve, particularly the question of Poland. The re-establishment of an independent Poland was important to both the USA and France. It would create a strong nation on Germany's eastern border, which would benefit France. As far as Wilson was concerned, independence for Poland was necessary to fulfil his principle of self-determination. However, Poland would need the economic means to maintain its independence – and this meant finding a way to give it access to the sea. German lands would thus need to be annexed by the new Poland. Lloyd George, in particular, was concerned about the bitterness and resentment this would generate in Germany.

51

Curzon Proposal Lord Curzon was the British foreign secretary from 1919 to 1924. He gave his name to the original boundary between Poland and Russia that was agreed at the peace conferences. This line was later moved further east following Polish seizure of land during the Russian Civil War.

Polish Corridor A territory defined by the Treaty of Versailles, made up of land that was formerly part of West Prussia. It was designed to give the new state of Poland access to the sea, and effectively separated Germany from East Prussia.

The new state of Poland was initially awarded the regions of Upper Silesia, Poznán and West Prussia from Germany. In addition, in December 1919, the **Curzon Proposal** attempted to mark out Poland's eastern borders with Soviet Russia.

Poland needed access to the sea and a port for its economic survival. Danzig, situated at the mouth of the Vistula River, was the best option; however, Danzig was mainly a German town surrounded by a Polish area. Lloyd George worked out a compromise by which Danzig would become a free city under the control of the League of Nations, but with its foreign policy decided by Poland. The '**Polish Corridor**' allowed access to this vital economic region.

As a result of the creation of Poland, the German nation was split in two. It lost around 2 million of its citizens in the east, along with large amounts of raw materials, particularly coal. In addition, Germany had to return all the land taken through the Treaty of Brest-Litovsk with Russia in 1918. As a consequence of Wilson's principle of self-determination, this resulted in the establishment of the Baltic states of Lithuania, Latvia and Estonia.

Former German colonies

The Allies all agreed that German colonies that were seized during the war should not be returned. However, the main powers had different opinions on exactly what should be done with them.

A map showing German colonies in Africa and whose mandates they became by the Treaty of Versailles

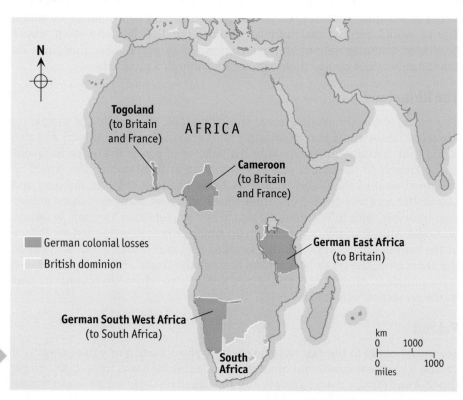

Activity

Carry out some further research on the impact on Germany of the loss of its colonies.

Wilson opposed the outright seizure of the colonies by the victorious nations, enforcing once more his belief in self-determination for colonial peoples. Instead, Wilson wanted these regions to be run as **mandates** by more politically advanced nations. These countries would help the former colonies develop into modern states under the supervision of the League of Nations.

Lloyd George agreed with Wilson, believing that the mandate system was 'virtually a codification of existing British practice'. However, the British dominions of South Africa, Australia and New Zealand were concerned about their own security, and wished to annex German South West Africa, New Guinea and Samoa respectively. Meanwhile, Japan had already secured British agreement to keep the former German lands it had seized north of the Equator. These demands caused conflict with the USA, as Wilson was determined to uphold Point 5 of the Fourteen Points (see page 25).

The South African prime minister, **Jan Smuts**, proposed a compromise. He suggested that the mandates should be divided into three categories based on the stage of development of the population, the economic conditions and the geographical situation of the territory. The dominions and Japan were willing to accept this, although they wanted the mandatory states to be named immediately. However, the USA objected – Wilson did not want to give the impression that the victorious powers were carving up lands as if they were the spoils of war.

Although Wilson was the first to suggest the mandate system, he was not happy with the terms on which they were to be administered, which favoured the British dominions and Japan. The US grew increasingly concerned about Japanese influence in the Pacific region (see page 9). In the end, however, the threat of Japan leaving the conference forced Wilson to accept the compromise. Smuts' ideas were adopted as a 'provisional decision', which would be reconsidered by the League of Nations once its constitution had been drawn up.

The mandates themselves were allocated in May 1919. Some historians have argued that it was decisions such as this that helped turn the **US Senate** against the Treaty of Versailles and ultimately led it to reject the post-war peace settlements.

The loss of its colonies (and also its trading rights in both China and Egypt), had a significant impact on the German economy, as the country lost access to vital raw materials and consumers for its industrial goods.

Disarmament

Disarmament was a crucial issue at the Paris Peace Conferences. It was widely believed that the arms race in the years leading up to the First World War had contributed to its outbreak in 1914. In particular, the size and power of the German military was of serious concern to the French, as their country had been invaded twice in just over 40 years. It was this that prompted France's unsuccessful call for the establishment of a Rhineland republic to provide a buffer zone between the two nations (see page 51).

mandates Territories formerly belonging to Germany or Turkey that were taken away following their defeat and placed under the administration of another country – often Britain or France – under the supervision of the League of Nations. The aim was to prepare the country for independence.

Jan Smuts (1870–1950)
Smuts had led the Boer forces during the Boer War between Britain and South Africa (1899–1902), but later supported co-operation with Britain. During the First World War, he led South African forces against German South West Africa. He was prime minister of South Africa 1919–24 and again in 1939–48, and fought for the British during the Second World War.

US Senate The Senate is part of the US central government. Along with the House of Representatives it makes up Congress. These two houses make laws and decide on issues such as taxation and war. Congress can accept or reject policies.

53

In general, the Allies agreed that Germany must reduce its armed forces 'to the lowest point compatible with internal security'. However, there was disagreement about what form this should take. Both Britain and the United States sought an end to conscription in Germany, but the French did not want Germany to have a professional army at all. In the end the US won the argument, and the following terms were decided:

- Germany was allowed an army of 100,000 professional soldiers (a quarter of the number that Britain had been willing to allow).
- Soldiers could serve for 12 years, which prevented the establishment of a well-trained reservist force.
- Restrictions were placed on the number and size of guns, and Germany was not allowed any armoured vehicles.
- The German navy was restricted to only six battleships of over 10,000 tonnes, six light cruisers, and 12 destroyers and motor torpedo boats; it was also forbidden to build any submarines and the base at Heligoland, an island in the North Sea off the German coast, was to be destroyed.
- The Germans were banned from having any military aircraft.

The Allies imposed these restrictions in order to make possible 'the initiation of a general limitation of armaments of all nations'. However, this global limitation was never carried out. The Disarmament Commission – part of the League of Nations – was established to oversee the reduction and destruction of the weaponry of the defeated powers.

Other elements of the Treaty of Versailles

Other features of the Treaty of Versailles were also designed to limit German power. Germany was forbidden to unite with Austria, for example (a measure that later had severe economic implications for Austria). German leaders – now called 'war criminals' – were to be punished for their part in starting the war. Kaiser Wilhelm II had fled to the Netherlands at the end of the war, but the terms of the treaty stated that he should be handed over to a tribunal to be tried for 'a supreme offence against international morality and the sanctity of treaties'. Despite widespread calls from the public to 'hang the kaiser', however, the Dutch government refused to hand him over, arguing that it was against international law. Those Germans who had violated the 'laws and customs' of war were also to be put on trial, and the Allies drew up a list of alleged war criminals. Most of these people were never arrested, though.

Activities

1 Imagine you are either a French or German journalist on the day that the Treaty of Versailles was published. Write an editorial for your newspaper on the subject of the treaty.

2 Create a summary chart to show the main terms of the Treaty of Versailles. You could set it out as shown in the example below.

Land losses	Colonial losses	Military reductions	Economic punishments	Other

Question

Do you think the terms of German disarmament were fair?

Discussion point

How different were the terms of the Treaty of Versailles to Wilson's Fourteen Points?

54

3 In light of the terms of the Treaty of Versailles, construct a spider diagram to show why the Germans resented it.

4 For each of the reasons you have identified in the spider diagram, award a mark to indicate how serious an issue it was for the German people. Which term caused the greatest hostility? Write a paragraph to justify your choice.

What was agreed in the other peace treaties?

Once the treaty with Germany had been agreed, the leaders of the Allied powers returned home and left their officials to draft the treaties with Germany's former allies. However, even before these had been drawn up and ratified, a settlement in Eastern Europe and the Balkans had been reached.

The Russian Empire disintegrated after the Bolshevik Revolution of 1917. This was followed by the collapse of the Austro-Hungarian Empire after the last Habsburg emperor abdicated on the day the armistice was signed. This led to the separation of Austria and Hungary, both of which argued that they were not the successors to the Austro-Hungarian Empire and, as a result, should not be treated as aggressors. The Poles and Czechs also declared their independence, whilst the South Slavs joined with Serbia to form what later became Yugoslavia. Despite these developments, the complexity of the ethnic frontiers in Europe meant that the final treaties were certain to cause conflict in the future.

The treaties all followed a similar pattern to the Treaty of Versailles, with the same five main areas of discussion (see page 44).

The Treaty of St Germain with Austria 1919

The Treaty of St Germain was submitted to the Austrians on 20 July 1919, but they did not sign it until 10 September. Despite the claims of the new state, the Allies regarded Austria as the successor to the old Austro-Hungarian Empire, and felt it should be punished in the same way as the other defeated powers. By formally accepting the treaty, Austria not only acknowledged the break-up and separation of the old empire, it also recognised the independence of the new republic of Czechoslovakia. Austria also accepted that it was forbidden to unite with other countries without the approval of the League of Nations. In practice, this meant that Austria recognised that union (*Anschluss*) with Germany would never take place – France would never approve such a move if it came before the League.

Like Germany, Austria was required to pay reparations. However, it had lost a great deal of land and nearly all its industry, and in 1922 the Bank of Vienna collapsed. As a result, Austria never made any reparations payments. In addition, the Austrian army was reduced to a force of just 30,000.

The loss of land after the break-up of the empire also meant that Austria lost a large part of its population (a decline of 15 million compared with the old kingdom of Austria). In the south of the region, the Italian border was moved to the Brenner Pass. Italy therefore took control of the former Austrian regions of South Tyrol, Trentino, Istria and Trieste, which contained large numbers of ethnic Germans.

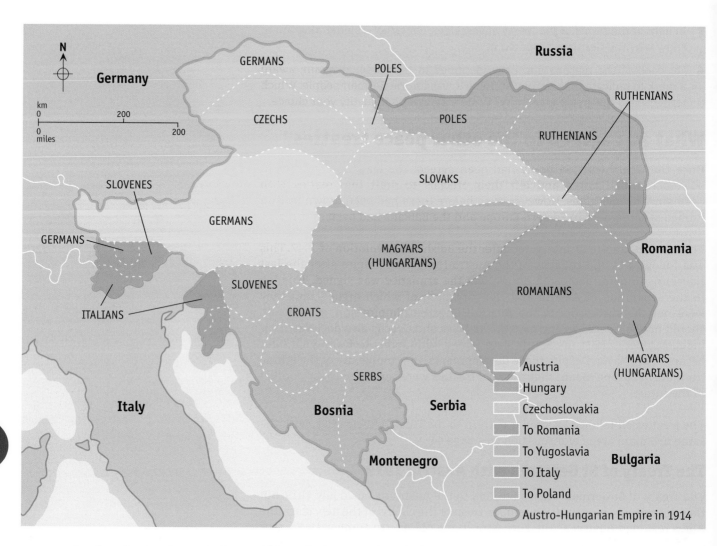

A map showing the break-up of the Austro-Hungarian Empire, the new successor states and the locations of the main nationalities

Napoleonic Wars These were the wars fought between France, under its ruler Napoleon Bonaparte, and several other nations – including Britain, Austria, Prussia and Russia. The wars ended in Napoleon's defeat at the Battle of Waterloo in 1815. The French defeat left Austria as the dominant power in mainland Europe, a position it maintained for just over 30 years.

Although these territorial changes had a significant impact on Austria, they were not intended to be a punishment. Rather, they were part of the creation of a series of self-determined 'successor' states that came to dominate eastern and south-eastern Europe. The Kingdom of Serbia, which became Yugoslavia in 1929, gained Bosnia and Herzegovina. Land was also taken from Austria to create both Czechoslovakia and Poland. Galicia was given to Poland. Bohemia and Moravia were granted to Czechoslovakia. One consequence of this arrangement was that 3 million German speakers found themselves in the Sudetenland in Czechoslovakia. This was part of the French plan to establish a strong ally in the region to protect them from future German or Austrian aggression.

The Treaty of St Germain ended any claim Austria had to be a great European power, which was a major change from its status at the end of the **Napoleonic Wars** in 1815. Austria objected to the treaty mainly because the principle of self-determination – which had been used to justify the break-up of the old state – was not applied to Austria itself. However, the Austrians had little choice but to accept the terms.

The Treaty of Trianon with Hungary 1920

As with Austria, the Allies regarded Hungary as a successor to the old Austro-Hungarian Empire. Despite Hungary's claims that it should not be considered an aggressor state, the Allies imposed similar punishments on Hungary as they had on Austria.

Although the Treaty of Trianon was drawn up in 1919, political problems meant that it was not signed until 1920. Firstly, Czech and Romanian troops moved in and occupied parts of Hungary they claimed for themselves. Meanwhile, within Hungary the revolutionary **Béla Kun** established a communist state in 1919. Initially he succeeded in driving out the Czechs, but Kun was overthrown by the Romanians in 1920 and his government was replaced by a military dictatorship under former naval commander Admiral **Miklós Horthy**. This brought greater stability to the country and eventually allowed the Treaty of Trianon to be ratified.

As with Austria, by signing the treaty Hungary acknowledged the break-up of the old empire and agreed to pay reparations (although the collapse of the Hungarian economy meant that these were never paid). The military terms of the Treaty of Trianon also limited Hungarian forces to an army of 35,000 for the purpose of internal security.

However, the loss of Hungarian territory was more significant even than that imposed on Austria, and many historians have argued that Hungary was the most severely treated of all the defeated powers. The new state lost land on all frontiers – amounting to around two-thirds of its pre-war territory – and nearly 42% of its population.

Béla Kun (1886–1938) Before the First World War, Kun worked as a journalist. He fought for Austria-Hungary in the war, was captured, and spent time as a prisoner of war in Russia, where his left-wing sympathies developed into full communism. After the war, Kun returned to Hungary and established a short-lived communist state there in 1919. Following his defeat he went into exile in Russia, before becoming a victim of Stalin's purges in the 1930s.

Miklós Horthy (1868–1957) During the war, Horthy was a commander in the Austro-Hungarian navy. In 1919, he helped to overthrow Béla Kun's communist state, and was named as regent of the Kingdom of Hungary, although he never allowed the monarchy to be restored. Horthy then headed a fascist-style dictatorship that lasted until 1944.

57

SOURCE G

C. A. Macartney, an expert on Hungary and the successor states, comments on the difficulties of applying the principle of self-determination in the drawing of new borders.

The ethnical line was practically nowhere clear cut. Long centuries of interpenetration, assimilation, migration and internal colonisation had left in many places a belt of mixed and often indeterminate population where each national group merged into the next, while there were innumerable islands of one nationality set in seas of another, ranging in size from the half-million of Magyars speaking Szekely in Transylvania through many interdeterminate groups of fifty or a hundred thousand down to communities of a single village or less. No frontier could be drawn which did not leave national minorities on at least one side of it.

Quoted in Williamson, D. 1994. War and Peace: International Relations 1914–45. London, UK. Hodder. p. 40.

Question

What problems does Macartney suggest there were in drawing up territorial boundaries after the First World War?

58

In the north, Slovakia and Ruthenia were given to the new state of Czechoslovakia. In the east, Romania gained Transylvania; whilst in the south Slovenia, Croatia and part of Banat were given to the Kingdom of Serbia (later Yugoslavia). However, it was the loss of the German-speaking area of Burgenland to Austria that caused the greatest resentment, and soured relations between the two nations for many years after the treaties.

The treaty created a great deal of bitterness in Hungary. Lost territory resulted in around 3 million Magyars coming under foreign rule, despite the principle of self-determination. Many Hungarians felt that whenever a conflict of interests about boundaries arose between Hungary and other states, the decisions always went against Hungary. At the same time, Romania – which had fought with the Allies since 1916 – seemed to be the main beneficiary of Hungarian losses, largely because of France's determination to prevent Russia from gaining access to the Mediterranean Sea. Thus, security concerns seemed to have superseded those of self-determination.

The Treaty of Neuilly with Bulgaria 1919

Bulgaria joined the war in 1915 in support of the Central Powers, and as a result it was treated as a defeated power at the Paris Peace Conferences. Most historians claim that Bulgaria was not treated as harshly as the other defeated nations, largely because it played only a small part in the war. However, some historians have suggested that the Allies were afraid that Bulgaria would take advantage of the new, weak states to dominate south-east Europe, creating future instability. These historians argue that as a result, the Allies aimed to restrain Bulgaria by reallocating some of its territory (to Romania in particular) and setting its reparations payments at £100 million.

As a result of the Treaty of Neuilly, Bulgaria was forced to formally recognise the new state of Yugoslavia and the borders between the two nations were also adjusted, restraining Bulgaria's influence in the region. More importantly, Macedonia and Western Thrace were given to Greece; this meant that Bulgaria lost its access to the Aegean Sea, although it was allowed to transport goods through the port of Dedeagach in Thrace. Some Bulgarian land was also given to Romania, as the Allies continued their policy of strengthening it as a buffer state. Most notably, the formerly shared region of south Dobruja was granted to Romania, even though the Romanian population there numbered just 7000 out of a total 250,000. Despite all these territorial losses, however, Bulgaria was the only defeated nation to also be *granted* land by the peace treaties – winning part of western Turkey.

Allied concerns over Bulgaria's potential dominance were also reflected in their decision to restrict the Bulgarian army to 20,000, which ensured that it would not be able to challenge the new regional balance that the Allies had established. By the end of the peace talks, Greece and Romania had replaced Bulgaria and Turkey as the major powers in the Balkans.

The Treaty of Sèvres with Turkey 1920

Turkey fought on the side of the Central Powers, but even before the First World War its empire was nearing a state of collapse; the war only hastened its decline.

The initial Treaty of Sèvres with Turkey was the result of a compromise between France and Britain. The aims were to ensure that Turkey would not cause Balkan unrest in the future and to settle the **Eastern Question**, which had dominated much of European diplomacy throughout the 19th century.

Lloyd George wanted Greece to fill the power vacuum created by the break-up of the Turkish Empire. He hoped to achieve this by depriving Turkey of its major European centre of Constantinople and taking away its control of the Dardanelles and the Bosphorus (see map), thus ending its control of access to and from the Black Sea. Lloyd George also wanted Turkey to be stripped of all territory that did not have an ethnic Turkish majority. However, this brought Britain into disagreement with France, which had invested heavily in Turkey before the First World War, and wanted to protect those investments by ensuring that the Turkish state remained viable. In particular, the French wanted the Turkish government to remain in Constantinople, where it would be easier to control.

Like the other defeated powers, Turkey had to pay reparations. However, economic interest in the state went much further than simply extracting money. An Allied financial committee was established, with the right to inspect Turkish finances and work out the scale of its debts. This intrusion angered the Turks, and was later successfully challenged.

In terms of land losses, Turkey suffered a large-scale break up of its former empire. In Europe, it was left with only a small area of land around the city of Constantinople as Smyrna and Eastern Thrace were given to Greece. In fact, encouraged by the Allies, the Greeks had already occupied Smyrna in May 1919 – an action that angered the Turks and did much to inspire the nationalist movement that later developed under the leadership of **Mustafa Kemal**.

> **Mustafa Kemal (1881–1938)**
> Kemal was a nationalist leader who led resistance to the Treaty of Sèvres. He became a national hero during the First World War when he helped defeat the Allies at Gallipoli (see page 60). Kemal objected to the loss of Turkish land through the Treaty of Sèvres, particularly Smyrna and Armenia. He successfully resisted the terms of the treaty and became president of the new republic. Kemal attempted to establish a secular state, encouraging westernisation. In 1934, he took the title 'Ataturk', meaning 'Father of the Turks'.

A map showing the break-up of the Turkish Empire, 1919

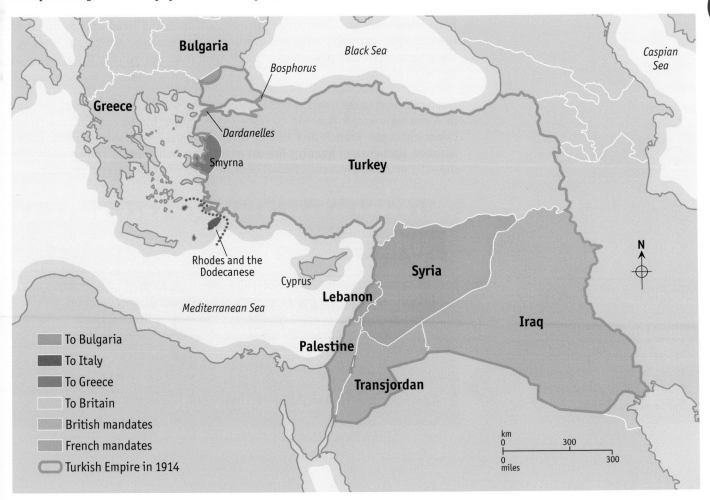

Fact

The Congress of Berlin was the second meeting that followed a crisis in the Balkans in 1875–78. There was a rising against Turkish rule, which resulted in Turkey being reduced in size and the establishment of a series of states that owed allegiance to Russia. However, this threatened Austria's influence in the region and the major powers met in Berlin to resolve potential conflict between Russia and Austria. The congress ensured that Russia's power in the Balkans was limited.

Gallipoli A military campaign in the First World War, which lasted from April 1915 to January 1916. Allied troops landed on the Gallipoli peninsula with the aim of marching on to Constantinople. The campaign was a failure.

Italy was also awarded land from Turkey, taking Adalia, Rhodes and the Dodecanese Islands. Britain officially gained Cyprus (although in reality the British had occupied the island since the Congress of Berlin in 1878). The important sea route of the Dardanelles and Bosphorus was placed under an international commission and opened to all ships, allowing access into the eastern Mediterranean.

Turkish land in both North Africa and the Middle East was also redistributed. Egypt, Tunisia and Morocco all became independent, under the protection of Britain and France. In the Middle East, Arabia gained independence, but Britain was granted Palestine and Iraq as mandates, providing it with valuable oil resources. France gained Lebanon and Syria as mandates, and was also granted shares in the Turkish Petroleum Company. The areas of Armenia and Kurdistan were granted independence, and Armenia also gained access to the Black Sea across Turkey. In line with Lloyd George's demands, Turkey lost all its lands without an ethnic Turkish majority. In addition, Turkish armed forces were reduced to just 30,000.

The terms of the Treaty of Sèvres were harsh and humiliating, and resulted in a growing Turkish nationalist movement led by Mustafa Kemal, the hero of **Gallipoli**. In order to enforce the treaty, the Allies decided to keep troops in Turkey, and a combined Allied force entered Constantinople in March 1919. The Allies also forced the sultan (the Turkish ruler) to dismiss his cabinet and declare Kemal a rebel. This decision pushed Kemal into a direct challenge of the government and the Allies, which threatened to become a full-scale war. Kemal's forces moved towards Constantinople, where Allied troops were stationed. France and Italy were unwilling to resist, but Lloyd George persuaded them to allow Greek forces to advance and head off the threat to the city. This was successful, and eventually Turkey signed the treaty. However, the government was powerless to implement it and eventually the sultan was forced to abdicate.

Over the next three years, Kemal continued to win support. By 1922, he was in a strong enough position to once again gather his forces and march on Constantinople. French and Italian troops left the city, leaving British forces isolated. Rather than fighting, Britain negotiated an armistice and agreed to the drawing up of a new treaty. Kemal became head of a new Turkish republic.

SOURCE H

The catastrophe which Greek recklessness and Allied procrastination, division and intrigue had long prepared now broke upon Europe. The signatories of the treaty of Sèvres had only been preserved in their world of illusion by the shield of Greece. That shield was now shattered.

Winston Churchill. Quoted in Williamson, D. 1994. War and Peace: International Relations 1914–45. *London, UK. Hodder. p. 43.*

Question

To what extent did events in Turkey during 1920–22 prove that Churchill's view, as expressed in Source H, was correct?

The Treaty of Sèvres had ignored the changes that were already taking place within Turkey, particularly the growth of nationalism and the dissatisfaction with the old system of government. In order for the treaty to be successful, the Allies needed to ensure it was signed before Kemal's support grew too great. However, as Source H shows, the fact that it was not signed until August 1920 meant that the treaty was impossible to enforce.

The new treaty was signed at Lausanne in Switzerland in 1923. It resulted in Turkey taking back some of the land it had lost. The clashes with Greece had already forced the Greek king to abdicate, and Turkey now regained Smyrna and Eastern Thrace, whose loss had been largely responsible for the outbreak of the conflict. Turkey also regained the Aegean islands of Imbros and Tenedos. All this went some way to restoring Turkish national pride, which had been so badly damaged by Sèvres.

The new treaty also resulted in the withdrawal of Allied troops from Turkey, and an end to reparation payments and checks on Turkish finances. The limits on Turkish armed forces were also abolished. Turkey won back control of the Dardanelles and the Bosphorus straits. However, as Kemal also wanted to avoid dependency on Russia, he agreed to the demilitarisation of both sides of the straits and freedom of navigation through its waters. In return for the settlement, Turkey renounced all claims to territory outside its new boundaries and guaranteed the rights of minorities living within its borders. A separate agreement was reached with Greece for the compulsory exchange of minorities, with Turks living in Greece being returned to Turkey and vice versa.

Although the threat of war was averted, the Treaty of Lausanne did not solve all the problems in the region, and was criticised within France, Britain and the USA. The treaty had not resolved tensions with Greece (a fact that became clear later in the 20th century, with the dispute over ownership of Cyprus). The Arabs were disappointed – they had expected the Allies to support their right to independence, and were worried by the emergence of Palestine. However, perhaps the greatest significance of Lausanne lay in the circumstances in which it came about. The Turks had overthrown the original Treaty of Sèvres by force within four years of Versailles. Turkish actions raised doubts about Allied willingness to enforce the treaties, and encouraged other states to use force as a means of resolving political issues.

How did the various nations react to the peace treaties?

As discussed in Chapter 2, the Allies entered the Paris Peace Conferences with very different motives and aims. These differences became increasingly apparent as the talks progressed.

The traditional view of the conferences is that there were frequent clashes between Clemenceau and Wilson, with Lloyd George acting as mediator and forcing through compromises. However, this view is too simplistic. France clashed with Britain over Lloyd George's desire not to treat Germany too harshly. Clemenceau stated: 'If the British are so anxious to appease Germany they should look overseas and make colonial, naval or commercial concessions.'

61

This conflict arose because Britain seemed to be content to show Germany leniency in Europe (where Britain would not be affected and France felt threatened), but was less willing to compromise over imperial and naval issues (which affected Britain more directly). There were also disagreements between Britain and the USA over some elements of the Fourteen Points, most importantly self-determination and free access to the seas for all nations.

The Treaty of Versailles was drawn up very quickly – by the end of April 1919 – and handed to the German representatives on 7 May. Its content represented compromises by all the major powers, and therefore no one was fully satisfied. Because of the extent of the debates and disagreements, the original plan of inviting the defeated powers to join the discussions after a preliminary peace had been drawn up was abandoned. The Germans were given 15 days (later extended by a week) to comment on the terms. They raised many objections, causing the British to push for modifications. These included Germany's immediate admission to the League of Nations, a reduction in the length of the military occupation of the Rhineland, and reduced reparations. However, the USA argued against making changes for reasons of political expediency. The Germans finally signed the original treaty on 28 June 1919.

The British reaction to the treaties

In many ways, Britain was the most satisfied by the terms of the peace treaties. Colonial issues had been resolved as the British had hoped, and the threat from the German navy had already been eliminated with its sinking at Scapa Flow (see page 30). Britain was not overly concerned about mainland Europe, although it did want to ensure that a balance of power was maintained there. This was mainly achieved by preventing the break-up of Germany, which would have left France as the dominant power on the continent.

SOURCE 1

A fair judgement upon the settlement, a simple explanation of how it arose, cannot leave the authors of the new map of Europe under serious reproach. To an overwhelming extent the wishes of the various populations prevailed.

Winston Churchill, speaking in 1919.

Discussion point

Churchill comments that the 'wishes of the various populations prevailed'. To what extent is history shaped by the wishes of the people rather than politicians?

Although Britain's main concerns were resolved by the Treaty of Versailles, the British were worried about the harshness of the terms imposed on Germany. The treaties of Trianon, St Germain and Neuilly caused fewer concerns for Britain, but the situation with Turkey was another matter. The initial Treaty of Sèvres had increased the size of the British Empire considerably, causing some to question Britain's motives at the peace conferences – particularly the Arabs, who gained little in return for their support of Britain during the war. However, the Treaty of Lausanne that replaced Sèvres did little to resolve the tension between Greece and Turkey, and caused concerns for Britain.

The opinions of France and the United States

Both France and the USA were unhappy with some elements of the Treaty of Versailles. Wilson had been forced to compromise many of his ideals, and the fair and just peace he had sought for Germany was modified at nearly every stage. As a result, the US refused to ratify the treaty or to join the League of Nations.

SOURCE J

Looking at the Conference in retrospect there is much to approve and much to regret. It is easy to say what should have been done, but more difficult to have found a way for doing it. To those who are saying that the Treaty is bad and should never have been made and that it will involve Europe in infinite difficulties in its enforcement, I feel like admitting it. But I would also say in reply that empires cannot be shattered and new states raised upon their ruins without disturbance. To create new boundaries is always to create new troubles. The one follows the other. While I should have preferred a different peace, I doubt whether it could have been made, for the ingredients for such a peace as I would have had were lacking at Paris.

Edward House, one of Woodrow Wilson's closest advisors, writing in his diary, 29 June 1919.

Activity

What was Edward House's opinion of the Treaty of Versailles? What does he mean by the comment, 'the ingredients for such a peace as I would have had were lacking at Paris'? Is it a valid comment? How similar is the view expressed in Source I (page 62) to this?

63

The French were far from satisfied with the Treaty of Versailles. They felt that it did not cripple Germany sufficiently, and that as a result their own security remained threatened. This was reflected in the results of the French election in January 1920 – Clemenceau was defeated because the French people believed that he had been too willing to compromise at the Paris Peace Conferences.

France was also concerned about the treaties in Central Europe. These had created many small successor states that might, should Germany recover its power, be unable to withstand German demands for revisions to the treaties. In the period after the treaties had been agreed, therefore, French foreign policy focused on preventing German recovery and developing a series of alliances with the new states, to protect against future German aggression.

The Italian response

The Italians were very unhappy with the results of the peace conferences. Italy achieved few of its territorial and colonial ambitions, and the prime minister, Vittorio Orlando, walked out of the talks in anger at the terms his country was offered. His protest had no effect on the outcome of the conferences, and his government was blamed for what the Italian people regarded as a 'mutilated victory'. This contributed to the downfall of the liberal government in Italy and the rise of Benito Mussolini's fascist dictatorship (see page 120), with its promise of making Italy 'great, respected and feared'.

Many Italians believed that the land they gained by the treaties was not adequate compensation for either their contribution to the war effort or the effect the war had on Italy, which included 600,000 war dead, huge debts and serious inflation. The failure of the Italian government to meet public expectations was made clear by events at the port of Fiume in 1919. Italy had hoped to win Fiume in the treaties and when this was granted to Yugoslavia instead, the Italian writer and nationalist Gabriele D'Annunzio led 500 troops to the city and and managed to maintain control of it for a year before being forced to surrender.

The Japanese response

The Japanese were also angered by the terms of the treaties. Many Japanese felt that the Allied states considered them inferior and that the peace treaties ensured Japan's role as a second-rate power. Wilson's ideas of democracy and humanitarianism were regarded as ways of maintaining Western domination.

The 'racial equality' clause (part of the League's covenant and, by extension, the peace treaties) caused the most controversy. This had great symbolic meaning to the Japanese, who wanted to be treated with respect as a world power. However, people in the white British dominions and the USA feared that the clause would result in waves of oriental citizens overwhelming Western civilisation. In Japan, public meetings were held demanding an end to the discrimination, but in the USA politicians warned of the dangers to the white race if the racial equality clause was accepted. There was similar opposition from the British Empire delegations; Australia in particular was concerned about large-scale immigration. The clause did not pass, and historians such as Macmillan have argued that this turned Japan away from the West and towards an aggressive nationalist policy.

However, having defeated the Japanese on this clause, the Allies were forced to compromise with them on other points. As a result, Japan gained all the territories promised to it during the war, even though this went against Wilson's ideals of self-determination.

The German reaction

The German response to the Treaty of Versailles was, unsurprisingly, outrage. They were shocked by the terms and regarded it as a betrayal of the Fourteen Points. Newspapers carried articles criticising the terms of the treaty and the German people took to the streets in protest.

Germans march in protest at the annexation of Danzig as part of the Treaty of Versailles, April 1919

Questions

What do Sources K and L tell us about German reaction to the Treaty of Versailles? How useful are they as evidence of this reaction?

SOURCE K

Today in the Hall of Mirrors the disgraceful Treaty is being signed. Do not forget it! The German people will, with unceasing labour, press forward to reconquer the place among the nations to which it is entitled.

Extract from an article in the German newspaper Deutsche Zeitung, *28 June 1919.*

This view was later built on by the leader of the Nazi Party, Adolf Hitler, who exploited the general dissatisfaction to develop a strong sense of nationalism and desire for revenge amongst the German people.

SOURCE L

What a use could be made of the Treaty of Versailles. How each one of the points of that Treaty could be branded in the minds and hearts of the German people until sixty million men and women find their souls aflame with a feeling of range and shame.

Adolf Hitler, in his book Mein Kampf ('My Struggle'), published in 1925.

There were a number of reasons why Germany disliked the treaty.

- **War guilt and reparations**. This was probably the most important reason for German resentment. Many people felt that blame for the outbreak of the war should have been shared among nations and not solely apportioned to Germany. War guilt also meant that Germany had to cover the cost of the war, and many believed that the already shattered German economy would not survive these reparations.

- **Disarmament**. Many Germans argued that the level of disarmament left them vulnerable to attack and invasion. The army and navy were symbols of German pride and their loss was seen not only as a humiliation, but also a clear sign that the Allies were intent on destroying Germany as a great power. They also objected to the fact that other nations were not required to meet the same level of disarmament. However, these complaints ignored the simple fact that in the aftermath of the war, no nation was in a position to threaten Germany and most were more concerned about economic recovery. Germany was now surrounded by a series of new, weak states, so it was not vulnerable to threats from a strong military alliance.

- **Loss of land**. Germany lost a significant amount of land and with it valuable raw materials. These losses had a damaging effect on the economy and were also seen as an insult to national pride, as German lands and colonies were shared among the victors. It should be noted, however, that German territorial losses were fewer than those Germany itself had imposed on Russia in the Treaty of Brest-Litovsk (see page 20).

- **The Fourteen Points**. The Germans argued that the treaty did not follow the principles of the Fourteen Points. The Baltic states of Estonia, Latvia and Lithuania had all been granted independence, which upheld the principle of self-determination. However, a similar principle was not applied where there were significant numbers of Germans, most notably in West Prussia and the Sudetenland. This complaint was also made by Austria, which had been denied the right of any kind of unification with Germany.

Theory of knowledge

History, ethics and moral relativism

All the peace treaties made after the First World War have been criticised as unjust by some historians. How can you determine whether an action is just or unjust? Are there any 'universal principles'? Today, action against other sovereign states requires the assent of the United Nations. Does the international community, as represented by the United Nations, have the right to determine whether an action is just or unjust? Is the UN governed more by the interests of its most important members than by 'universal principles'?

The Germans were given the treaty on 7 May 1919, and soon demanded revisions to the terms. They wanted immediate membership of League of Nations, the establishment of a neutral commission to consider the issue of war guilt, and the opportunity for Austria and the ethnic Germans in the Sudetenland to decide if they wanted to join Germany.

Some minor changes were made to the treaty in response to German demands, but none was significant and the overall tone of the treaty remained the same. The Germans were presented with the final version on 16 June, and given five days to sign it. No one in Germany wanted to pay the political price of doing so – those who had signed the armistice had already been branded the 'November Criminals' and accused of having 'stabbed the country in the back'. The issue of whether or not to sign the Treaty of Versailles split the cabinet and caused the chancellor, Philipp Scheidemann, to resign. However, Germany was so weak it had little choice but to accept the terms. When the Germans finally signed the treaty, they did so noting that it was under duress.

Activity

Read Source M. Explain what the German government meant by 'surrendering to superior force but without retracting its opinion regarding the unheard of injustice of the peace conditions'.

SOURCE M

Surrendering to superior force but without retracting its opinion regarding the unheard of injustice of the peace conditions, the government of the German Republic declares its readiness to accept and sign the peace conditions imposed by the Allied and Associated governments.

Statement from the German government on the signing of the Treaty of Versailles. Quoted in Schultz, G. 1972. Revolutions and Peace Treaties 1917–1920. London, UK. Methuen. p. 189.

Most Germans did not feel that they had started the war, and many did not feel that they had lost it. They did not understand the scale of the defeat, and believed that the terms would be lenient because Germany had asked for the armistice. The Treaty of Versailles was therefore a great shock, and had an enormous psychological impact on the nation. This was later exploited by nationalists such as Hitler.

SOURCE N

The mistake the allies made, and it did not become clear until much later, was that, as a result of the armistice terms, the great majority of Germans never experienced their defeat at first hand. Except in the Rhineland, they did not see occupying troops. The Allies did not march in triumph into Berlin, as the Germans had done in Paris in 1871. In 1918 German soldiers marched home in good order, with crowds cheering their way; in Berlin, Frederich Ebert, the new president, greeted them with, 'no enemy has conquered you'.

Macmillan, M. 2001. Peacemakers: Six Months that Changed the World. London, UK. John Murray. p. 168.

There was a strong feeling that because Germany had agreed to a ceasefire, it should have been represented at the peace conferences to participate in the negotiations. According to the contemporary writer in Source O, the Allies made mistakes and were responsible for the hatred the treaty created.

SOURCE O

The Allies could have done anything with the German people had they made the slightest move toward reconciliation. People were prepared to make reparations for the wrong done by their leaders … Over and over I hear the same refrain, 'We shall hate our conquerors with a hatred that will only cease when the day of our revenge comes.'

Blücher, E. An English Wife in Berlin. 1920. London, UK. Constable and Co. pp. 302–4. Princess Evelyn Blücher was an Englishwoman who had married a member of the German royal family.

Activity

Margaret Macmillan (Source N) and Princess Evelyn Blücher (Source O) offer different interpretations of the possibilities of German acceptance of the treaty. Explain the views put forward by Macmillan and Blücher. Why do you think they differ? Blücher was writing at the time. Does that make her opinion more or less reliable?

Many historians now argue that it would not have mattered what the terms were: the Germans were simply unwilling to accept defeat or their role in the outbreak of the war. Indeed, they have been accused of double standards. In addition to the harsh terms imposed on the Russians by the Treaty of Brest-Litovsk, there was other evidence to suggest that if Germany had won the war it would have been equally severe on the Allied powers. The most compelling example of this is the 'September Memorandum' or 'September Programme', which Germany issued before the First World War and which appeared to set out its war aims. The memorandum suggested that these aims included the establishment of a central European customs and economic union, or *Mitteleuropa*, which involved the annexation of Luxembourg and some of France, and also control over Belgium and the Channel ports. In addition, the programme envisaged the release from Russia of the Baltic states and Poland, which would then come under German influence. A similar scheme was outlined for Africa. Such plans went far beyond the terms imposed on Germany at Versailles.

Were the Germans treated too harshly?

The Treaty of Versailles is one of the most controversial documents in history, and it was not only the Germans who considered it unfair. Many others at the time believed the terms of the treaty were too harsh.

SOURCE P

The impression made by the Treaty is one of disappointment, of regret, and of depression. The terms of peace appear immeasurably harsh and humiliating, whilst many of them seem to me impossible of performance.

Lansing's Memorandum, 8 May 1919. From Lansing, R. 1921. The Peace Negotiations, A Personal Narrative. London, UK. Constable and Co. pp. 244–45. Robert Lansing was US secretary of state and a member of the US delegation at the Paris Peace Conferences.

67

Much of the criticism of the treaty centred on two key issues: firstly the 'War Guilt' clause, which ignored the contribution of the Allied powers to the outbreak of war – notably Russian mobilisation; and secondly, the level of reparations that Germany was required to pay. Many argued that the reparations created great bitterness and prevented Germany regaining political stability in the post-war world, which led to serious problems for the new Weimar government.

Other complaints focused on the issue of disarmament. The defeated powers were the only nations that were disarmed, which left them feeling vulnerable and insecure. Critics have argued that the treaty was motivated by revenge and that this was clearly seen in the popular calls to 'make Germany pay' and 'hang the kaiser'. The nature of the proceedings – excluding the defeated powers from the negotiations – added to the feeling that the treaty was simply a *diktat*.

The politicians responsible for the treaty acted in very difficult circumstances. They had to find quick solutions to a range of complex problems. Europe was already in a state of crisis, so lengthy negotiations were not an option. It is also apparent, particularly from the results of the French election in 1920 (see page 63), that less harsh terms would have been unacceptable to the public in both France and Britain. The treaty should also be placed in a wider context and its terms compared with those that Germany imposed on Russia in the Treaty of Brest-Litovsk.

Nonetheless, since 1919, most historians have expressed the view that the terms of the Treaty of Versailles were too harsh and were likely to lead to another war. The French general Foch prophetically stated: 'This is not peace. It is an armistice for fifteen years.'

PEACE AND FUTURE CANNON FODDER

The Tiger: "Curious! I seem to hear a child weeping!"

A British cartoon published in May 1919 showing the leaders of Britain, France, Italy and the USA leaving the peace talks; in the background a child is crying

Activity

The caption underneath this cartoon reads: The Tiger [Clemenceau]: 'Curious! I seem to hear a child weeping!' Why would Clemenceau have been surprised to hear a child crying after the conferences? Who or what does the child represent? How far does this cartoon support Foch's view that Versailles was simply an armistice?

The peace treaties: an assessment

When assessing the merits and failures of the Treaty of Versailles it is important to consider a number of points. To begin with, the First World War was the most terrible conflict the world had experienced at that time, and the peacemakers were determined that war on this scale should never occur again. As a result, they wanted to weaken Germany so that it could not invade France again. In 1918, many were convinced that German military ambition had been a main cause of the war; the German military thus had to be so severely reduced that it could not threaten peace again.

Secondly, the terms could have been a great deal more severe, especially in view of the strong desire for revenge among the victorious nations. The Germans were spared the creation of a Rhineland republic, while a call to put the kaiser on trial was rejected. Thirdly, it could be argued that many of the terms would not have come as a surprise to the Germans. When they signed the armistice in November 1918 they knew that they would lose territory, pay reparations and have their armed forces reduced. This always happened to defeated powers at the end of a war. The Germans had imposed similarly harsh terms in the recent past. In 1870, they made the French pay 5 billion francs and placed German troops in France until the payment was made. The Treaty of Brest-Litovsk took away a quarter of Russia's farmland and population.

SOURCE Q

If they could have done better, they certainly could have done much worse. They tried, even cynical old Clemenceau, to build a better order. They could not foresee the future and they certainly could not control it. That was up to their successors. When war came in 1939, it was a result of twenty years of decisions taken or not taken, not of arrangements made in 1919.

Macmillan, M. 2001. Peacemakers: Six Months that Changed the World. London, UK. John Murray. p. 500.

However, some historians still believe that Versailles was a failure. They consider that the terms were so harsh that the decisions made at the conferences were responsible for the outbreak of the Second World War only 20 years later.

SOURCE R

The historian, with every justification, will come to the conclusion that we were very stupid men. I think we were. We came to Paris, confident that the new order was about to be established; we left it convinced that the new order had merely fouled the old. We arrived determined that a Peace of justice and wisdom should be negotiated: we left it, conscious that the treaties imposed upon our enemies were neither just nor wise.

Nicolson, H. 1933. Peacemaking 1919. Safety Harbor, USA. Simon Publications. p. 186.

SOURCE S

In the end, Versailles proved a colossal failure for Woodrow Wilson, for the United States, and for the future of a world that had hoped it might be governed by the principles of freedom and self determination – even today. Covenants of peace were not openly arrived at. Freedom of the seas was not secured. Free Trade was not established in Europe; indeed, tariff walls wound up being erected, higher and more numerous than any yet known. National armaments were not reduced. German colonies and the land of its allies, Austria Hungary and the Ottoman [Turkish] Empire, were distributed among the victors as spoils – from the Saar to Shantung, from Serbia to Syria – the wishes, to say nothing of the interests, of their population flagrantly disregarded. Russia was not welcome in the society of nations. Territorial settlements in almost every case were mere adjustments and compromises between the claims of rival states. Even the old system of secret treaties remained untouched.

Andelman, D. A. 2008. *A Shattered Peace – Versailles 1919 and the Price We Pay Today.* London, UK. David Wiley.

Discussion point

Compare the views about Versailles offered by Margaret Macmillan (Source Q, page 69) and David Andelman (Source S). Which opinion do you find the most convincing? Why?

The other treaties have caused less controversy amongst historians. These treaties certainly transformed central and southern Europe, but it must be remembered that many of the new states had already been established by the time the treaties were ratified, and they received much popular support from citizens in these states. Nonetheless, it was impossible to construct borders that resolved *all* ethnic divisions. The issues raised by the creation of the new states are examined in Chapter 4.

In the long term, the treaties created a series of weak successor states that were unable to withstand an aggressive Germany in the 1930s. The peacemakers at Versailles cannot be blamed for failing to anticipate the rise of German nationalism two decades in the future; however, they could have foreseen certain difficulties. The break-up of Hungary was particularly severe, and many Magyars found themselves outside Hungary's new national borders.

The economic difficulties facing all the successor states were in part the result of the treaties and the break-up of the Austro-Hungarian Empire, but they were also made worse by the world economic problems that developed in the 1920s and 1930s.

Was the peace settlement doomed from the start?

Writing in 1944, historian Etienne Mantoux put forth the argument that the production levels of German industry in the 1930s, particularly its armaments industry, were a clear indication that Germany was able to meet the reparations demands fixed in 1921. His work began to challenge earlier writing that condemned the peacemakers for the harshness of the treaties. Mantoux's view was reinforced by Maurice Baumont in his book *The Origins of the Second World War* (1978). Here, Baumont argued that, 'As a whole the treaties righted age-old wrongs', particularly the issue of the different national groups in Central Europe.

Anthony Adamthwaite took a slightly different view. In *The Making of the Second World War* (1977), he suggested that it was not the results of the peace conferences that created problems, but the unrealistic hopes with which most nations went to the talks – they were almost certain to be disappointed. Adamthwaite argued: 'No peace settlement could have fulfilled the millennial hopes of a new heaven and a new earth. It was the destruction of these Utopian hopes that provoked the denunciations of the settlement.' It might also be suggested, as later chapters will discuss, that it was the failure to enforce the treaties that created future problems.

Activities

1 Copy the chart below to evaluate the harshness of the Treaty of Versailles. One example has been given. Complete the chart, giving other examples of evidence of the harshness or fairness of the treaty.

Evidence that the Treaty of Versailles was harsh	Evidence that the Treaty of Versailles was fair
Germany was the only country that was disarmed and was therefore insecure	

2 Create a similar chart for the other treaties arising from the Paris Peace Conferences.

3 Review the two charts you have made. How harsh were the peace treaties? In order to reach a supported judgement about the treaties, you should copy and complete the table below. Award each treaty a mark out of 10 based on how harsh it was, ranging from 0 for very lenient to 10 for very harsh. In the third column, explain the mark you have awarded. When you have completed the table, write a paragraph explaining which treaty you think was the harshest and why.

Treaty	Mark	Supporting evidence
Versailles		
St Germain		
Trianon		
Neuilly		
Sèvres		

End of chapter activities

Summary

This chapter has outlined the terms of the peace treaties drawn up at the end of the First World War. You are now in a position to compare the aims and motives of the major powers with the actual conditions contained in the treaties, and consider to what extent these aims were satisfied. You should be aware of the reaction of the defeated nations to the treaties, and consider whether their reactions were justified. This is particularly the case with Germany, where you should understand the historical debates surrounding the punishments, particularly the issue of war guilt and subsequent reparations. You should now be in a position to make a judgement about how fair the peace treaties were, and reach a conclusion about their relative success.

You should understand how the former empires of Austria-Hungary and Turkey were replaced with successor states. The next chapter will look at the problems that the treaties caused, to develop your understanding of how successful the treaties were in resolving the problems created by the collapse of the old empires. This chapter has also explained what happened to the colonies of these former states, and the next chapter will allow you to examine whether the mandate system achieved Wilson's goals.

Summary activity

In order to complete this activity you will need to refer back to Wilson's Fourteen Points on page 25. Copy the chart below to compare the terms of Wilson's Fourteen Points with the actual terms of the peace treaties. In the first column you should write in the terms of the Fourteen Points. In the second and third columns you should look at the terms of the peace treaties and add evidence that supports the view that the Fourteen Points were either upheld or not upheld. The first has been done for you as an example.

Wilson's Fourteen Points	Evidence it was upheld	Evidence it was not upheld
The establishment of the League of Nations	The League of Nations was set up	The USA did not ratify the treaties and therefore did not join

Once you have completed the chart, assess the extent to which Wilson's Fourteen Points were upheld by the peace treaties.

Paper 1 exam practice

Question

According to Source A opposite, what was the reaction within Germany to the Treaty of Versailles?
[2 marks]

Skill

Comprehension of a source

SOURCE A

Today in the Hall of Mirrors the disgraceful Treaty is being signed. Do not forget it! The German people will, with unceasing labour, press forward to reconquer the place among the nations to which it is entitled.

Extract from an article in the German newspaper Deutsche Zeitung, *28 June 1919.*

Student answer

Source A shows that there was a feeling of resentment about the treaty, made clear by the use of the word 'disgraceful'. The source also claims that Germany was entitled to be a great power and resents having its status taken away, implying that the people will work to restore their position in the world, and hinting at the possibility of future conflict in response to the treaty. Although Source A gives only the reaction of a German paper, the feelings expressed were fairly common within Germany, as was shown later by Hitler's ability to exploit dislike of the treaty in his rise to power.

Before you start

Comprehension questions are the most straightforward questions you will face in Paper 1. They simply require you to understand a source and extract two or three relevant points that relate to the question. Before you attempt this question, refer to page 212 for advice on how to tackle comprehension questions, and a simplified markscheme.

73

Examiner comments

The candidate makes good use of the source to support the argument. The answer does not simply paraphrase the source, but uses key words and phrases, such as 'disgraceful' to support their overall argument. Although the question does not ask for a comment about the reliability of the source, a valid point relating to the question is made in mentioning that the paper was fairly typical of feelings within Germany, and this is supported by reference to later developments. The student also explains why the German people would object to the treaty, again with specific reference to the source. This question carries two marks and the candidate has made two valid, well-developed points, and would therefore gain full marks.

Paper 2 practice questions

1   In what ways was the Treaty of Versailles unfair?

2   Assess the view that the Treaty of Versailles was too lenient.

3   Analyse the arguments of the Big Three for and against punishing Germany at Versailles.

4   Assess the reasons for the failure of the Paris Peace Conferences.

5   Analyse the problems facing the peacemakers at Versailles.

6   For what reasons and with what consequences were small successor states established in Eastern Europe?

7   Discuss the view that Hungary suffered most out of the defeated nations by the terms of the peace treaties.

4 The impact of the peace treaties 1919–30

74

Timeline

1918 Nov: Hungarian Republic proclaimed

Dec: creation of the Kingdom of Serbs, Croats and Slovenes

1919 May: Chinese protests about Japanese gains at the peace conferences

Aug: Romanian forces occupy Budapest

Dec: Poles reject frontier based on Curzon Line

1920 Jan: Poland invades Ukraine

1921 Feb: Franco–Polish agreement

Mar: Treaty of Riga – Poland gains land in Belorussia and eastern Ukraine; Little Entente between France and Poland; Romanian–Polish Pact

Nov: Polish–Czechoslovakian Neutrality Pact

1924 entente between France and Czechoslovakia

1926 entente between France and Romania

May: Piłsudski takes control of Poland, ending parliamentary government

1927 Demonstrations in Vienna; entente between France and Yugoslavia

1929 Croats demand a federal state

Jul: king of the Serbs, Croats and Slovenes proclaims royal dictatorship and bans political parties

1930 right-wing groups in Austria reject democracy and adopt fascist programme

Key questions

- What were the main political effects of the peace treaties on Europe?
- What were the main economic effects of the peace treaties on Europe?
- How successful was the mandate system?

Overview

- The political impact of the treaties on central, eastern and southern Europe was far-reaching, as the new states were often weak and politically unstable.
- The Russian Revolution and the ensuing civil war meant that it was even harder to bring stability to the region.
- The states of central and eastern Europe faced ethnic, cultural, political and economic problems, and their success in dealing with these varied considerably.
- The weakness of the successor states had a serious impact on the balance of power within the region. Therefore, although Germany had lost the war, it was in a relatively stronger position than before the war.
- The war had created economic difficulties, particularly as a result of increased borrowing; these debts now had to be repaid. A brief economic boom followed the ending of hostilities, but this was followed by economic decline.
- All the states in central, eastern and southern Europe faced economic problems – most notably inflation. Germany was particularly badly hit, but Austria and Hungary also faced crises.
- The mandate system was established to administer the colonies and imperial possessions of the defeated powers, but some saw this as simply the continuation of imperialism under a different name.
- The mandate system allowed the victorious powers of Britain and France to maintain and even increase their influence throughout the world.

What were the main political effects of the peace treaties on Europe?

The situation in Europe as a whole

At the end of the First World War, the political situation in Europe was both complex and confused. The war, and a growing nationalist feeling that had been evident even before the war, resulted in the break-up of the old Austro-Hungarian Empire and its decline as the centre of European diplomacy and trade. The impact on the **geopolitical** situation in the region was even greater because of the collapse of the other two empires in central and southern Europe – those of Turkey and Russia.

The peace treaties drawn up in Paris during the course of 1919–20 did not create political stability within Europe, and failed to resolve many of the problems that had confronted the peacemakers. Instead of three large, stable empires dominating the region, a series of small, weak and unstable states emerged from the Paris Peace Conferences. Indeed, in some places new states had been established even before the formality of the peace treaties. These new states not only had to find a sense of national identity (often among competing ethnic groups), but they also had to develop their economies, which was a major challenge in the aftermath of the war. The weaknesses of these states made them more vulnerable to the aggressive policies of Adolf Hitler in the later 1930s.

Meanwhile, in states such as Germany and Russia, struggles took place to establish new regimes. Even some of the liberal governments, such as that in Italy, faced political difficulties. Throughout much of central and southern Europe, these problems were made worse by fears of the spread of communism from Russia. Even some of the more secure democracies, such as Britain, experienced a rise in support for left-wing parties.

Russia, the Baltic states and Poland

The Russian tsar was overthrown in 1917, but this did not bring about political stability. The communist seizure of power that resulted from the removal of the provisional government in October/November 1917 did not end the unrest. Communist support was not widespread, and initially the communists only had two centres of control – Moscow and Petrograd. It took a violent civil war that lasted until 1921 for the communists to gain greater control, and stability within the region was difficult to achieve whilst the civil war was going on. It was essential that Russia agreed to the treaties arising from the Paris Peace Conferences and to the borders of the new states – particularly in Eastern Europe, but also in the **Near East**. However, this agreement was difficult to secure since various ethnic groups took the opportunity to exploit the unrest caused by the civil war to make territorial gains of their own.

This instability was most apparent in the Baltic states and Poland. Latvia and Estonia were occupied by Bolshevik forces in the winter of 1918–19, but an alliance of White Russians (opponents of the communists, or Reds), Swedes, Finns and even a brigade of German nationalists drove out the Bolsheviks and occupied these states. Concerned that a victory for the Whites in the Russian Civil War would result in Latvia and Estonia becoming part of Russia, the wartime Allies ordered that troops should be withdrawn. This demand was ignored. It was only the victory of Bolshevik forces in 1920 that finally secured independence for the Baltic states.

geopolitical This term describes a combination of geographical, demographic and political factors within a state, region or the world as a whole.

Near East This is a term that was once used to describe the lands of south-eastern Europe or the Balkans. However, it is now more commonly applied to the land between the Mediterranean and India, or the Middle East.

75

Similar political instability and attempts to seize land occurred in Poland. The Russian Civil War encouraged the Poles to take as much land as possible in the east at Russia's expense. In December 1919, the Poles rejected the eastern border suggested in the Curzon Proposal (see page 52), and in early 1920 they invaded Ukraine.

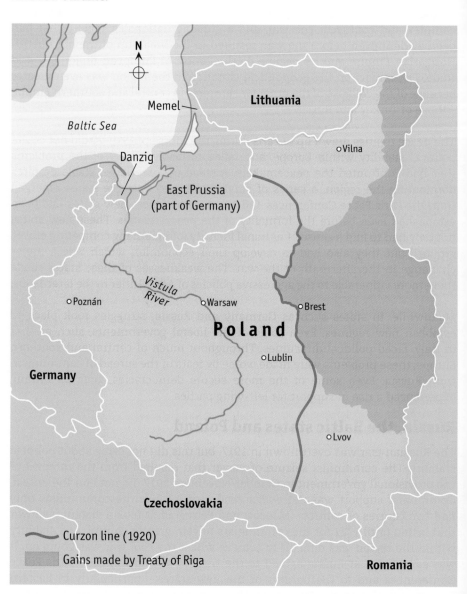

A map showing the boundaries of the Polish states as outlined by the Curzon Proposal, the land seized from Russia by the Poles and the new boundary line gained by the Treaty of Riga

However, by August 1920 Bolshevik forces had pushed the Poles back as far as the capital, Warsaw, and there were fears that Poland would collapse. This would have had serious implications, destroying the terms of the Treaty of Versailles. In order to prevent this, France supplied aid to Poland and the Bolshevik forces were finally defeated. As a result, a new military balance was established in Eastern Europe, and the Treaty of Riga was signed between Russia and Poland in March 1921. Poland made considerable territorial gains in the east, including a large part of Belorussia and eastern Ukraine – all at Russia's expense.

SOURCE A

The Polish Government and the French Government, both desirous of safeguarding, by the maintenance of the Treaties both have signed or which may in the future be recognised by both Parties, the peace of Europe, the security of their territories, and their common political and economic interests have agreed as follows:

In order to co-ordinate their endeavours toward peace the two Governments undertake to consult each other on all questions of foreign policy which concerns both states, so far as those questions affect the settlement of international relations in the spirit of the Treaties and in accordance with the Covenant of the League of Nations.

If, notwithstanding the sincerely peaceful views and intentions of the two contracting States, either or both of them should be attacked without provocation, the two Governments shall take concerted measures for the defence of their territory and the protection of their legitimate interests within the limits specified in the preamble.

Extract from the Franco–Polish agreement of 19 February 1921. From Thomson, D. (trans.) Le Livre Jeunes Francais: Documents Diplomatiques. 1938. Paris, France. Imprimierie Nationale.

Questions

According to Source A, what was the aim of the treaty? What do you think were the benefits to France and Poland? In light of this document and your own knowledge, how far do you agree with the view that Poland would not be able to survive without the support of the Allied powers?

Germany

In Germany, instability was created by the very act of signing the Treaty of Versailles. The German people blamed the leaders of the new Weimar Republic for the treaty, and accused them of betraying the army. The association of the new government with the terms of the treaty only added to its problems, and contributed to the political and economic difficulties faced by the new democratic regime. The territorial losses caused great resentment, and protests began the day the treaty was signed, both within Germany and in areas that had been lost but which contained significant German minorities. The German people were also angry at having to pay reparations; they had hoped to receive compensation from the nations they had defeated in the war to help repay Germany's own war loans.

The sense of bitterness in Germany was aggravated by the poor economic and social conditions. The shortage of food caused by the Allied naval blockade, combined with a lack of fuel and power, made the winter of 1918–19 particularly severe. The return of demobilised soldiers did little to quieten the country, as many discovered that they had returned to a nation where there was no work. As a result, many ex-soldiers joined nationalist groups or enlisted in irregular army units, which were involved in fighting in the Baltic and along the Polish border.

In the face of so much unrest, the German government found it difficult to limit its armed forces to 100,000 and show the Allies that it was actively disarming. These problems were heightened by the resentment many Germans felt at the disarmament clauses of the Treaty of Versailles.

Nazi Party The National Socialist German Workers' Party (NSDAP), or Nazi Party, was formed in 1920 after Adolf Hitler persuaded the small German Workers' Party (DAP) – an extreme nationalist party – to change its name. In 1921, Hitler became leader of the NSDAP. Despite its name, it was a strongly anti-left, extreme nationalist and anti-Semitic party.

coalition A form of government in which two or more political parties share the role and responsibility of running a country.

Historical debate

Traditionally, historians have argued that the problems facing the Weimar Republic and its constitution helped the Nazis in their rise to power. Proportional representation increased the influence of small parties and made the formation of strong governments difficult. However, historians such as Richard Evans have suggested that this view is exaggerated, and that despite frequent changes in cabinets there was considerable continuity in some German ministries throughout this time. For example, Gustav Stresemann was foreign minister from 1924 to 1929, Heinrich Brauns was minister of labour from 1920 to 1928, and Otto Gessler was army minister for the same period.

The communist unrest that affected Germany in late 1918 and early 1919 (see page 36) continued after the signing of the Treaty of Versailles. However, the challenge from right-wing groups within Germany was arguably even greater, as hardline conservatives also blamed the government for Germany's humiliation. Although the treaty had reduced the size of the army, many former soldiers simply joined the Freikorps (see page 36), and by early 1920 the Allies were becoming concerned about the growing membership of these groups.

The Allies ordered the German government to disband the Freikorps, but when it attempted to do so, a man named Wolfgang Kapp led several Freikorps units on a march to Berlin, and there declared a new government. The existing government was forced to flee and, lacking forces to put down the rising, appealed to the workers for help. A general strike began, bringing the capital to a halt as there were no supplies of power or water, and no transport. Within days the rising collapsed. It is significant, however, that the German army refused to act against the Freikorps and that those who participated in the rising were not punished.

Post-war economic problems also had political repercussions in Germany. The apparent surrender of the government over the invasion of the Ruhr (see page 141) encouraged another right-wing uprising. In November 1923, the leader of the **Nazi Party**, Adolf Hitler, led a rebellion in the Bavarian city of Munich. The police crushed the rising and Hitler was arrested. However, his punishment was lenient – he was sentenced to five years' imprisonment, but served only nine months. Hitler used the trial to gain publicity for his party, and established himself as the leader of Germany's extreme right-wing nationalist element.

After 1923, Weimar Germany became more stable as the economy began to strengthen. The period from 1924 to 1929 saw a growth in support for democratic parties at the expense of extremist parties, and neither the communists nor the Nazis made a significant electoral breakthrough. However, despite this apparent stability, no political party was ever able to achieve a majority in the German parliament, and governments were often short-lived **coalitions**.

The rise in economic stability ended with the Wall Street Crash in 1929 (see page 16). The subsequent Great Depression had a severe economic impact on Germany – greater than anywhere else in Europe – but it also had huge political implications. A series of governments were unable to deal with the problems it created. Most significant of these problems was unemployment, which reached 6 million in 1932. As the situation worsened, many people turned to extremist parties such as the communists or Nazis, who appeared to offer simple solutions to the difficulties (see page 164). There was growing electoral support for the Nazis: their representation rose from 14 seats in the German Reichstag (parliament) in 1924 to 107 in 1930, and 230 by July 1932. In such circumstances – and under pressure from former political leaders – the German president finally asked Hitler to form a government in January 1933.

The successor states

In the period immediately after the signing of the peace treaties, the greatest problems and instability emerged in Eastern Europe, where the new successor states struggled with internal ethnic conflicts, challenges to their governments and even external warfare.

The peacemakers at Versailles hoped that the new states would be democratic, and act as a defence against the spread of communism. The French also intended them to provide protection against a resurgent Germany. The reality was very different, though. The new states of Poland, Czechoslovakia and Yugoslavia (as it was known after 1929) had been created by the victorious powers, and were therefore involved in the peace process. However, the states of Austria and Hungary were the heirs of the Austro-Hungarian Empire and were treated as defeated states. The 'victorious' states wanted to preserve the Versailles settlement, whilst the defeated states wanted to overturn the peace treaties. These conflicting desires eventually created two blocs – a division that had serious consequences for international relations in the interwar period.

In many of the new states, conflicts emerged based on ethnic and cultural differences. This created rivalries and tensions that the new governments often found difficult to resolve. The inhabitants of the new states had to learn to live together, and new geopolitical relations needed time to develop. Many of these problems were a direct result of the failure or, in some instances, the impossibility of fully implementing the ideal of self-determination. Although self-determination was desirable, it was not always practical, as the need for economic stability was far greater than the wishes of minorities. As a consequence, many sizeable minorities found themselves in other countries after the post-war borders were drawn. For example, in the Polish Corridor (see page 52) – created to allow Poland access to the sea and to avoid a landlocked state squeezed between Germany and Russia – 2 million Germans came under Polish rule. A similar situation developed in Czechoslovakia, where there were around 3 million German speakers (previously subjects of the Austro-Hungarian Empire) in the Sudetenland. Here, despite president **Edvard Beneš'** promise to ensure that the new state was 'racially harmonious', racial tensions arose that Hitler was able to exaggerate and exploit in the later 1930s.

In some instances these difficulties were resolved by plebiscites (see Chapters 2 and 3). However, in many cases the minorities had to rely on their new states agreeing to and enforcing minority treaties, by which they agreed to act fairly towards the ethnic groups living within their borders. This was supervised by the League of Nations.

The break-up of the Austro-Hungarian Empire also created significant economic problems, not just for Austria but for many of the successor states, too (see map on page 56). Several states in the region were very weak and instead of having a large free-trade area, as the empire had enjoyed, the new states imposed taxes on trade. This made economic development in the region difficult. The situation was not helped by the transport network in this part of Europe, particularly rail lines, which did not fit in with the new territorial boundaries.

The balance of power

The establishment of the new states had a profound impact on the balance of power across the continent – and on wider international relations. Before the First World War, the major powers in the region were Germany, Austria-Hungary and Russia. Germany and Austria-Hungary were allies, while Russia was supported by France. This ensured that there was a balance between the powers, which stopped any one of them dominating the region. France was particularly worried that, following the collapse of Austria-Hungary and the Bolshevik victory in Russia, the balance of power would be upset and that French security would decline. France had lost its Russian ally, which had become one of the **outcast states** of Europe following the communist revolution. This, combined with the emergence of weak successor states, meant that Germany might be able to recover and dominate the region.

Edvard Beneš (1884–1948)
Beneš was a leader of the Czech independence movement, and prime minister of the new state of Czechoslovakia from 1921 to 1922. He became president in 1935, and led the government in exile during the Second World War. Beneš returned to lead Czechoslovakia after the war, before he was removed by the communists in 1948.

Discussion point

Geography is a separate academic subject from history, with different skills. You have seen how geography created problems for the peacemakers at Versailles. How useful is an understanding of geography in assessing historical developments?

outcast states This term is used to describe Russia and Germany after the First World War. Russia was called an 'outcast state' because of its communist regime, which was viewed with distrust. Germany earned the title because of its responsibility for the war. As a result, neither country was allowed to join any of the international agreements or the League of Nations, as they were not trusted by the other powers.

Discussion point

Was France in a weaker or stronger position in Europe after the war than it had been before it?

French fears

There was also a general fear – felt particularly by France – that the two outcast states, Russia and Germany, would form an alliance. These fears were confirmed by the 1922 Treaty of Rapallo, which re-established diplomatic relations between Germany and Russia (see page 141). This meant that although Germany had lost a significant amount of land through the peace treaties, it was no weaker in the region than it had been before the First World War. The question of security for France was therefore of great significance. The successor states offered no protection against a resurgent Germany, and France's hopes for a British–US guarantee of support in case of future invasion collapsed when the US refused to ratify the Treaty of Versailles.

The Little Entente

On all its eastern borders, Germany was actually in a stronger position than it had been before the war began. The successor states were therefore concerned to protect their gains. They feared that those countries that had lost land in the peace treaties – or which had not gained what they felt they deserved – might use force to secure the territory they wanted. As a result, the new states entered into a series of alliances to protect themselves. These treaties were known as the Little Entente. In 1920–21 the 'victorious' states of Czechoslovakia, Romania and Yugoslavia formed an alliance to protect themselves against future aggression from Hungary and Italy. The three signatories were afraid that both these nations would try to reverse the terms of the Treaty of Trianon, by which Hungary had lost large amounts of territory and Italy had failed to gain all the land it had expected, particularly in the Adriatic.

France supported this alliance, seeing an opportunity to establish friendly relations with the new states and to prevent German recovery and expansion in the east now that Russia could no longer be relied upon to fulfil that role. The French government negotiated a series of agreements with the Little Entente states, as well as with Poland. The French promised assistance to these nations in upholding the 1919 settlements and boundaries.

80

Questions

Why did the Little Entente develop?
How strong was this alliance?
Why did France support the Little Entente?

SOURCE B

Fear of Hungarian revisionism resulted in the formation of the Little Entente between Czechoslovakia, Romania and Yugoslavia in a series of alliances in 1920 and 1921. This alliance system was extended with the conclusion of the Romanian-Polish pact in March 1921, which was specifically aimed against the Soviet Union, and the Polish-Czechoslovakian Neutrality Pact in November. From the outset the little Entente was closely linked to France. France sent weapons and military missions to the Little Entente and there was a clear understanding that all four states would work together to uphold the treaties. France was now committed to defend Poland against both Germany and Russia, to thwart Hungary's revisionist ambition and support Yugoslavia against Italy. France thus not only undertook to be the principal guarantor of the Treaty of Versailles but also of the entire peace settlement.

Kitchen, M. 2006. Europe Between the Wars. London, UK. Longman.

Despite these developments, the situation in Eastern Europe was still not as stable as it had been before the First World War. It could therefore be argued that the balance of power in Eastern Europe favoured Germany. In addition, the French were concerned that the agreement with Poland might drag France into future conflicts between Poland and either Germany in the west or Russia in the east.

Political stability in the successor states

US president Woodrow Wilson hoped that the new states established in Central and Eastern Europe would be democratic. He strongly believed that democracy in the region would help to restore peace and stability in the long term. However, although the new states often adopted a democratic constitution, in practice the political systems that emerged were often far from democratic.

There were two main reasons for this. Firstly, like Germany, many of the new states did not have a democratic tradition upon which to build a new constitution, but were more accustomed to authoritarian rule (see page 13). Secondly, the racial tensions in many new states – often heightened by the development of political parties that represented particular racial groups – meant that there was widespread political dissent.

Yugoslavia

The greatest challenges were faced by the two new states of the Kingdom of Serbs, Croats and Slovenes (which became Yugoslavia in 1929) and Czechoslovakia, as they were made up of a wide range of ethnic and cultural groups. In Yugoslavia, the Serbs soon dominated the state and ensured that their monarch, Peter, was proclaimed king of the new country. The assembly that drew up the constitution for the new state was led by two Serbian parties, so the final constitution favoured the Serbs. When it came to the vote on whether to adopt this constitution, the Croats and Slovenes staged a **boycott**. Despite this, the constitution was still approved.

boycott An act of protest in which those participating withdraw from commercial or social relations with another group or nation.

This was not a good start for the new kingdom, and events in the early 1920s only confirmed the difficulties. There was frequent hostility between the Croat Peasant Party and the Serbian Radical Party, which dominated the government based in Belgrade. The Croats complained that taxes were too high and that the central government had too much power. This culminated in 1923 with Croat deputies declaring that laws passed in Belgrade did not have any force in Croatia. The government responded in 1924 by declaring that the Peasant Party was illegal because of its communist principles.

In 1925 there appeared to be a move towards reconciliation, when the Croats were invited to join the government. In reality, however, this did not reduce tensions; the leader of the Peasants Party scarcely co-operated with the government and referred to fellow ministers as 'swine'. These attempts at co-operation ended in 1926, when the Croats left the government. After this it became increasingly difficult to govern the country.

federal A system of government in which several states join together as a nation but retain some independence in internal affairs.

Finally, in 1928, a deputy from Montenegro opened fire in parliament and killed some members, including Croats. This increased hostility, and in 1929 the Croats demanded a **federal** state and established their own government in Zagreb. In response, the king declared a royal dictatorship. He assumed responsibility for government and banned all political parties.

Question

What was the greatest political challenge for the Kingdom of Serbs, Croats and Slovenes?

Discussion point

This section has discussed the problems caused by diverse cultures living in close proximity. What are the difficulties in studying cultural history? Is it possible for a historian to understand and empathise with other cultures?

Activity

Compare the success of the government in the Kingdom of Serbs, Croats and Slovenes with the government of Czechoslovakia in resolving the ethnic problems each state faced.

Discussion point

Why do you think a democratic government developed in Czechoslovakia but not in Poland?

Czechoslovakia

Despite the difficulties Czechoslovakia faced in the period after the peace talks, it was in fact the only new state to develop into a constitutional democracy. Unlike the Kingdom of Serbs, Croats and Slovenes, Czechoslovakia was successfully ruled by coalition governments from across the main political parties. The language issues, which reflected the ethnic divisions within the country, were also partly resolved. The 1920 Language Law declared Czech to be the official language, but it also allowed other nationalities to use their own language in schools and law courts in areas where they accounted for more than 20% of the population. The only complaint came over the voting procedures to decide the proportions in different areas. However, even this was mainly resolved and relations between the different ethnic groups improved to such a degree that in 1925 some German-speakers even joined the government. Tensions were further eased in 1927, when the country was split into four 'lands' – Bohemia, Moravia-Silesia, Ruthenia and Slovakia. Each state had its own governor and local parliament, which provided a degree of autonomy (self-rule).

Poland

The formation of the Polish state was complicated by its history of occupation by both the Central Powers and Russia, each of which supported a different provisional government. There was also a provisional government in exile in Paris. Eventually, Marshal Józef Piłsudski was appointed provisional head of state. However, Piłsudski's reputation as an authoritarian leader raised concerns that he might try to establish a dictatorship, so the powers of the president were severely limited, causing Piłsudski to refuse the position.

The greatest problem facing the new Polish state was its economy (see page 87). Attempts to resolve economic and other problems raised opposition from different groups, with the result that between 1919 and 1926, 13 different governments were formed. On 11 May 1926, Piłsudski published an attack on the new government, and the following day he led troops into Warsaw. The government ordered the army to oppose them, but many refused and instead joined Piłsudski's rebellion. By 14 May, the government had resigned and Piłsudski became virtual dictator of Poland until his death in 1935.

Armoured trucks amongst the crowds at a rally in Warsaw in support of Piłsudski's rebellion, May 1926

Austria

Austria faced similar problems to the newly formed states in Central and Eastern Europe. Although union with Germany was expressly forbidden by the terms of the Treaty of St Germain (see page 53), the Austrian **constituent assembly**, which replaced the old imperial government, voted to be part of the German Empire. In addition, the provinces of Salzburg and Tyrol voted to join Germany in 1921 and were only prevented from doing so by threats from the Allied powers. The new Austrian government also faced serious economic problems (see page 88), which had political implications. The country experienced food shortages, a large influx of immigrants and serious inflation (a rise in the cost of goods), which was only managed by loans from the League of Nations – granted in return for an agreement that Austria would not try to unite with Germany.

The main political conflict that developed in Austria was between the left and right wings, both of which had their own private and uniformed armies. There was frequent political unrest, which reached a climax towards the end of the 1920s. In 1927, demonstrations were held in Vienna after the alleged murder of two socialists by right-wingers. During the demonstrations, 85 protestors were killed and many more wounded. In 1928, the right-wing forces joined together to brutally suppress 'any attempt to set up a Red dictatorship'. In 1929 the prime minister, Ignaz Seipel, resigned and his successors found it even more difficult to maintain political stability. This was evident when right-wing groups proposed a march on Vienna; in the region of Styria, a demonstration resulted in even more deaths. Finally, in 1930, the right wing adopted a fascist programme that included the 'rejection of democracy and parliament'.

Hungary

Although Hungary was in theory a democracy, the regime that emerged under Admiral Horthy (see page 57) from 1926 was in practice authoritarian, verging on dictatorial. In the old Austro-Hungarian Empire, the Hungarian kingdom had been dominated by wealthy landowners. In the new Hungarian republic a major conflict arose between these landowners – who wanted to retain political control – and the peasants. Fascist groups also began to emerge at this time, adding to the problem of opposition from other nationalities, who made up nearly half the population of the new state.

Hungary was plunged into chaos after the First World War. With no recognised government there, it was impossible for the Allies to agree a peace treaty with the country until 1920 (see page 57). After the downfall of Béla Kun's communist government, Admiral Horthy seized power and took revenge on communist and left-wing supporters. Although elections were finally held in January 1920, the Social Democrats boycotted them because of Horthy's brutal actions. As a result, parliament was dominated by conservatives and farmers, who declared the actions of both Karolyi (the leader during the short-lived period of democracy) and Kun illegal. The Hungarian king, Karl, had abdicated, but the monarchy still existed with Horthy as regent, ruling on the king's behalf. In 1921, Karl made two unsuccessful attempts to regain the throne, but the threat died with him in 1922, ending any chance of the monarchy being restored in Hungary.

The king's defeat and death in exile did not end the political problems. The struggle between the landowners and the left wing resulted in revisions to the franchise. Many peasants and members of the working class lost their right to vote, and the electorate was reduced to 27% of the population. The landowners therefore came to dominate the voting system in Hungary.

constituent assembly An assembly, or organisation, that is formed with the purpose of drawing up a country's constitution.

83

Fact
The revisions to the franchise in Hungary were accepted because the government was able to reach a deal with the socialists. In return for socialist support, the government agreed to release union funds that had been seized, and to free socialists who had been imprisoned for opposing the regime.

During the 1920s, Hungarian politics were dominated by the desire to abolish the Treaty of Trianon. Hungary had suffered the greatest territorial losses of all the defeated powers, with Romania, Yugoslavia, Czechoslovakia and Austria winning their claims against Hungary. As a result, around 2 million Hungarians now lived in Romania, 700,000 in Slovakia and lesser numbers in Austria and Yugoslavia. The most significant attempt to revise the frontiers agreed in the treaty was an alliance with Italy in 1927, by which Hungary was allowed port facilities at Fiume and received arms from Italy. However, when this agreement was discovered in 1928 there was an international outcry. Hungary also attempted to undermine the Little Entente, as all the powers who had signed it had gained Hungarian land. Hungary tried to negotiate a treaty with Yugoslavia, but Yugoslavia delayed talks, and nothing came of it.

> **Questions**
>
> How serious were the political problems facing the new states of Austria and Hungary? Which state was more successful in solving these problems?

> To complete activities 2 and 3 you might find it helpful look ahead to the next section, which covers the economic impact of the peace treaties in these states.

Activities

1   Imagine you are a League of Nations official in 1920. Write a report outlining the difficulties and prospects facing one of the new states.

2   It was very difficult to establish democracy in the new states. Below is a list of reasons for these difficulties. For each of the five states – Yugoslavia, Poland, Czechoslovakia, Austria and Hungary – decide which of the following statements apply and then place them in order of importance for each state.

    a   the absence of established political parties

    b   democracy was imposed on the new states

    c   the economic weakness of the country encouraged political extremism

    d   ethnic divisions encouraged the emergence of regional and ethnic parties that were concerned with protecting their own interests

    e   dominant groups wanted to maintain their position

    f   peasants made up the majority of the population and they had no political experience

    g   there was no tradition of democracy within the country – they were accustomed to authoritarian rule.

3   In the activity above you considered the inherent problems in the new and successor states. However, in some states it was problems that developed during the 1920s that brought about an end to democracy. For each of the five states, decide to what extent the following factors apply.

    a   the effects of the Great Depression and the inability of the government to deal with the problems

    b   immediate post-war economic problems, such as inflation, and the inability of the governments to deal with the problems

    c   internal problems that developed after 1919

    d   growing political and ethnic extremism.

What were the main economic effects of the peace treaties on Europe?

The situation in Europe as a whole

At the end of the First World War, much of Europe faced low levels of production, shortages of both food and raw materials, large debts and rapidly rising inflation. The economies of many of the powers declined dramatically. They had lost trading opportunities to nations beyond Europe that were not involved in the war, and now found it very difficult to win back those markets. In addition, the economies of many states had been geared towards war production; now that the war was over, they were not in a position to meet the needs of the post-war world. Immediately after the war there was a brief economic boom as nations replaced goods lost during the conflict, but this was short-lived and many European nations soon faced the prospect of a shrinking economy.

War debts worsened the economic situation, particularly in France and Germany, which had borrowed heavily to finance the war effort. To pay back these debts they had to cut back their spending, which slowed economic recovery. Most nations had very little money to spend on trade, and international trade severely declined throughout the 1920s. Many nations also suffered from a period of rapid inflation, particularly in the period 1921–23, as the amount of money in circulation increased.

SOURCE C

Industrial output in Eastern Europe 1920–29

Country	1920–21	1925	1929
Czechoslovakia	69.8	136.4	171.8
Hungary	64.0	76.7	113.9
Poland	35.1	63.1	85.9
Romania	47.2	92.2	136.9
Yugoslavia	n/a	n/a	140.0
Europe	66.9	89.6	110.7

The index is based on 1913 = 100. Figures below indicate a fall in production (69.8 means a fall of 30.2% from 1913) and figures above the percentage rise (171.8 means a 71.8% increase).

From a report by the League of Nations, Industrialisation and Foreign Trade. *1945. Geneva, Switzerland. pp. 136–37.*

Russia

The Russian economy had grown at a dramatic rate before the outbreak of the First World War, but this changed as production became geared towards the war effort. The outbreak of the civil war in 1918 worsened the situation. Industry was destroyed as a result of either the fighting or through neglect, as many workers were forced to join the army. Communist seizure of industry and the ending of private ownership did nothing to stimulate production, and the new communist government faced a substantial decrease in production levels in the key industries in the post-war period. The agricultural problem was even worse. The communists used requisition squads to seize grain in order to feed its soldiers and people in urban areas, but this resulted in peasants hiding their produce or simply not growing food, as they were not paid for their efforts.

Peasant farmers in Russia in 1923

Germany

The economic situation in Germany was particularly bad at the end of the war and throughout the early 1920s. Before the war, Germany's main trading partners were Britain and the US, both of which ceased trading with Germany during the conflict. The naval blockade prevented goods from entering Germany, which caused severe economic and social problems. Like other countries involved in the fighting, Germany also lost colonial and other overseas trading markets during the war, and was unable to win these back. However, Germany was also hit by the loss of territory and colonies, which had provided raw materials and a market for German goods.

This poor situation was heightened by Germany's financial problems. The country had financed the war by borrowing money in the belief that once it won the war it would be able to pay back the debts by imposing reparations on the defeated powers. With its own defeat came a double blow – Germany not only had to cover its own war debts, it also had to pay reparations to the victorious powers. In order to meet the costs the government printed more money, causing inflation. This gathered pace soon after the end of the war, hitting drastic levels (hyperinflation) in 1923, after the invasion of the Ruhr (see page 141).

The invasion of the Ruhr and the subsequent loss of vital raw materials had a serious impact on economic production in Germany. Levels dropped to well below those just before the First World War and did not return to pre-war levels until 1927. Only a series of loans from the USA in the period after 1923 allowed Weimar Germany to enter a period of relative economic stability. This collapsed when the US recalled its loans in the aftermath of the Wall Street Crash.

The successor states

The newly established states experienced similar economic difficulties, mainly due to the underdeveloped nature of their industry and agriculture. Added to this, trade with Russia had all but ended, and the new states therefore needed to widen the scope of their trading. They were greatly dependent on world economic growth; however, several key nations – including the USA – began to introduce **tariffs** in order to protect their own industries as the world economy started to shrink. At the same time, the successor states – which had benefited from the lack of internal trade barriers while they were part of the Austro-Hungarian Empire – imposed their own tariffs as they tried to protect their new and vulnerable industries from foreign competition. This made imported goods more expensive and increased the difficulty of exporting their own products. In the period between 1928 and 1933, exports in Hungary, Poland and Yugoslavia all fell by over 60%.

At the same time, it was impossible for the treaties to share out economic resources fairly and equally. Poland, for example, was divided economically: the land in the west of the country that was gained from Germany was much more economically advanced than the land taken from Russia in the east, which was more agricultural. Austria had an even bigger problem, as the Treaty of St Germain had taken away nearly all of its industrial resources, leaving it reliant on agriculture.

Fact

The dramatic rate of inflation in Germany can be seen in the rising cost of a loaf of bread in Berlin. This had stood at 0.63 marks in 1918, but had reached 163 marks by 1922 and 201,000,000,000 marks by November 1923.

---

tariffs These are trade barriers and taxes imposed on imported goods to protect domestic industries, so that the price of home-produced goods is usually cheaper than imported goods. Tariffs became an important issue in the Great Depression of the 1930s.

Yugoslavia

The economic problems facing the Kingdom of Serbs, Croats and Slovenes (Yugoslavia) were severe. Serbia had been at war since 1912, first in the Balkan Wars and then the First World War. The country was in debt, and relied almost entirely on agriculture. Around 10 million of its 14 million inhabitants made their living from the land. The new boundaries created by the peace treaties disrupted established trade routes, as Croatia had traded with Hungary and Macedonia with the south Balkans and Turkey. Rail links were also poor, which made transporting goods difficult. The hostility between the various states also caused problems, resulting in either trade barriers or no trade at all.

Despite these issues, the Yugoslav economy experienced a brief recovery until 1929. Agricultural goods earned a fair price on the world market, and healthy harvests allowed an export trade to develop. There was also some foreign investment, which resulted in the development of a steel industry. However, the economy remained heavily reliant on agriculture and its success depended upon high prices. The decline in world food prices after 1929 therefore wrecked the Yugoslav economy and caused widespread unemployment.

Czechoslovakia

The new state of Czechoslovakia had economic potential. It contained large supplies of raw materials, especially coal and iron ore in Silesia and Bohemia. Czechoslovakia also gained much of the former industrial areas of the old Austro-Hungarian Empire. Where there were not large-scale mineral resources, the land was often fertile and the state contained rich agricultural lands. As a result, the Czech economy developed throughout the 1920s, avoided the inflation crises that affected many European states after the war, and was not dependent on foreign loans.

By 1923, production levels in the country were higher than those in the same regions before the war. Industries flourished and Czechoslovakia was able to develop its markets both at home and abroad. It was only with the advent of the Great Depression in 1929 that the Czech economy began to suffer, as other nations cut their overseas trade.

Poland

The Polish economic experience was varied. As we have already seen, most people in eastern Poland earned their living from farming, and they suffered badly at the onset of the Great Depression. However, western areas experienced a different situation. At first, the whole country was hit by high inflation, with prices rising 2.5 million-fold. The government responded to this with spending cuts, increased taxes and wage freezes – all of which resulted in a decrease in the standard of living for Polish workers.

Despite this, there were areas of growth and development. Poland gained the industrially rich area of Upper Silesia through a plebiscite in 1921. With American gold also lent to Poland, it could obtain foreign loans. The coal industry benefited from a miners' strike in Britain in 1926, which increased international demand for Polish coal. The result of all this was a growth of 38% in the Polish economy between 1925 and 1928 – a figure that was exceeded in Europe only by Russia.

Austria

Austria suffered badly from both the post-war problems and from the onset of the Great Depression. The first crisis to hit Austria was hyperinflation, which reached similar levels to that of Weimar Germany. The value of the Austrian currency fell to one-15,000th of its pre-war level by 1922. The economy was only saved by large loans organised by the League of Nations and financed by countries such as Britain, France, Italy and Czechoslovakia. To address the problem of high levels of inflation, wages were cut – which caused social problems such as low living standards and poverty. This encouraged the growth of political extremism, as the Austrian people became more and more dissatisfied with their government.

There were some signs of economic recovery towards the end of the decade, with agricultural improvements and the development of hydro-electric power in an attempt to reduce the reliance on and cost of foreign coal. However, as elsewhere, hopes of economic recovery were dashed by the Depression.

Hungary

At the end of the war, the Hungarian economy was not as weak as Austria's, mainly because Hungary was self-sufficient in food. However, the establishment of the new state's boundaries by the Treaty of Trianon seriously damaged the economy, as lines of communication were destroyed and raw materials were lost. Between 1921 and 1923, Hungary experienced rapid inflation. Despite these early difficulties, however, the Hungarian economy began to recover. In return for guarantees to uphold the Treaty of Trianon, Hungary was granted a loan by the League of Nations. The loan encouraged industrial investment and the country enjoyed a period of economic development. New industries were built and mines opened, which reduced unemployment levels. Industrial production almost trebled in the period 1921–28, while the number of factory workers rose from 137,000 to 236,000. Meanwhile, the agricultural sector also prospered. Demands for food both at home and overseas allowed farmers and landowners to make large profits.

As in Weimar Germany, however, much of Hungary's recovery and prosperity was dependent upon foreign loans. As the 1920s progressed, Hungary was borrowing simply to repay the interest on its loans. Most of its exports were still agricultural goods and, although this was profitable at the start of the decade, income began to fall as agricultural prices on the world market declined before the major collapse of 1929. The Depression ended overseas loans, and Hungary was soon in a desperate situation. Spending cuts created political instability, which resulted in the fall of the government in 1931.

Analysis

All the states that emerged from the peace treaties faced economic problems. The treaties often created unintentional difficulties through the construction of the new boundaries. These were aggravated by inflation, which gripped most of the states. Even where these problems were overcome in the mid 1920s and production levels rose, the Depression that began in 1929 had serious consequences and added to the political problems. The much-needed period of economic stability never fully materialised, and the successor states faced the challenges of the 1930s in a much weaker position than they might have otherwise.

Activities

1 For any one of the states you have studied in the 1920s, find out what political developments took place in the 1930s and how far they were the result of the economic problems caused by the Great Depression.

2 You have now considered both the problems that the new states inherited and the problems that developed during the 1920s. Earlier, you wrote a report on the prospects and difficulties facing one of the new or successor states (see page 84). Now imagine you are a League of Nations official in 1931. Write a report on the same country, explaining how and why the position has changed.

3 What economic problems did the new European states face? Make a list of the difficulties facing each country to compare them. How similar were the problems they faced? Why do you think this was the case? Compare the issues faced by the successor states with those faced by Germany. How similar were they? Write a summary paragraph explaining the extent of the problems.

How successful was the mandate system?

In the period before the First World War, many European countries embarked on what has been called the **Scramble for Africa**. European powers sought to extend their power, influence and status by seizing land, principally on the African continent. This land provided many nations with raw materials and a market for their goods. The colonial system was confirmed by the 1884 Berlin Conference, at which the major European powers divided up Africa into **spheres of influence**. However, this formality did not diminish tensions between the powers and there was a series of conflicts between them in the years before the First World War. Britain clashed with France at Fashoda in the Sudan in 1898 (the two countries came to the brink of war). Germany came into conflict with France over influence in Morocco in both 1905 and 1911. However, an empire was a significant status symbol, and all the powers were determined to maintain or increase their influence in Africa. By the eve of the First World War, almost all of Africa was under foreign rule.

The tension created by the old colonial system undoubtedly contributed to the outbreak of the First World War. This was recognised in Wilson's Fourteen Points, which called for 'A free, open-minded and impartial adjustment of all colonial claims, based upon a strict observance of the principle that the interests of the population concerned must have equal weight with the equitable claims of the government whose title is to be determined.'

> **Scramble for Africa** This term is used to describe the events by which European nations seized land in Africa in the 19th century.

> **spheres of influence** Regions or countries whose development is influenced by other countries.

A map showing foreign powers and their rule in Africa on the eve of the First World War

89

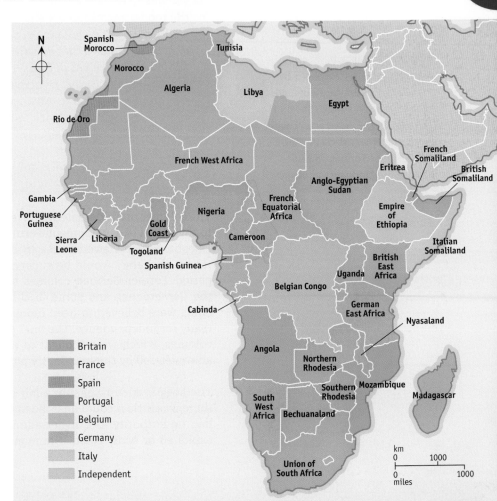

If the colonies of the defeated nations were simply divided amongst the victorious powers, it would go against this declaration and give further credibility to the belief that the treaties were simply a way of rewarding the victors. However, any attempt to implement the principle of self-determination among the empires that already existed would cause conflict. The system that emerged, therefore, was accused of double standards. In reality, even the colonies of the defeated powers gained very little independence from the arrangements made by the peace treaties. This has led some historians, including David Fieldhouse, to suggest that the colonial system after the First World War was merely a continuation of imperialism, just under a different name.

At the Paris Peace Conferences, the Allies agreed to a mandate system (see page 53) to administer the former colonies of the defeated powers. These colonies would be mandated by the victorious powers under the supervision of the League of Nations. The mandatory powers were responsible for the wellbeing of the people in the colonies and were accountable to the League of Nations' Mandates Commission. This development was outlined in Article 22 of the Covenant of the League of Nations.

SOURCE D

To those colonies and territories which as a consequence of the late war have ceased to be under the sovereignty of the States which formerly governed them and which are inhabited by peoples not yet able to stand by themselves under the strenuous conditions of the modern world, there should be applied the principle that the well-being and development of such peoples form a sacred trust of civilisation and that securities for the performance of this trust should be embodied in this Covenant. The best method of giving practical effect to this principle is that the tutelage of such people should be entrusted to advanced nations who by reason of their resources, their experience or their geographical position can best undertake this responsibility.

Article 22 of the Covenant of the League of Nations.

Questions

According to Source D, why was the mandate system established? In what ways does Article 22 uphold Point 5 of Wilson's Fourteen Points (see page 25)? In what ways could it be argued that Article 22 still allowed the victorious powers to increase their influence and power?

The colonies of the defeated powers were divided into three categories according to their level of development. Former Turkish colonies (Syria, Mesopotamia and Palestine) were viewed as the most developed and placed in Category A. This meant that they would be supervised by Britain and France for only a short period. Former German colonies in Africa (German East Africa, Togoland and the Cameroons), and some in the Pacific, were placed in Category B. These lands were believed to need more time and supervision before they would be ready for independence. The final group, Category C, included the other Pacific colonies, which were thought to need even closer supervision, and would be administered by the mandatory power as an integral part of their territory.

The League tried to ensure a fair administration of the mandates, but in fact there was little it could do if the mandatory power failed in its role – the League had no authority to transfer administration to another state if a colony was exploited or badly ruled. The mandatory powers were required to send in an annual report to the League's Mandates Commission. This organisation soon earned a reputation for being thorough in its supervisory role. Whenever unrest broke out in the mandates, the commission established a successful Committee of Enquiry, which required the mandatory power to account for itself. This was clearly seen in 1923, when the South Africans were criticised for their handling of the Bondelswarts Uprising in German South West Africa.

The mandate system affected Africa, the Middle East and China. Whether it achieved its goal, or whether it was just another form of imperialism, has been the subject of much debate.

Africa

In Africa, Britain took control of German East Africa, whilst Togoland and the Cameroons were split with France; further south, German South West Africa was placed under the supervision of South Africa. A study of the map below shows that these developments strengthened the British position, particularly in East Africa, whilst France was clearly the dominant power in the west. This seems to support the argument that the mandate system was simply a new form of imperialism. However, it must be recognised that the mandated territories *did* gain independence. For example German East Africa, or Tanganyika, became independent in December 1961 and British Togoland became part of Ghana and independent in 1956. However, the mandate system did not reduce the gap between those regarded as 'advanced' peoples and 'backward' peoples, and it therefore failed in its aim of establishing racial equality.

Fact

The Bondelswarts Uprising was a rebellion among the mixed-race Bondelswarts in what was formerly German South West Africa. It was provoked by the actions of the South African government, which continued and even extended the harsh rule of the pre-First World War period. However, the long-term cause was the brutal rule of the Germans before the war. The Bondelswarts had hoped that the mandate status imposed on the region would improve conditions, restore to them their lost tribal lands, and allow tribal leaders to return to their former positions. None of these changes took place under the South African mandate.

Activity

Research the history of one of the mandated African territories during the inter-war years. Decide if the mandate system helped or hindered its development.

91

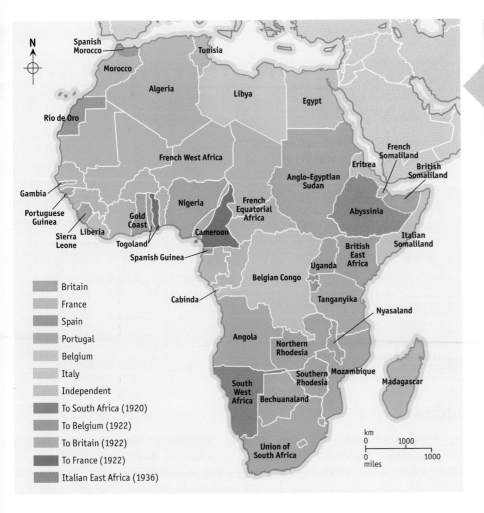

A map of Africa in 1922 showing the regions ruled by the colonial powers and the mandated territories; Abyssinia was independent until Italy's victory over it in 1936

Theory of knowledge

History and lessons for the future

The German philosopher Georg Hegel (1770–1831) said: 'The only thing we learn from history is that we learn nothing from history.' The history of the problems in the Middle East is a clear indication of the value of understanding the past to prevent the same problems arising in the future. To what extent can an understanding of the past prevent similar events from recurring?

The Middle East

The former Turkish (Ottoman) territories were placed under the supervision of Britain and France. Britain was mandated Palestine, Iraq and Transjordan, whilst France gained control over Syria and Libya as well as access to oil in Mosul, Iraq. It was in these areas that Britain and France encountered the greatest problems. The French were never able to pacify Syria, and the country proved very costly to administer. Meanwhile, Britain pulled back as quickly as it could from both Transjordan and Iraq.

The greatest problem arose in Palestine, because of a series of contradictory promises and actions made by the British. In return for Arab support in the war, Britain promised the Arabs independent states. At the same time, however, Britain sought to partition lands in the Middle East between itself and France. The Arabs therefore felt betrayed by the settlements reached in the peace treaties.

The situation was further complicated by the Balfour Declaration of 1917, in which the British promised support for a Jewish national home in Palestine. This caused dismay amongst the Palestinian Arabs. The British government stated that there was no intention that the Jews should occupy the whole of Palestine and there would be no interference with the rights of Palestinian Arabs. Instead, the British hoped to persuade Arabs and Jews to live together peacefully in the same state, demonstrating a catastrophic lack of understanding about the deep divide that existed between these two peoples. The failure of the British mandate in Palestine became clear when the former British prime minister Arthur Balfour visited the region for the first time in 1925.

Questions

What can we learn from Source E about Arab reaction to the terms of the peace treaties? Why was there such hostility to the terms?

SOURCE E

In Jerusalem he [Balfour] opened the new Hebrew University with a stirring speech in which he talked proudly of his own share in the establishment of a Jewish home. He was touched by the reception he received throughout Palestine from Jews but failed to notice the Arabs in mourning and the shops closed in protest. His private secretary destroyed the hundreds of angry telegrams from Arabs before he could see them. When he and his party moved on to Syria to do some sight-seeing, the French authorities mounted a guard round him, much to his annoyance. In Damascus his hotel was surrounded by an excited crowd of 6,000 Arabs. As the paving stones started to fly and the French cavalry fired back, Balfour watched bemused.

Macmillan, M. 2001. Peacemakers: Six Months that Changed the World. London, UK. John Murray. p. 437.

concessionary rights The rights to conduct trade and other commercial activities within certain areas of China. These rights had been gained by Germany in the late 19th and early 20th centuries.

China

In April 1919, the victorious powers informed China that Germany's **concessionary rights** in the Chinese province of Shantung would not be returned to it, but were instead being given to Japan. This went against the promises that the victorious powers had made to China to persuade the country – at considerable cost – to enter the war on the Allied side. Ultimately, the Allies were unwilling to extend to China the right of democracy or self-determination, and this decision had far-reaching consequences. The Chinese people felt humiliated, and this contributed to the growth of a strong sense of nationalism within the country. It resulted in the emergence of the nationalist 4th of May Movement and protests on the streets. Government ministers were physically attacked because they had agreed to the terms of the treaties, and there were anti-Japanese boycotts in both Beijing and Shanghai.

SOURCE F

This movement is the strongest move of its kind that the Chinese have made. Not only has it spread all over China, but in Australia, Singapore, Hong Kong, Vladivostok, and even as far as America. Already it has caused great alarm in Japan. This boycott is different to all others. On previous occasions it has been the Chinese merchants who have been the mainstay of such attempts, but this time it is the consumer who is carrying it on. The students not only shamed the people into a refusal to purchase Japanese goods, but each one of them took a certain part of the street and explained why they should not. Millions of dollars have been collected to start making articles which have heretofore been purchased from Japan. It will not surprise me if this boycott within the next eighteen months does not cost the Japanese four hundred million dollars.

A Western observer comments on the Chinese reaction to the terms. Quoted in Lynch, M. 1996. China: From Empire to People's Republic 1990–49. London, UK. Hodder. p. 33.

Perhaps the most significant aspect was the response of Chinese students. They began to turn to revolutionary ideals to justify their resistance, inspired by the communist seizure of power in Russia. While Japan retained control of mineral rights in Manchuria and Inner Mongolia, it seemed that the old imperial exploitation remained. In Russia, Bolshevism had attacked the idea of imperialism, which appeared to be at the very heart of China's present humiliation. It is therefore perhaps not surprising that communist cells were soon established in major Chinese cities, and that in 1921 the Chinese Communist Party was formed.

The losses resulting from the treaties did little to improve Sino–Japanese relations. They provided the long-term basis for a dispute between the two countries that culminated in the invasion of Manchuria (see Chapter 9) and ultimately full-scale war in 1937.

Fact

Before 1911, China had been ruled by emperors but, in that year, a nationalist revolution overthrew the imperial dynasty. In 1913, the new nationalist party the Guomindang (GMD) – led by Sun Zhougshan – won a majority in elections to a new National Assembly. However, a military dictator then took over and, from 1916, central government collapsed and rival warlords ruled different parts of China. This situation continued until 1927.

Questions

What can we learn from Source F about the reaction of the Chinese to the terms of the peace treaties? How useful is the source as evidence for Chinese reactions to the gains made by Japan?

93

Activities

1 Choose one of the mandated territories. Research its history from the time of the peace conferences until it was granted its independence.

2 On a map of the world, shade the countries that were made mandates and use a colour key to indicate which country was responsible for them.

3 Organise a class debate to consider whether the mandate system was anything more than imperialism by another name.

End of chapter activities

Summary

You should now have a good understanding of the impact of the peace treaties on international relations, and how they affected regional developments in the immediate post-war period. You have read about the problems encountered in establishing the new states, and examined how successful these new countries were in meeting the immediate challenges they faced. You should now be able to judge the extent to which the aims of the peacemakers were met when they established these states. You have also considered the stability of the successor states and should now be able to assess how successfully democracy was established in the region, and to consider whether it was the immediate post-war problems or later developments that were a greater challenge to democratic forms of government in these states.

In studying the establishment of the mandate system, you have looked at the reasons for the problems in managing the former colonies of the defeated powers. You have also examined the extent to which the mandate system brought about an end to imperialism and was successful in bringing stability, prosperity and future independence to the areas concerned. You should also be aware of some of the issues that remained unresolved by the peace treaties.

Summary activity

The successor states faced both political and economic problems. Copy the chart below, and then complete it to assess the extent and severity of the problems. For each problem, award a mark out of 5 to show how serious you think the problem was – the higher the mark, the more serious the problem. The overall total will allow you to see which state faced the most serious problems. Write a paragraph to summarise your findings.

State	Political problems	How serious?	Mark/5	Economic problems	How serious?	Mark/5	Total/10
Austria							
Hungary							
Czechoslovakia							
Poland							
Yugoslavia							

Paper 1 exam practice

Question

Compare and contrast the views expressed in Sources A and B about the impact of the Treaty of Trianon on Hungary.
[6 marks]

Skill

Cross-referencing

SOURCE B

Hungary won only a few minor concessions from the allies: more patrol boats on the Danube, for example. On June 4 1920, in a brief ceremony at the Trianon Palace, its representatives signed the Treaty. In Hungary the flags flew at half mast. Trianon became shorthand for allied cruelty and its memory fuelled an almost universal desire among Hungarians to undo its provisions. Horthy and his supporters toyed with improbable plans to restore Hungary to its pre-war boundaries, for example by gassing Czech soldiers in their barracks and rushing in with Hungarian troops.

Macmillan, M. 2001. Peacemakers: Six Months that Changed the World. London, UK. John Murray. p. 278.

SOURCE A

A map produced in Hungary just after the Treaty of Trianon; the caption reads: 'The arbitrary dismemberment of the Kingdom of Hungary, forming a geographically and economically united territory' (clockwise from top: Czechoslovakia, Romania, Yugoslavia and Austria)

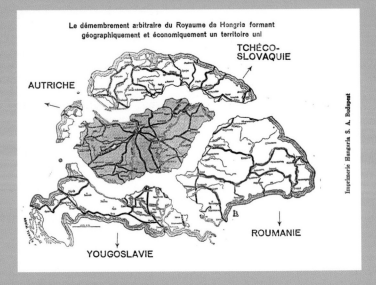

95

Student answer

Both Sources A and B put forward the view that the Treaty of Trianon was harsh on Hungary. Source A suggests that the major impact on Hungary was the loss of land and the economic losses associated with the territory, as Hungary lost its only rich industrial areas. However, although Source B also puts forward the view that the treaty created disquiet in Hungary, shown through the flying of the flag at half mast, it does not give any specific reasons for this reaction, except to argue that the treaty was seen as a symbol of allied cruelty.

Before you start

Cross-referencing questions require you to compare and contrast the information/content/nature of **two** sources. Before you attempt this question, refer to pages 212–13 for advice on how to tackle cross-referencing questions and a simplified markscheme.

Despite this, it could be argued that Source B implies that territorial losses were the main reason for the disquiet, as it suggests that Horthy's government considered trying to take back some of the lost land. This agrees with the feelings expressed in Source A, which concentrates on showing the sheer scale of the land lost, indicating clearly that Hungary had territory taken at every point, reducing it to about half its former size. This would explain the reaction expressed in Source B, that the flags flew at half mast. Source B also suggests that it was the loss of land that caused the greatest anger, as it refers to the universal desire to undo the provisions and restore the pre-war boundaries. Source B therefore supports the view expressed in Source A that the territorial losses provoked considerable opposition. However, Source A does link this reaction to the economic losses associated with the territory, which is not considered in Source B.

Examiner comments

This answer successfully links the two sources, rather than dealing with them individually, and the candidate compares the points of similarity. This is usually supported by precise evidence from the relevant source, which is a good approach to take. The candidate starts by giving an overall comparison, showing that the sources are very similar in their view, and concludes by linking the material. However, the student could have made greater use of the map in Source A, pointing out that it was produced just after the treaty and therefore reflects the immediate reaction of the Hungarian people, as does the flying of the flag at half mast in Source B. However, a point-by-point comparison of the two sources has been made, and the links between them are clearly outlined. The candidate has therefore done enough to earn 5 of the 6 marks available. In order to gain full marks, more detailed use of Source A would be needed.

Paper 2 practice questions

1   What were the aims of the peacemakers in establishing the successor states and how far did they achieve these aims?

2   Examine the view that the most serious problems facing the new states in Central and Eastern Europe were economic.

3   Assess the success of the Allied powers in establishing democratic states in Central and Eastern Europe.

4   Evaluate the causes of instability in Eastern Europe in the years 1919–23.

5   'Economic problems, rather than political changes, were the most important cause of the problems in Eastern Europe after the war.' To what extent to you agree with this assertion?

6   Analyse how far the problems facing the successor states were resolved in the period from 1919 to 1923.

7   Analyse the success and failures of the mandate system.

5 The role and structure of the League of Nations

Timeline

1919 Feb: draft constitution of League of Nations agreed

Apr: covenant of League of Nations produced

1920 Mar: US Congress votes against USA joining League; first meeting of League of Nations

1921 establishment of Permanent Court of International Justice in the Hague

1922 Apr: Treaty of Rapallo between Russia and Germany

1926 Sep: Germany joins League of Nations

Key questions

- What was the intended role of the League of Nations?
- In what ways were the League's weaknesses the result of its covenant and structure?
- How successful was the work of the League's organisations and commissions?
- How important was the absence of Germany, the USA and Russia from the League of Nations?

Overview

- The League of Nations was the organisation set up to ensure that peace was maintained after the First World War. Its role was to resolve conflicts and remove many of the issues that were believed to have led to the war.
- The League was intended to prevent aggression through 'collective security', where all members acted together against an aggressor.
- The League also aimed to bring about the disarmament of all nations, as many people believed that the arms race had been a significant cause of the First World War.
- Member nations hoped that co-operation, through the development of trade, would reduce the amount of conflict in the post-war world.
- The League's structure and the need for all member nations to agree on any action to be taken meant that decision-making was both difficult and slow. This reduced the effectiveness of the League right from the start.
- The League was made up of three major bodies – the Assembly, the Council and the Secretariat.
- The work of the League's commissions was probably its greatest success. Particularly important were the commissions that dealt with the issues of refugees, slavery, health and education.
- The USA's absence from the League seriously weakened the organisation; most historians regard this as a major cause of the League's ultimate failure.
- Germany and Russia were not allowed to join the League when it was established, and this strengthened the impression that it was no more than a 'club' for the victorious powers.

arbitration This is when two sides explain their differences to an independent body, which judges who is right or has the best claim. In some cases, the arbitrator's decision is not binding.

congress system A term used to describe a series of meetings held between the leaders of Austria, Britain, Prussia and Russia in the period after the Napoleonic Wars. At these meetings they discussed European and international issues, such as the revolution in Spain.

98

Questions

What can we learn from Wilson's speech in Source A about the challenges facing the League of Nations? What do you think was the purpose of Wilson's speech?

What was the intended role of the League of Nations?

The peacemakers were aware that the treaties resulting from the Paris Peace Conferences had not solved all the problems of the post-war world. Their major hope for a lasting peace lay in the establishment of the League of Nations. The formation of an international peacekeeping organisation was difficult, because it was the first major attempt to set up an institution for international diplomacy and **arbitration**. In the past, organisations or meetings, such as the **congress system**, had met only to deal with particular issues. These were attended by just a few nations and were not a permanent framework for solving international disputes. There was therefore no precedent for the League of Nations, and it faced a series of difficult issues. These included border disputes (a common result of the peace treaties and the collapse of four major empires), social and economic chaos in many states, the problem of minorities within these states, disarmament, and the governing of the mandates.

SOURCE A

For the first time in history the counsels of mankind are to be drawn together and concerted for the purpose of defending the right and improving the conditions of working people – men, women and children – all over the world. Such a thing as that was never dreamed of before, and what you are asked to discuss in discussing the League of Nations is the matter of seeing that this thing is not interfered with. There is no other way to do it than by a universal league of nations, and what is proposed is a universal league of nations.

Woodrow Wilson, speaking to an American audience about the establishment of the League and its purpose, 1919.

The covenant of the League of Nations set out several clear aims. These were:

- to discourage aggression between nations
- to encourage nations to disarm
- to encourage nations to co-operate, particularly in matters of trade and business
- to improve people's working and living conditions.

If these aims could be carried out, they would help to create a better, more stable world. Certainly many of the articles contained in the League's covenant attempted to address issues that had contributed to the outbreak of war in 1914. However, despite initial optimism, the aims of the League were always difficult to achieve in practice.

A cartoon entitled 'Ready to Start' depicting a plane leaving the 'old order'

Discouraging aggression: collective security

One of the main aims of the League was to preserve peace and international order. This was clearly stated in Article 11, which offered member states the sense of security they so desperately needed after the First World War.

SOURCE B

Any war or threat of war, whether immediately affecting any of the members of the League or not, is hereby declared a matter of concern to the whole League, and the League shall take any action that may be deemed wise and effectual to safeguard the peace of nations.

Article 11, The Covenant of the League of Nations.

Despite these strong words, the article did not actually specify what action would be taken to safeguard this peace. Initially, disputes were to be submitted to arbitration by the League, and Article 15 allowed the League to set up an enquiry even if the dispute had *not* been submitted for arbitration. There would then be a three-month cooling-off period, during which time the nations involved in the dispute awaited the League's verdict. However, this did not address the problem of how to force states either to wait for the three months or to accept the League's verdict on the dispute.

Article 10 made it clear that the League would uphold the independence of states. According to President Wilson, this was 'the heart of the matter and strikes at the taproot of war'. However, the idea that the League would 'advise' on the means by which the obligations should be fulfilled was challenged by a Canadian resolution, which proposed that Article 10 should be completely removed from the covenant. In the end the article remained, but in 1923 the League agreed that individual governments could decide for themselves how to meet their own obligations.

> **Question**
>
> Why do you think Article 11 of the League of Nations covenant did not specify *what* action or procedure was to be taken in order to safeguard the peace?

> **Question**
>
> Why do you think the Canadian government introduced a resolution to delete Article 10 from the covenant, and why was the 1923 decision made?

99

SOURCE C

The Members of the League undertake to respect and preserve as against external aggression the territorial integrity and existing political independence of all Members of the League. In case of any such aggression or in case of any threat or danger of such aggression the Council shall advise upon the means by which this obligation shall be fulfilled.

Article 10, The Covenant of the League of Nations.

International order was to be preserved through a process known as collective security. This guaranteed protection for all nations that were members of the League, and was particularly important for smaller states. Article 16 explained that if any country belonging to the League was attacked, the other members would come to its aid and protection.

SOURCE D

Should any Member of the League resort to war it shall ipso facto be deemed to have committed an act of war against all other Members of the League, which hereby undertake immediately to subject it to the severance of all trade or financial relations and the prevention of all financial, commercial or personal intercourse between the nationals of the Covenant-breaking State and the nationals of any other State, whether a member of the League or not. It shall be the duty of the Council in such case to recommend to the several Governments concerned what effective military, naval or air force the Members of the League shall severally contribute to the armed forces to be used to protect the covenants of the League.

Article 16, The Covenant of the League of Nations.

Activity

Rewrite Article 16 in your own words to make clear the aims and methods by which the League would guarantee collective security.

The threat of the combined force of other nations against an aggressor state was designed to stop nations from carrying out acts of war. In theory, this meant that there was no longer any need for countries to form individual alliances to guarantee security. Wilson believed that this would remove another of the causes of the First World War – secret treaties between different countries. However, as discussed in Chapter 4, many smaller states in Central and Eastern Europe still looked to the old system of alliances for protection against attack from nations that wanted to change the peace treaties. More significantly, France was involved in these alliances. From the start, therefore, a leading member of the League seemed unconvinced of its ability to safeguard collective security. In fact, during the whole time that the League existed, it never used armed force to prevent aggression.

Disarmament

At the end of the First World War, there was a general feeling that the arms race had played an significant role in the outbreak of the conflict. Most nations therefore agreed that disarmament was desirable. This was reflected in Article 8 of the covenant.

SOURCE E

The Members of the League recognise that the maintenance of peace requires the reduction of national armaments to the lowest point consistent with national safety, and the enforcement by common action of international obligations.

Article 8, The Covenant of the League of Nations.

Discussion point

What do you understand by 'the lowest point consistent with national safety'? Why do you think this made it difficult to bring about disarmament?

Despite the general desire for a reduction in arms levels, it was difficult to achieve in practice and a Disarmament Conference did not meet until February 1932. The major problems with disarmament were self-interest and a lack of trust. No one was willing to be the first to disarm, in case other nations then refused to honour the agreement. There was also ambiguity in the phrase 'the lowest point consistent with national safety'. As a result, only the defeated nations disarmed – a fact that gave rise to a sense of unfairness and discrimination.

International co-operation

Most countries believed that if there was global co-operation over matters such as trade and business, conflicts were less likely to arise. Strong international trade bonds would make nations realise that they had too much to lose by going to war and destroying the economic and financial benefits that were available through trade. Britain and the USA were particularly keen to restore trade links with Germany, and this was one of the reasons why they both supported German recovery after the war. It also encouraged the USA to lend Germany money through the Dawes and Young Plans (see pages 146 and 153) during the 1920s. The recovery of trading relations between states reduced international tensions, and it was no coincidence that when trade collapsed after the Wall Street Crash, some nations took aggressive measures to solve their economic problems.

 Theory of knowledge

History and hindsight
Historians know that the League of Nations failed to stop the outbreak of the Second World War. They have the benefit of hindsight when writing. How might this affect their interpretation of events? Does it make a historian's task more difficult? What are the advantages and disadvantages of hindsight?

The fourth aim of the League was to improve working and living conditions. Its successes in this area are covered on pages 105–7.

Activities

1   Imagine you are President Wilson. Write a speech to be given to the American people explaining why they should support the League of Nations.

2   Construct a spider diagram to show evidence of all the ways in which the aims of the League might be regarded as idealistic.

3   Design a poster to uphold the principle of collective security.

4   Imagine you are a League of Nations official. Write a letter to the leaders of the governments in Central and Eastern Europe explaining why they do not need to make alliances. What might their reply be?

In what ways were the League's weaknesses the result of its covenant and structure?

The structure of the League and the rules governing each of its internal bodies were set out in its covenant. The covenant also explained the situations in which the League would become involved and how its decisions would be both reached and implemented. One major issue the organisation faced was how to enforce its aims and uphold its decisions, and a series of measures against aggressor states were decided on. These were:

- moral persuasion
- economic sanctions
- military force.

Steps against aggressor nations

In the first instance, the League would use moral persuasion or condemnation. It would decide which nation was the aggressor and would try to persuade this state to stop its activities. In reality, there were always going to be limits to the effectiveness of moral persuasion, as aggressor states were unlikely to listen to arguments that differed from their own perspective. At the time, though, many people believed that after the horrors of the First World War, all states would favour peaceful resolutions and would listen to reason.

If moral persuasion failed, economic sanctions would be imposed: member states would refuse to trade with the aggressor. However, although economic sanctions could be effective, there were always other nations outside the League – including the USA – that might continue to trade with the aggressor. The use of sanctions also depended upon the willingness of member nations to include *all* goods within the trade embargo, which was necessary if it was to have the desired effect. Once again, this was not always the case, particularly during the Great Depression when trade embargos badly affected member nations' economies. The idealism with which the League was formed eventually gave way to economic reality, and member states were unwilling to sacrifice their own interests for a greater good.

The final option available to the League was military force. However, the organisation did not have its own army and depended on the willingness of member nations to contribute troops. Many states were reluctant to commit their own forces – most nations were in debt from the war and, as economic conditions worsened, the cost of military intervention became a pressing concern. The main contributors both militarily and financially were likely to be the major powers, but not even Britain and France had the resources available after the war.

Even more importantly, the structure of the League made it very difficult for military action to be agreed upon. The League could only act if war had been officially declared, and there was no plan for League action if the aggression took the form of a **guerrilla war**. This further limited the likelihood of League involvement or its success in resolving conflicts. The League could also only intervene if either the Council or International Court agreed (see page 104). If they did not agree on a course of action, the states could 'legally' continue the conflict.

Although these three steps were outlined in the covenant, there were no specific details so it was easy for countries to avoid following League decisions concerning individual acts of aggression. This made it difficult for the League to take effective action, especially during the 1930s.

The institutions of the League

The League was made up of two major institutions – the Assembly and the Council. These were supported by the Secretariat, which also had specialist departments responsible for issues such as health care. Some historians have suggested that the structure of the League condemned it to failure from the start. They argue that the decision-making process was too slow, given the difficulties of reaching a unanimous decision before action could be taken. The Assembly had to recommend action to the Council, and this also slowed the process. Moreover, even when matters reached the Council, each permanent member had a **veto** and could therefore block action, even if all the other members of the Council agreed.

The Assembly

Wilson's desire that the League should be like a 'world parliament' that upheld democracy was reflected in the Assembly. This was the League's parliament and every member state had three representatives, regardless of the size of that country. The Assembly had a number of important functions, including admitting new members to the League, deciding on how much money each state should contribute so that a budget could be agreed, and appointing temporary members to the Council. However, the Assembly met only once a year, so it was unable to deal immediately with any developing crises. The greatest weakness of the Assembly was its **unanimity** rule.

guerrilla war This is where the regular army of a country is involved in fighting against unofficial or irregular forces. The guerrilla forces are usually much smaller than the regular army, but are often difficult to defeat because they know the area well and avoid full-scale battle, using tactics such as ambushing their enemy to achieve victory.

veto The power to prevent something from being done. Each of the permanent members of the League of Nations Council had the right of veto, which meant that any one nation could halt proceedings.

unanimity In order for a decision to be taken, *all* members – or those with the right to vote – have to agree.

The structure of the League of Nations

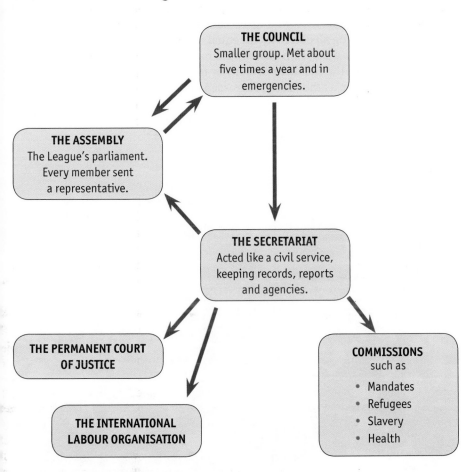

There has been some difference of emphasis on the reasons for the failure of the League. David Williamson has focused on the structure of the League, with the unanimity clause and veto being the main reasons that the League was unable to take effective action. Ruth Henig and Xenia Eudin have blamed the absence of major powers, such as the USA, Germany and Russia. However, A. J. P. Taylor suggested that it was the self-interest of member states that hindered the effectiveness of the League.

103

SOURCE F

Except where otherwise expressly provided in this Covenant or by the terms of the present Treaty, decisions at any meeting of the Assembly or of the Council shall require the agreement of all the Members of the League represented at the meeting.

Article 5, The Covenant of the League of Nations.

Article 5 of the League's covenant stated that decisions must be unanimous. The article's purpose was to remove any controversy and ensure that all states agreed to a response. However, in reality it was very difficult to get such a large number of countries to agree, particularly over controversial or disputed issues. In 1920, there were 42 members of the League of Nations; by 1934 this had risen to 60 members. This enlarged membership made it even harder to achieve unanimity. Decision-making was inevitably very slow, and aggressor states often completed their acts before the League agreed on what action to take. This eventually destroyed faith in the organisation, and encouraged smaller nations to look elsewhere – often to traditional alliances – for protection.

It was also difficult to achieve unanimity because of the problem of overcoming the self-interest of member states. Although all agreed that another war must be avoided, they were less willing to set aside their own interests for the common good. Giving all countries an equal number of votes meant that small nations could block a decision that would have a far greater impact on larger states. Once again, the idealism evident at the League's foundation proved to be a stumbling block as the 1920s progressed and nations put self-interest first.

The League of Nations at its opening session in Geneva, Switzerland, 15 November 1920

The Council

The Council was the main body within the League. It effectively became the **executive** committee or 'cabinet' of the Assembly, working out the details and implementation of the policies that had been approved, at least in principle, by the Assembly. In part, the Council's key role in the League came about because it was in session almost constantly, and was therefore able to deal with incidents as they occurred.

Despite this, there were several weaknesses in the structure of the Council. It was dominated by Britain and France, both of which had a permanent seat as the major founding powers. They were joined as permanent members by Italy and Japan. This meant that these four nations (and Germany from 1926) controlled the decision-making and could veto any action they disapproved of. As decisions normally required a unanimous vote, the states involved in the disputes under discussion were not allowed to participate, so that they could not block decision-making.

The Council also included a number of temporary members; however, they did not have the power of veto. The number of non-permanent members varied from an initial four to nine at various times during the history of the League.

executive The part of an organisation that has the power to put plans into action. This is often contrasted with the institution that draws up the plans and policies – in the case of the League of Nations, the Assembly.

Temporary members were elected by the Assembly for a period of three years. Despite this aim of involving a wider range of nations in the decision-making process, the permanent members still had the last word.

The Secretariat and the League's commissions

The Assembly, Council and other commissions of the League (see below) all needed to keep records of their meetings and find information to assist in their decision-making. This was provided by the Secretariat, which acted as the League's **civil service** or administrative body. Unlike the Council and the Assembly, the Secretariat was successful in its role, although it was often overworked because it was made up of relatively small numbers. The Secretariat's job was to provide other departments with the information they needed, to keep records of discussions, to produce reports for either the Council or Assembly to help them understand a particular situation, and to provide interpreters for meetings. The Secretariat included specialist sections covering areas such as health, disarmament and economic issues, and could therefore provide the detailed information required by the Assembly and Council.

The Secretariat worked closely with the other agencies of the League. These agencies included organisations such as the Permanent Court of International Justice, the International Labour Organisation, the Mandates Commission, the Refugees Commission, the Slavery Commission and the Health Committee. Their work is described in the following section.

> **civil service** The permanent and professional administrators within an organisation or state. They are non-political and their job is to provide information for those who hold office and to give impartial advice on decisions.

Activities

1   Copy and complete the chart below to summarise the strengths and weaknesses of the League's organisation and structure.

Institution	Strength	Weakness
Assembly		
Council		
Secretariat		

2   For each of the major institutions of the League, explain how the weaknesses you have outlined in the chart above might be overcome and what difficulties your solutions might face.

3   Why do you think it was impossible to strengthen the League's institutions?

How successful was the work of the League's organisations and commissions?

The Council and Assembly were often weak and ineffective, but the League's various organisations and commissions were much more successful in their work. They helped introduce many changes to the social and economic conditions of large numbers of people throughout the world.

The Permanent Court of Justice

The Permanent Court of Justice, based in the Hague (in the Netherlands), played a key role in the League's purpose of settling international disputes peacefully. It was made up of judges from a range of member states, whose job it was to consider disputes and to give legal advice to both the Council and Assembly. However, there was a weakness in its procedure. The Court could only intervene and arbitrate on a dispute if it was *asked* to do so; it also lacked the power to enforce its decisions and could not ensure that nations followed its rulings. Therefore, although the Court was a force for preventing and resolving conflicts in theory, in practice its effect was limited.

The International Labour Organisation

The International Labour Organisation brought together employers, workers and government representatives once a year. The scale of its operation meant that it had its own organisational structure to manage it and keep records. The aim of the organisation was to improve the living and working conditions of workers in member states, and in many areas it was successful. The organisation limited the number of hours that young children were allowed to work, and succeeded in banning poisonous white lead in paint. It also collected large amounts of information about working conditions and encouraged governments to improve in this area. The International Labour Organisation campaigned for a maximum 48-hour working week and eight-hour working day, but this was supported by only a few member states; most argued that such restrictions would damage their economies by raising the cost of industry. Once again, this limitation suggests that when self-interest and prosperity were at stake, member nations were less willing to carry out decisions.

The commissions on refugees and health

The most notable of the League's commissions was the Mandates Commission, whose work was discussed in Chapter 4. The League also had commissions to deal with refugees and health issues, and these were very successful in bringing about change, even in countries that were not members of the League.

Refugees

Refugees were a major problem at the end of the war – thousands of people had fled their homes during the conflict and thousands more were prisoners of war in need of repatriating. Under the leadership of the High Commissioner for Refugees, the Norwegian Fridtjof Nansen, the League oversaw the return of some 400,000 prisoners of war to their homelands. In 1922, the Refugee Commission successfully aided the refugee crisis that hit Turkey and Greece, when thousands were made homeless.

Health

The League was also successful in preventing the spread of diseases such as cholera, smallpox and dysentery in the refugee camps. The Health Commission, which later became the World Health Organisation, was also very effective in its work. Not only did it start an education programme to make people aware of dangerous diseases and how to prevent them spreading, it also limited the spread of leprosy and launched a worldwide campaign to eradicate mosquitoes, which significantly reduced cases of malaria and yellow fever. Perhaps the most obvious sign of the Health Commission's success was when Russia – which was not a member of the League at the time – asked for advice on how to prevent the plague in Siberia. Russia usually opposed the work of the League; the fact that it turned to a League organisation for help was an indication of the respect the Health Commission had earned.

Slavery and drugs

The League's record was encouraging in terms of other social problems, too. The Slavery Commission helped to abolish slavery in a number of regions, most notably in Sierra Leone, where some 200,000 slaves were freed. The commission also organised raids against both slave owners and traders in Burma, and helped to reduce slave labour in the building of the Tanganyika railway in East Africa, where the death rate dropped from 50% to 4%. In addition, the League took action over the illegal drugs trade, naming companies that were involved in such practices, which helped to discourage others from pursuing similar policies.

Fact
Following the Greco–Turkish War of 1919–22, a refugee crisis occurred involving nearly 2 million people. Nansen travelled to the region to co-ordinate a huge relief effort that supplied aid to both Turkish and Greek refugees, who had been crowded into refugee camps. The League then helped organise the transfer of populations between Greece and Turkey, and assisted the refugees in settling in their new countries.

The success of the League's organisations was far-reaching and improved the lives of millions, yet many historians ignore this work and focus instead on issues such as border disputes, disarmament and the resolution of conflicts, where the League had less success.

Activities

1 Carry out some additional research, and then copy and complete the chart below, to add to your summary of the strengths and weaknesses of the League's organisation and structure.

Institution	Strength	Weakness
Permanent Court of Justice		
International Labour Organisation		
Mandates Commission		
Refugees Committee		
Slavery Committee		
Health Committee		

2 Conduct a class discussion on the following points:

• Why was the League concerned about resolving social issues?
• The League had great success in resolving several social and economic issues. Does this change the view that the League of Nations was a failure?

Theory of knowledge

History and bias
The historian Keith Windschuttle said that historians sometimes find that the evidence 'forces them, often reluctantly, to change the position they originally intended to take'. As the task of the historian is to explain and make sense of the past, he or she should consider the widest possible range of events and issues. However, when writing about the League of Nations, historians have tended to focus on its weaknesses rather than its social and economic achievements. Is this an example of 'confirmation bias'? Can you find other examples where historians have ignored events in their writing, with the result that their interpretation is less balanced? Does this make their writing less useful?

How important was the absence of Germany, the USA and Russia from the League of Nations?

When the League first met in 1920 there were 44 member states. Of these, 32 were the Allied nations from the First World War and 12 were neutral countries. The defeated powers were not allowed to join until they had clearly demonstrated that they were willing to honour the terms of the peace treaties and to abide by international agreements. In the end, Germany was accepted into the League in 1926. However, to begin with, the absence of the defeated powers made the League look like a 'club of victors' that would uphold only the interests of Britain and France. The League was also seriously weakened by the absence of two former Allied powers – the United States and Russia.

The Republican victory 1919

The League of Nations had been conceived by Woodrow Wilson, and US membership was considered crucial to its success. The USA's refusal to join the League was thus a crushing blow right at the start. The United States emerged from the war in a much stronger position than either Britain or France, having been only actively involved from 1917. Although the USA had lent money to the Allies, it was financially stronger than either Britain or France. As a result, the USA was in a position to help the League both financially and militarily in ways that Britain and France simply could not afford. American membership of the League was also essential for the success of economic sanctions, which would carry far more weight if the US withdrew trading rights from an aggressor state.

Democrats One of the two major political parties in America. Democrats are usually in favour of government intervention in public affairs and the economy, and support issues such as health reform and welfare.

Republicans The other major political party in America. Republicans are usually more conservative than Democrats, and do not believe in government intervention, believing that it is individuals' responsibility to look after themselves.

Monroe Doctrine The doctrine put forward by the US president James Monroe in 1823, which stated that intervention in the affairs of the Americas by other powers could be regarded as an act of hostility.

Warren Harding (1865–1923)
Harding took office as president in 1921. He was a Republican and defeated the Democrat candidate by 16 million votes to 9 million. Harding's presidency is often associated with corruption and scandals, as he appointed a number of dubious figures and friends to high office. He died whilst in office and was succeeded by his vice-president, Calvin Coolidge.

Wilson tried hard to convince the US Congress to approve the peace treaties and American membership of the League, but ultimately both he and his successor as the **Democrats**' presidential candidate failed. The Democrats had been in power in the United States for eight years, since 1913. US entry into the First World War provoked controversy, despite Wilson's rhetoric about the ideals of freedom and democracy. During his period in office opposition had grown, and Wilson's political opponents regarded the peace conferences and the establishment of the League of Nations as an ideal opportunity to defeat him.

In 1919, the mid-term elections resulted in victory for the **Republicans** under the leadership of the forceful but conservative Henry Cabot Lodge. This meant that there was now a Republican majority in the US Senate. When Wilson returned to the USA in the spring of 1919 to sign legislation, there were calls for revisions to the League. The Senate was particularly concerned about Article 10 of the covenant, which promised protection for member nations against aggressor states; they feared that such a commitment would drag the USA into a range of conflicts. Lodge called for an amendment that would allow the US government to decide what issues it should or should not be involved in. There were also worries that the League would interfere in the affairs of the Americas, which had previously been shielded from outside intervention by the **Monroe Doctrine**.

When Wilson returned to the peace talks he won three concessions from the other Allied leaders, which he hoped would earn approval for the treaties and the League back home:

- The validity of international agreements and regional understandings was confirmed; in practice this meant that the Monroe Doctrine would be upheld and the League would not interfere in affairs within the the USA's sphere of influence.
- States that wanted to leave the League were allowed to, as long as they gave two years' notice.
- The League would not consider disputes that arose from domestic sources.

However, these concessions were not enough to win Wilson sufficient public support in the USA. Despite increasing ill-health, he embarked on a nationwide tour to speak to the American people about his vision for the League, but in 1919 Congress voted against the proposals. In 1920, Wilson suffered a stroke but he did not give up campaigning for approval of the League. He took the proposal back to Congress in March 1920, but it was defeated again by 49 votes to 35.

The Democrats were concerned that if the United States was not involved in world affairs then another war would break out, and were therefore determined to continue pushing for approval of the League. Membership of the League was adopted as a central part of the presidential election campaign in 1920. However, with Wilson ill and public opinion against US involvement in European affairs, it was the Republican **Warren Harding** who won the election, campaigning under the slogan of returning America to 'normalcy'.

The USA's refusal to join the League

The USA's decision not to join the League was the result of political opposition within Congress, as the Republicans reflected public opinion against membership. Many Americans disliked the terms of the peace treaties, believing them to be unfair and ineffective in solving problems in Europe.

They feared that the terms would lead to further conflicts as the defeated nations sought to right what they saw as wrongs. The US public did not want its soldiers involved in foreign wars defending treaties that most believed were flawed and morally wrong. Nor did they want the US to be involved in potential future conflicts aimed at preserving British and French imperialism. In addition, with European economies so weak, the US feared that it would have to fund any wars that might arise.

A US illustration from 1920 showing American concerns about the League of Nations

The idea of trade embargos was another point of contention. The US economy was growing and the country experienced a period of prosperity in the immediate post-war years. However, much of this depended on international trade. If the US joined the League, it would be obliged to honour League rulings on economic sanctions for aggressor states, which would damage the US economy.

There were also a significant number of US citizens who had German ancestors, which gave them a particular reason to dislike the international peacekeeping system outlined by the peace treaties and the League of Nations covenant. These people viewed the terms as a way of preventing German recovery and keeping it out of world affairs. The same was true of American Italians: there was much dissatisfaction in America about how Italian claims had been dismissed at the peace conferences. For politicians, association with a system that antagonised sizeable groups in America was a guaranteed vote-loser.

Vladimir Ilyich Lenin (1870–1924) Lenin started on a revolutionary path after his brother was executed for the attempted assassination of the tsar. Expelled from university, he was imprisoned in Siberia but escaped to Western Europe. Lenin became a writer, detailing communist and Marxist principles, and explaining how socialism could be achieved in Russia. He remained in exile until April 1917, when he returned to Russia. Lenin then pushed for the Bolsheviks to overthrow the provisional government, which was determined to keep Russia fighting in the First World War. He was the leader of the Bolsheviks until his death in 1924, following a series of strokes.

Questions

What reasons does Eudin give for the Soviet distrust of the League? Using your own knowledge, what evidence is there to support this interpretation? Why might the Russians have this view of the League?

The isolation of Russia in the 1920s

The Allied powers were bitterly opposed to Bolshevism, and at the time of the Paris Peace Conferences Allied forces were fighting on Russian soil to prevent the establishment of a communist or Bolshevik state. They particularly wanted to isolate the new regime because it was trying (with some success in Hungary, see page 57) to start communist revolutions in other nations. For this reason, Russia was not permitted to join the League of Nations.

In fact, it is unlikely that Russia would have accepted an invitation to join. The leader of the Russian Revolution, **Vladimir Ilyich Lenin**, regarded the League as a capitalist club, formed to prevent the spread of communism. Lenin also believed – as did many Germans – that the League's high ideals were designed to give moral authority to an unfair treaty. In a series of speeches in the early 1920s, Lenin accused the League of upholding capitalism and colonialism.

SOURCE G

In its drive for security and legal recognition, Soviet diplomacy again and again came up against the League of Nations. Here, as in other areas of diplomacy, the Soviets followed a dual policy: on the one hand they denounced the League as a coalition of predatory imperialist powers; on the other, they demanded to take part in such conferences of the League as affected Russian interests. The Soviet attitude towards the League had been influenced by the fact that Soviet Russia had not been invited to become a member, by the communist idea of capitalist encirclement, by the fear of any coalition or alliance of which Russia was not a member.

Eudin, X. 1957. Soviet Russia and the West 1920–1927, A Documentary Survey. Stanford, USA. Stanford University Press. p. 121.

The significance of Germany's absence

The decision not to allow Germany to join the League was made during the peace talks. Before membership would be considered, Germany had to demonstrate that it had abandoned its aggressive attitude and was ready to take its place among the 'civilised' nations of the world. In other words, Germany was on probation for good behaviour – once it had proved that it was willing to behave peacefully, it could join the League.

Germany's absence from the League fuelled bitterness within the country and reinforced the view that the League was a club of victors, who would use it to keep Germany subdued, prevent its recovery, ensure its isolation from Europe and condemn it to a position as a second-rate power. In fact, Germany's absence had exactly the opposite effect. Far from being isolated, Germany signed the Treaty of Rapallo with Russia in 1922, and used this to bypass several military clauses of the Treaty of Versailles (see page 141). In some ways, it was this treaty that encouraged Britain and France to change their attitudes towards Germany and, after the invasion of the Ruhr, to work towards its integration into world affairs in the hope that improved relations with the Western powers of Britain and France would cause Germany to turn its back on Russia.

The significance of the USA's and Russia's absence

Without the USA, Russia and Germany, the League was dominated by Britain and France, strengthening the view that this was an organisation run by and for the benefit of the victorious powers. The League would have gained greater credibility by allowing Germany's membership from the start; in the event, it ultimately drove Germany into an alliance with Russia.

The direction of the League was guided by Britain and France, which had very different views about its aims and purpose. As the 1920s progressed, these differences became more noticeable and were heightened by Italy and Japan – the two other major powers on the Council – which had their own expansionist and aggressive ambitions. British and French dominance further weakened the League, as both powers had suffered severe damage during the war. Neither nation was strong enough, financially or militarily, to act as the 'world's policeman'.

Britain and France were divided by their post-war priorities. France was concerned about future German aggression. Believing Britain would be unwilling to lend support should this occur, France acted outside the League to protect itself from the German threat, signing alliances with the new states in Central and Eastern Europe (see Chapter 4). Britain, on the other hand, was more concerned with rebuilding trade to aid its economic recovery and secure its empire, as nationalist independence movements began to stir in different regions of the world. Some British politicians even stated that Britain should not have joined the League after the US had refused membership.

> **Fact**
> During and after the First World War, nationalist movements developed within the territories of the former Turkish Empire and also across parts of the British Empire. These movements sought to establish their own countries, free from foreign or colonial rule. In the British Empire this was most noticeable in India, where Mohandas (Mahatma) Gandhi led the Congress movement in its call for independence.

111

A cartoon from the British magazine Punch, *10 December 1919*

THE GAP IN THE BRIDGE.

> **Activity**
>
> What is the message of this cartoon? Explain your answer with reference to details of the cartoon and your own knowledge. What impression does the cartoon give of the USA? Carry out some research into US foreign policy in the 1920s. How valid is the view of this expressed in the cartoon?

From the very beginning, the League of Nations was not a global organisation, a fact that made it much more difficult for the League to deal with conflicts outside Europe. This can be seen by events in Manchuria in 1931 (see page 181). A region such as this was a long way from Europe and of little immediate concern to either of the leading League powers. The situation would have been very different if a Pacific power, such as the USA or Russia, had been a member.

The USA's absence – to a greater extent than that of Germany or Russia – has often been blamed for the League's weakness and ultimate failure, prompting Sally Marks to argue that 'in its larger role the League foundered on the twin rocks of the unanimity clause and the absence of America'.

The strengths and weaknesses of the League: an analysis

From the outset, attempts to strengthen the powers of the League were defeated by self-interest. France wanted the League to be able to direct members to adopt specific policies or to provide an established number of troops to deal with a crisis. However, member states were not willing to give up their sovereignty and freedom of action.

This was seen most clearly in the attitude of Britain towards the Geneva Protocol (see page 126), when it refused to accept the proposal that nations involved in a dispute should accept the Council's decision. As a result, the League never functioned as a military alliance, but rather as a loose association of nations. Despite these weaknesses, however, the League promoted greater international co-operation than ever before. Consequently, the 1920s witnessed a large number of international agreements, which will be examined in the next chapter.

Historians such as Ruth Henig have been dismissive of the performance of the League. In Henig's view, the post-war problems made it very difficult for the League to succeed.

SOURCE H

Given the unstable and impoverished condition of large parts of Europe after 1919, and the growing antagonism between Britain and France, it is hardly surprising that the League, on which so many hopes rested in 1919, should have failed to make a significant political impact.

Henig, R. 1984. Versailles and After 1919–33. London, UK. Methuen. p. 41.

Some historians have also suggested that the very structure of the League doomed it to failure from the start, whilst others have argued that the absence of major powers such as the USA and Russia made its task even more difficult.

Although Wilson's hopes that all major powers would join the League, that they would willingly disarm, accept the decisions of the organisation and take any conflict or dispute they had to the League were largely idealistic, there was still a great deal of support for principles behind the League of Nations. Many people believed that if nations joined together it would be enough to deter others from aggression. This attitude was particularly strong in the 1920s and helps to explain, at least in part, why there were no major conflicts in this period. However, this must be balanced against the fact that few countries had the economic strength to become involved in another conflict, even if they had wanted to.

There were some who resented that they saw as Wilson's conviction that he alone knew how to solve the world's problems. Others believed that his ideas were too vague or had been put together too hastily. Despite this, it appeared as if the world had entered a 'new age', as the League gathered for its first session in 1920. It is easy with the benefit of hindsight to argue that these hopes were an illusion.

Many nations, even those such as Japan and Italy who were members of the League, were dissatisfied with the peace treaties and wanted to change their terms. This, along with the absence of major powers such as America and Russia, made it much harder for the League to survive and presented it with a serious challenge in the period after the Great Depression, when large-scale conflicts broke out.

It was very difficult to persuade nations to sacrifice their own interests and to accept decisions made by other countries. This issue will be examined in detail in the next chapter, but even in the 1920s the League struggled to resolve disputes where the interests of major powers such as France and Italy were involved. States were not willing to give up their independence, and the League had no power to intervene in internal issues. It therefore relied on the goodwill of its member states to accept decisions.

Activities

1 Construct a spider diagram to show the reasons why the USA did not join the League of Nations.

2 Imagine you are a French diplomat in the early 1920s. Write a letter to the government explaining what you think France should do to improve its security now that the USA has not joined the League of Nations.

End of chapter activities

Summary

In this chapter, you have considered Wilson's motives in establishing the League of Nations and his hopes and aims for it. These aims have been contrasted with those of France to show that there were already tensions at the start of the League's work. You should now have a clear understanding of the terms of the covenant and the extent to which they were practical or driven by idealism. In particular, you should be aware of the cornerstone of Wilson's drive for peace and international order: collective security.

You should be able to explain the strengths and weaknesses of each body within the League, which will help you to understand the League's later failings, particularly in the 1930s. You should now realise why some people take the view that the League was doomed from the start. This was partly because of the membership of the League, most significantly the USA's absence. You have seen the importance of this absence and the resultant domination of the League by Britain and France, and should be able to describe the problems this created.

Summary activity

Consider the following two views about the League of Nations.

View A: *The League of Nations appears impressive but it is idealistic and has severe weaknesses in its structure.*

View B: *The League of Nations can secure peace and bring protection to small nations, preventing future wars.*

Using the information in this chapter, find examples and evidence that support each of the statements. Using this evidence, write a paragraph explaining which of the views about the League of Nations you think is the most valid and why.

Paper 1 exam practice

Question

With reference to their origin and purpose, assess the value and limitations of Sources A and B on page 115 for historians studying the origins of the League of Nations.
[6 marks]

Skill

Value and limitations (reliability/utility) of sources

SOURCE A

A cartoon published in America in January 1919

Citisen.] [Brooklyn, U.S

An Expected Arrival.
Will the stork make good as to this infant ?

SOURCE B

In all the League had to do during the first year of its existence it was profoundly affected by the refusal of the United States of America to become a member. It had been assumed that a project so American in origin and its originality would, of course, be accepted in Washington. The news of its rejection in the United States created feelings of discouragement and even disgust in Europe. For a time men doubted if the League would go on without support from a great nation who was rich enough to soothe Europe's wounds.

Bassett, J. S. 1930. The League of Nations – A Chapter in World Politics. New York, USA. Longmans, Green & Co. p. 31.

115

Student answer

Source A was produced at the time the League was being discussed, and therefore shows the hopes and aspirations associated with it. As it was produced in America, which later rejected joining the League, it does show that at this early stage there was some optimism about the League, and support for it, although the caption also makes us aware that there were doubts as it states 'will the stork make good to this infant?' This is useful to the historian, as it suggests that even before the League came into existence there were doubts about its ability to succeed, and as this was produced before the League had experienced any failures or America had decided not to join, it does not have the benefit of hindsight. The cartoon appears to reflect the divisions in the USA about Wilson's dream of a League of Nations. The caption 'An Expected Arrival' makes it clear that the Americans were expecting Wilson to push for a League at the peace conferences, but that there were some doubts about its likely effectiveness.

Before you start

Value and limitations (utility/reliability) questions require you to assess **two** sources over a range of possible issues – and to comment on their value to historians studying a particular event or period of history. You need to consider both the **origin and purpose** and also the **value and limitations** of the sources. You should link these in your answer, showing how origin/purpose relate to value/limitations.

Before you attempt this question, refer to pages 213–14 for advice on how to tackle these questions, and a simplified markscheme.

On the other hand, Source B was written by a historian and is an extract from a book on the League. It was published at a time when the League was struggling, and this might explain why the historian is trying to assess the difficulties the League faced in terms of America's absence. This book was written in 1930, before the impact of the Depression had been fully felt and this may explain why the writer places the emphasis for the failure of the League on the USA, rather than other events. However, it was written by an expert and will have been thoroughly researched. Despite this, as it was written in 1930 Bassett was unable to see the full reasons for the failure of the League, as other events had not yet unfolded.

Examiner comments

The question requires the student to consider the origin and purpose of the two sources in order to assess their value and limitations. Although it is not expected that answers will consider all these elements, the student does not address the *purpose* of either source, although this is hinted at with Source B. However, the answer does provide strong consideration of both the strengths and limitations of the sources as evidence. The student makes some important comments about Source B, linking the date of its publication to the line of argument that is pursued. However, as with Source A, there is little direct consideration given to its *purpose*. As a result, the student has done enough to get into Band 2 and earn 4 marks out of the 6 available.

Activity

Look again at the two sources, the simplified markscheme on page 214, and the student answer above. Now try to rewrite the answer to push it into Band 1 and so obtain the full 6 marks. Remember to give due consideration to the *purpose* of each source.

Paper 2 practice questions

1   Were the aims of the League of Nations realistic?

2   Discuss the view that the League of Nations failed because of the absence of the USA.

3   Assess the reasons why the USA did not join the League of Nations.

4   Assess the view that the League of Nations was doomed to fail from its foundation.

5   Examine the extent to which structural weaknesses were the main reason for the failure of the League of Nations.

6   Analyse the extent to which the self-interests of Britain and France were to blame for the failure of the League of Nations.

6 The League of Nations: collective security in the 1920s

Key questions

- What problems were there in enforcing the peace treaties?
- How successful was diplomacy in the 1920s?
- How successful was the League of Nations in resolving border disputes and other conflicts in the 1920s?

Overview

- There were many problems in enforcing the peace treaties during the 1920s. This situation was not helped by the absence of the USA from the League of Nations, which created a sense of insecurity among many nations.
- Disarmament was difficult to achieve: states did not trust one another; they were still concerned about their own lack of security, and feared being attacked if they did disarm.
- France and Britain had their own priorities, and appeared to be more concerned about these than upholding international interests. France was preoccupied with the question of its own security should Germany recover its strength. Britain focused on problems within its empire.
- The attitudes of both Italy and Japan towards the settlements undermined the treaties as, despite being members of the League, both powers sought to obtain land and influence that they believed had been denied them at the peace talks. This was a particular problem in the Far East, because of China's political instability.
- Despite these difficulties, some progress was made in fostering international co-operation in the 1920s.
- During this period, the League of Nations had mixed results in resolving border disputes, but was more successful when dealing with smaller and less powerful nations.

Timeline

1905 Japanese defeat Russia in Russo–Japanese War

1912 revolution in China; Chinese emperor abdicates; civil war breaks out in China

1919 Treaty of Versailles; Japan and Italy feel they do not gain sufficient rewards for their sacrifices

Jun: Anglo–American guarantee signed at Versailles

1920 conflict over Vilna

1920–21 Aaland Islands dispute

1921 Mar: plebiscite in Upper Silesia

May: revolt in Upper Silesia

Oct: League hands most of industrial area of Upper Silesia to Poland

1921–22 Washington Naval Agreements

1922 League of Nations organises financial assistance for Austria

1923 League of Nations organises financial assistance for Hungary; conflict over Memel

Aug: Italian forces ambushed and killed whilst surveying border between Greece and Albania

1924 Italian occupation of Corfu; Geneva Protocol; conflict over Mosul

1925 conflict between Greece and Bulgaria

1928 Japanese army assassinates warlord in Manchuria

Aug: Kellogg–Briand Pact signed

Italian nationalists invade the port city of Fiume in 1919 – one of the first signs of the failure of the peace conferences

What problems were there in enforcing the peace treaties?

The question of how to ensure that the peace treaties were upheld was a difficult one. The USA's refusal to ratify the treaties seriously weakened international security and created major problems in making sure they were enforced. America's absence from the League meant that responsibility for upholding the agreements fell mainly to Britain and France, with some help from Italy and Belgium. However, both Britain and France had agreed to the terms of the treaties in the belief that they would have US support, and neither country was strong enough to meet the challenge alone.

The problem of disarmament

Disarmament posed the greatest challenge throughout the 1920s. The peace treaties stated that the defeated powers must disarm, and indeed all nations were encouraged to do the same, in line with the aims of the League of Nations. However, it had already proved difficult to ensure that Germany disarmed to the level specified in the treaty, and it was an even greater challenge to persuade the victorious nations to reduce their arms.

Disarmament was a key feature of Wilson's Fourteen Points. It was supported by the public because of the horrors of the First World War, and was desirable in the post-war economic climate due to the high cost of rearming. In practice, though, little progress was made in reducing weaponry. Countries were concerned about their own security – even more so after the USA refused to join the League, as most states believed that America was the only nation powerful enough to ensure world peace.

In the longer term, disarmament was further threatened by the rise of nationalist movements in Japan, Italy and Germany, as well as the problems created by the Wall Street Crash and the Great Depression. As a result, although a number of disarmament conferences were held throughout the 1920s and early 1930s, little progress was made.

The absence of the USA

To begin with, the USA's withdrawal from the international scene caused the greatest concern. When France failed to ensure the division of Germany and to have the Rhineland removed from German control, Britain and the USA offered France an Anglo–American guarantee of security. This was signed at Versailles on 28 June 1919. Despite this agreement, the USA intended that the League would deal with any threats to French security, whilst Britain hoped that if a German resurgence threatened France, the USA would lead any action against it. Therefore, even at this early stage neither power was really willing to commit itself to protecting France. In practice, the USA's refusal to ratify the treaties meant that the guarantee was not binding for either party. This pleased the British public, who were reluctant for their government to make foreign commitments so soon after the war, but it pushed France into developing the Little Entente with the new Central and Eastern European powers (see page 80).

There was a growing feeling in the USA, particularly among Republicans, that America should avoid further foreign entanglements or commitments that could lead to US involvement in future conflicts. Traditional accounts have argued that this isolationist approach continued throughout the 1920s, as the US feared that European commitments would have a detrimental effect on its own booming economy. Such historians have argued that US policies throughout the 1920s were driven by an urge to retain its global economic power, but in practice this approach conflicted with the policy of isolationism.

Although the USA wanted to remain internationally isolated, its desire to protect its own trade and economy meant that a certain level of involvement in international affairs was necessary – a fact demonstrated by the Washington Conference (see page 123) and the Dawes Plan (see page 146) – while still maintaining a freedom of action to protect its own interests. More recent writing has therefore described American policy in this period not as 'isolationism' but as a policy of 'independent internationalism'. This aimed to create a world order in which US interests could flourish. US policy in the 1920s therefore focused on two key issues: preventing future conflict by limiting arms, and maintaining US economic superiority.

The attitude of Britain and France

A further difficulty in upholding the treaties was the attitude of the two main powers who were now responsible for the process – Britain and France. These nations each took a different approach to implementing the treaties. Britain wanted to re-establish a balance of power in Europe to prevent French dominance on the continent. In order to achieve this, Germany must be allowed to recover some of its power. Britain also believed that this was in the best interests of European economic stability – a prosperous Germany would, after all, be more able to pay reparations. In addition, there were many in Britain who believed that the Treaty of Versailles had been too harsh on Germany and that revisions to the terms of the treaty should be considered. Britain also faced other issues that it considered more urgent, including unrest in Ireland and India. For the French, the main concern was security against future German aggression, and they were unwilling to consider any moves that might lead to German recovery.

Fact
By the time of the peace conferences, there had been civil unrest in Ireland for some years, with the south demanding independence from the UK and much of the north wanting to remain united. There was a feeling in southern Ireland that self-determination had not been applied there. However, the growing nationalist feeling ultimately resulted in the partition of Ireland in December 1921 in an attempt to solve the problem. Meanwhile, nationalist feeling was also developing in India, creating a further challenge to the stability of the British Empire.

Fact

The Conference of Ambassadors was an inter-Allied organisation formed in January 1920, which took over from the War Council. It was responsible for supervising the implementation of the Treaty of Versailles and mediating over disputes. It consisted of the ambassadors of Britain, Italy and Japan who were based in Paris, and the French foreign minister, with the US ambassador present as an observer. The Conference of Ambassadors lost its importance after Locarno in 1925 (see page 148) and was later incorporated into the League of Nations.

Benito Mussolini (1883–1945)

Mussolini worked as a journalist for a socialist newspaper, *Avanti*, and during this time he learnt the value of propaganda. However, he was expelled from the socialist movement for supporting Italy's entry into the First World War, and this led to his founding the fascist movement. Mussolini won the support of many landowners and industrialists, who most feared socialism and communism and did not believe the weak liberal governments in Italy could keep order. In 1922, Mussolini was appointed prime minister and by 1925 he had become a virtual dictator, having banned opposition parties. He remained in power until his execution in 1945 towards the end of the Second World War.

Although neither Britain nor France was strong enough to enforce its wishes, the lack of agreement about how to deal with Germany allowed the Germans to exploit these divisions to delay honouring the terms of the treaty. This caused even greater insecurity.

The final difficulty was the French attitude towards how the treaties should be upheld. They did not think that responsibility for enforcing the treaties should lie with the League of Nations, believing that the League would show sympathy towards the defeated powers. This had two important consequences.

Firstly, it meant that right from the start the League of Nations struggled to establish itself as an international organisation. Its credibility was challenged by one of its own key members and this caused problems later, particularly when faced with the issue of border disputes (see page 128). Secondly, France's attitude meant that many disputes were referred to the Conference of Ambassadors. Because this group was dominated by the major powers it was much easier for France to ensure that decisions went in its favour, as happened in the case of Italy over Corfu (see page 131). This raised further doubts about the League's role, as it appeared that major powers could find a way around League rulings in order to protect their own interests.

Political developments in Italy

Italy regarded the Treaty of Versailles as a 'mutilated victory', in which it did not gain all the land it expected. Many Italians also felt that the treaties did not sufficiently reward the sacrifices that their forces had made in the war, reinforcing the view that the imperial powers of Britain and France were determined to deny Italy equal treatment.

The weakness of Italian governments after the war, and the social and economic problems the country faced, also allowed the anti-socialist, anti-liberal, nationalist fascists to emerge as a major political force, led by **Benito Mussolini**. Mussolini exploited his country's fear of socialism and communism to win support. In 1922, the king asked Mussolini to form a government in an attempt to end the political chaos. At first, the fascists were a minority, but gradually Mussolini created a dictatorship by changing the electoral laws and merging the fascists with the nationalists in Italy.

SOURCE A

The whole country has to become a great school for perpetual political education which will make Italians into complete Fascists, new men changing their habits, their way of life, their mentality; their character and finally, their physical make-up. It will no longer be a question of grumbling against the sceptical, mandolin-playing Italians, but rather of creating a new kind of man who is tough, strong-willed, a fighter; a latter-day legionary of Caesar for whom nothing is impossible.

Benito Mussolini, speaking in 1931. Quoted in Thomson, D. 1991. State Control in Fascist Italy, Culture and Conformity 1925–1943. Manchester, UK. Manchester University Press. p. 99.

Mussolini's rise to power in 1922 brought a new approach to Italian politics and a determination to make Italy a great power, in line with Mussolini's nationalist ambitions. His aim was to make Italy 'great, respected and feared'. Seeing the popularity of Gabriele D'Annunzio's actions at the port of Fiume (see page 64), Mussolini sent in an Italian military commander to rule the territory. In January 1924, Yugoslavia agreed hand over Fiume to Italy, ensuring Mussolini's popularity.

Problems in the Far East

The origins of Japanese aggression

In 1905, Japan defeated Russia in the Russo–Japanese War. This victory resulted in Japan gaining control of the Korean Peninsula and the lease over the South Manchurian railway, giving the country a strong foothold in the region. In order to protect the railway, Japan was allowed to station 15,000 troops – known as the Kwantung – in the area. This, along with mineral rights in the region, gave Japan a vested interest in Manchuria, which became increasingly important as its investments there increased.

Although Japan had been slow to modernise, by the 1920s it was rapidly becoming the major power in Southeast Asia. During the First World War, Japan fought with the Allies and won German colonies in the Pacific, further increasing its influence there. However, despite these gains, Japan still needed to import both food and raw materials, as it was unable to support its own rapidly increasing population. There was therefore a growing feeling in Japan that the Pacific region should be subject to Japanese demands, and that foreign influences such as Britain and the USA should be removed from the area.

The peace treaties angered the Japanese, who felt that the Allies had not treated them as equals in deciding the terms. Japan was also refused equal status at the Washington Naval Conference in 1922 (see page 124), being permitted only three ships for every five allowed to the USA and Britain. This encouraged the Japanese military to extend its influence, in the belief that the civilian government had failed to protect the nation's interests.

The public shared the army's view that the government was weak and corrupt, so when the government adopted a policy of disarmament and cuts in military spending there was widespread resentment in Japan. The 1920s were difficult years for the Japanese people, as even before the start of the Great Depression they faced serious economic problems. Most notably, there was a dramatic fall in the price of rice, the major agricultural product, which hit the Japanese economy hard.

Political instability in China and its impact on Japan

In 1911–12, the **Qing dynasty** in China was overthrown, marking the end of the Chinese Empire. The republic that replaced it was unable to keep order and there followed a period of decline as China descended into a state of civil war. As a result, the period between 1916 and 1927 was dominated by a series of **warlords**, who fought among themselves for influence and who in reality had more power than the new national government. Eventually this disorder was brought under control by an alliance between communists and nationalists, but the nationalists later turned on the communists and defeated them in 1927. However, nationalist control was limited and disorder was nearly always present.

Historical debate

Historians have disagreed over the problems of enforcing the peace treaties and the subsequent consequences. Writing in the aftermath of the Second World War, Winston Churchill argued that the major problem was the 'rise and collision of embarrassed demagogues', who undermined the new order, rather than any fundamental flaws in the treaties. However, the Frenchman Jacques Neré suggested that the problems were the result of the Allies' unwillingness to enforce the actual terms, rather than the rise of the dictators or other problems.

Question

Why did Japan believe that it should be the dominant Pacific power?

121

Qing dynasty Chinese history is divided into dynastic periods. The Qing dynasty was the 12th dynastic period. The Qing had ruled China since 1644, but in 1912 the six-year-old emperor abdicated and China became a republic.

warlords The nationalist Guomindang (GMD) republican government that followed the fall of the Qing dynasty in 1912 was unable to impose its will on Chinese provinces. As a result local regions fell under the domination of private armies, whose commanders ran the government. The military commanders became known as warlords.

Nationalist officers inspect communist dead during the Chinese Civil War

Question

Why did political stability collapse in China?

The Japanese were concerned by the chaos in China, fearing that it would damage their economic investments. By 1920, this fear had become increasingly justified as atrocities were carried out against foreigners in China, and a growing sense of nationalism in the country led to strikes and boycotts of Japanese companies. This was partly the result of a growing number of Japanese who had moved into the area (seven out of every ten foreigners in Manchuria were Japanese). Tensions increased because many Chinese had also moved to Manchuria to seek employment in Japanese-funded industries. Japanese resentment grew over attacks on their citizens, which they claimed the Chinese government had not investigated. At the same time, the Japanese feared that the nationalist leader in China, Jiang Jieshi, would take away the concessions that had been granted to Japan in Manchuria, further threatening their investments.

Activity

Find out more about the challenges to order in either Ireland, India or China. What was their impact on international affairs?

By the end of the 1920s, there were signs that the Japanese military was ready to take action to protect Japanese interests in China. In 1928, Japanese troops assassinated a warlord in Manchuria, believing that their government's policy of friendship towards him was wrong and that the warlord would support Jiang's nationalist policies. This was a clear indication that the military would act independently of the civilian government. Tension in the region was thus high even before the Depression of the 1930s. As Chinese resentment grew over Japanese domination of Manchuria, Japan realised that China would soon make moves to regain influence in the region.

Activities

1 Construct a spider diagram to show the problems there were in enforcing the peace treaties in the 1920s. Having drawn the diagram, list the factors in order of importance with the most serious first, then write a paragraph to explain the order you have chosen.

2 Imagine you are either an Italian or Japanese journalist. Write an editorial for your newspaper in which you explain why your nation is dissatisfied with the peace process and what you think needs to be done to rectify it.

3 Hold a class discussion on why there was so much support for nationalist movements in Italy and Japan.

4 Research the Chinese nationalist leader Jiang Jieshi, then write a summary profile of him.

How successful was diplomacy in the 1920s?

From 1920 to 1933, the League of Nations held a series of meetings to discuss the process of disarmament, with varied results. The meetings ended with the disastrous Disarmament Conference of 1933, when Hitler withdrew Germany from both the conference and the League of Nations, and began a military programme that broke the terms of the Treaty of Versailles. As well as the issue of disarmament, diplomacy in this period focused on efforts to strengthen the powers of the League, to encourage acceptance of the national borders established by the peace treaties, and to renounce aggression as a way of solving disputes.

The Washington Naval Agreements 1921–22

Although the USA had not ratified the peace treaties or joined the League of Nations, its new president, Warren Harding, was still anxious to reduce naval armaments. He also wanted to settle potential difficulties in the Far East, where Japan was an increasing threat to US interests. Harding was particularly concerned to avoid the expense of a naval race in the region. Japan was already the third largest naval power in the world and had started an ambitious naval building programme. Harding knew that Congress would not approve a programme on the same scale, so unless an agreement could be reached, America's position as a leading naval power would be weakened.

Plans to develop a US Pacific fleet pushed Britain – reluctantly – into developing its own naval rearmament programme in 1921. The British hoped that this would allow them to maintain parity (equal status) with the US by agreeing a one-to-one ratio through negotiation without the cost of building new vessels, which it could not afford after the war. The US was willing to agree to this suggestion on the condition that Britain did not extend its alliance with Japan, which was due for renewal. Both Britain and the USA put pressure on Japan to agree to talks about naval armament.

Although Japan now had the opportunity to catch up with the USA and Britain through its new naval building programme, it was also reluctant to spend too heavily on its navy, fearing that high expenditure there would damage other areas of its economy. In addition, all three countries realised that investing in naval power might be a waste of resources, as developments in other military areas, particularly air power, were starting to make large battleships obsolete. Thus, all three major naval powers would benefit from reaching an agreement.

Fact

The USA had gained control of Hawaii in 1867, but it was the ending of the Spanish–American War in 1898 that resulted in America emerging as a major power in the Pacific, as it won control of the Philippines and Guam. This area provided the USA with an entry point into the lucrative Chinese market, which it wanted to protect. Although Japan had strong trading ties with the USA, The Japanese were concerned that China was a rival for American support. The chances of a clash between the USA and Japan increased, as many Japanese resented the limitations on Japanese immigration into the United States.

Fact

Britain had signed an alliance with Japan in 1902 in order to help protect British interests in the Far East. Britain had been concerned about possible Russian expansion in the area. In the agreement, if one nation was attacked by a single aggressor, the other country could maintain its neutrality. However, if more than one state attacked either Britain or Japan, the other country was committed to providing support.

Talks were held in Washington from November 1921 to February 1922, and discussions included both naval disarmament and issues in the Far East. The foreign ministers of the USA, Britain, France, Japan and Italy led the delegations during the discussions on disarmament. They were joined by Belgium, Portugal, the Netherlands and China when Far East issues were discussed, as all these powers had interests in the area.

The Four Power Agreement

The first agreement reached at the Washington talks was the Four Power Agreement, between the USA, Britain, Japan and France. This was signed in December 1921, and guaranteed the territorial rights of these four nations to their respective possessions in the Pacific. They also agreed to defend each other in the event of attack by another country. The Four Power Agreement brought stability to the region and relieved US concerns about the potential Japanese threat.

The Five Power Agreement

The second agreement was the Five Power Agreement, signed in February 1921, by which Italy joined the alliance. This agreement dealt more specifically with the size of naval forces. The five powers agreed to limit their naval strength by establishing a ratio for the size of their fleets – 5:5:3 for the USA, Britain and Japan, with France and Italy having fleets half the size of Japan. In practice, this meant that Britain and the USA could have 525,000 tonnes of **capital ships** and Japan 315,000 tonnes; France and Italy were limited to 175,000 tonnes. The states also agreed not to build battleships for a period of ten years, and to destroy any ships that took them above the ratio. The agreement was to last for 14 years. It stopped the building of capital ships for ten years and also resulted in the scrapping of some battleships and cruisers.

However, the Five Power Agreement went much further than just capital ships. It also limited the use of submarines and banned the use of poison gas as a weapon of warfare. Many people regarded this as the first step towards international disarmament.

124

capital ships These are the most important warships in a navy – usually those with the greatest firepower.

SOURCE B

At the time the Washington conference was widely hailed as a significant step towards international stability. The prospect of a financially crippling naval arms race had been prevented, the first substantive arms control treaty had been agreed, the navies of the great powers were to be limited, a clash between the major powers for dominance in east Asia and the Pacific had been avoided, and the Anglo-Japanese alliance that had filled other states with such unease had been replaced by a broader agreement. It would prove to be only a short term solution. Within ten years, the Washington system had collapsed, largely due to the renewed Japanese bid for hegemony.

Goldstein, E. 2002. The First World War Peace Settlements 1919–25. London, UK. Pearson. p. 79.

Activity

What is Goldstein's view of the Washington Agreement? Support your argument with reference to the passage. Goldstein's view is not completely optimistic. What negative feature does he point out?

An expensive naval race had been avoided. However, not all the nations were entirely happy with the terms of the agreement. The Italians were pleased to have achieved parity with the French, but the ratio ensured that France remained a second-rate naval power. After the Washington Conference, in order to try to appease the French and to address some of their concerns about the German threat, they were allowed to build some light ships and submarines. However, French demands did cause concerns, as the cartoon below from a British newspaper shows.

A cartoon entitled 'Torpedoed', from the British newspaper the Daily Star, *December 1921; it shows the French submarine policy blowing up the naval peace*

Discussion point

Why was it possible to achieve agreement on naval reduction?

125

Activity

What is the message of this cartoon? Use details from the cartoon to explain your answer. In light of the comments in Source B on page 124 and from the information contained in this section, how accurate do you think the view in the cartoon is?

The Nine Power Agreement

The final issue discussed at Washington was the problem of the Far East which, in reality, meant China. All nations present at the conferences were concerned that China's political instability would encourage other powers to extend their influence in the region, which could lead to international conflict.

SOURCE C

The treaties signed at the Washington Conference served to uphold the status quo in the Pacific: they recognised existing interests and did not make fundamental changes to them. At the same time, the United States secured agreements that reinforced its existing policy in the Pacific; including the Open Door in China and the protection of the Philippines, while limiting the scope of Japanese imperial expansion.

From the US Department of State, Office of the Historian.

Questions

Why do you think the USA supported the Washington Agreements? How useful is Source C to the historian studying international relations in the 1920s?

Frank Billings Kellogg (1865–1937) Kellogg worked as a lawyer and politician before being appointed US ambassador to Britain in 1924. The following year he became secretary of state for US president Calvin Coolidge. Kellogg's position in charge of foreign affairs in the decade after the First World War allowed him to negotiate the Kellogg–Briand Pact, and he was awarded the Nobel Peace Prize in 1929 for promoting world peace.

In order to deal with the problems created by Chinese instability, the Nine Power Agreement was signed. This agreement confirmed an 'open door' policy, by which all nations were able to trade within China. The states also agreed to protect Chinese territory and to strengthen the country financially by giving it greater control over customs income. Japan also agreed to return to China the Shantung Peninsula, which had previously been a German concession and had been granted to Japan at the peace conferences (see page 53).

Why were the Washington Agreements successful?

There were two main reasons for the success of the Washington Agreements. Firstly, it was much easier to find common ground and reach an agreement when only a small number of nations were involved. Secondly, naval rearmament was expensive and most countries were not in a position to embark on a costly building programme after the war. All were therefore keen to find a solution to the problem. However, it can also be argued that the process of developing a navy was much slower than expanding an army – and more difficult to do without the knowledge of other nations – so the various powers were more willing to agree to naval limitations than they might be to other military restrictions. The success of the Washington Agreements did not, therefore, guarantee success in other areas of disarmament.

Further attempts to achieve disarmament in the period 1926–27 were unsuccessful. A Naval Conference held in Geneva in 1927, between the USA, Britain and France, ended without agreement (although eventually, in 1930, some additional limitations were agreed). A Preparatory Commission for a Disarmament Conference began work in Geneva in 1926, but disagreements caused it to be postponed until 1932 (see page 172).

The Geneva Protocol 1924–25

Throughout the 1920s, the League of Nations tried to strengthen its powers and encourage countries to renounce the use of aggression. The first aim took the form of the Geneva Protocol. This arose as a result of two separate events: the Corfu Incident in 1923 and the settlement of the reparations issue with the Dawes Plan of 1924. The Corfu Incident (see page 131) dramatically highlighted the weaknesses of the League, showing how its decisions could be undermined by its own members. This particularly worried the French, who had always wanted the League to act more as a military alliance. After the Corfu Incident, France and Britain both applied pressure to broaden the powers of the League. The French were also concerned by the Dawes Plan, by which the US offered huge loans to aid the reconstruction of German industry. This money came from individuals and banks, and was not guaranteed by the US government – nor was it accompanied by offers of US military support to curb German aggression. In practice, this meant that if there was an economic crisis, the USA could stop paying these loans, leaving France to face a strengthened Germany without international support. For the French, therefore, the Geneva Protocol was a way of gaining military security.

A Treaty of Mutual Assistance was drafted in 1923–24, but was never signed. After this, the Geneva Protocol of 1924–25 was drawn up by France and Britain, where a Labour government under Ramsay Macdonald was more willing to strengthen the powers of the League than previous administrations had been.

By the terms of the Geneva Protocol, members of the League to come to the help of any state on the same continent that fell victim to aggression. However, before the Protocol could be put into effect, a general election in Britain brought a Conservative administration to power. The new government was not prepared to commit Britain to the role of the 'world's policeman'. As a result, the British foreign secretary, Austen Chamberlain, vetoed the Geneva Protocol in March 1925. Once again, the self-interests of a nation had triumphed over the wider powers of the League.

The Kellogg–Briand Pact 1928

The Kellogg–Briand Pact was largely the work of **Frank Billings Kellogg** (US secretary of state, see page 126) and **Aristide Briand** (foreign minister of France), and concerned the rejection of war as an instrument of national policy. It also had an influence on disarmament, for, as Churchill commented, nations would not disarm unless they felt secure. Although some historians have described the pact as naïve, it did help to create a climate – at least in the short term – in which nations were more willing to consider disarmament. By fostering a spirit of co-operation, the League of Nations also contributed to this climate.

The Kellogg–Briand Pact was partly the result of the public pressure in the USA, where there was a great desire for disarmament and peace. This was reflected in the growth of **pressure groups** such as the American Committee for the Outlawry of War and the Carnegie Endowment for International Peace. On 27 March 1927, Professor Shotwell, the head of the Carnegie Endowment, visited Paris and persuaded the French foreign minister to send a message directly to the American people, proposing an agreement between France and the USA outlawing war.

As French foreign policy was dominated by the desire for security – and seeing the opportunity to bring France into the USA's sphere of protection – Briand sent the message. The US government realised that it could not ignore public opinion, but wanted to avoid a definite commitment to France. In December 1927, the US issued a cautious reply, suggesting an agreement that involved as many nations as possible, not just France and the USA. Although this did not fulfil French aims, France still believed that any agreement that might strengthen its security was better than nothing.

SOURCE D

1 The high contracting parties solemnly declare in the names of their respective peoples that they condemn recourse to war for the solution of international controversies, and renounce it an instrument of national policy in their relations with one another.

2 The high contracting parties agree that the settlement or solution of all disputes or conflicts of whatever nature or of whatever origin they may be, which may arise among them, shall never be sought except by pacific means.

3 This treaty shall remain open for adherence by all the other Powers of the world.

The three articles of the Kellogg–Briand Pact, 1928.

Aristide Briand (1862–1932)

Briand was prime minister of France no fewer than 11 times, the first in 1909–10. He resumed the role during the war, but resigned over disputes about French offensives in 1917. Returned once more in 1921, he left office again after failing to resolve the issue of German reparations. Briand was reinstated after the Ruhr invasion, when his policy of conciliation was more in tune with public opinion. Briand was foreign minister in 1925, and won the Nobel Peace Prize for his part in the Locarno Pact.

127

pressure groups These are non-elected groups that operate outside parliament or other elected bodies, but try to influence government policy.

Discussion point

What should the role of pressure groups be? Do they strengthen or weaken democracy?

Activity

Explain in your own words the meaning of the three articles in the Kellogg–Briand Pact. What is the main weakness of the pact? Why do you think this weakness was present? What can we learn from the terms about attitudes towards the implementation of security and disarmament?

The pact was signed by 15 nations on 27 August 1928; by 1933 a further 50 nations had agreed to it. Of the 65 nations invited to sign the agreement, only two – Brazil and Argentina – refused to do so. There were attempts to link the pact to the League of Nations, but those failed. However, many politicians and political commentators believed that, by outlawing war, it did support the League's covenant, whilst the League had the power to establish commissions of enquiry and implement cooling-off periods if a dispute broke out. It could also be argued that the pact reinforced the concept of collective security, by suggesting that the best way to avoid conflict was for all nations to act together.

Despite this optimism, the Kellogg–Briand Pact was little more than a statement of good intentions – there were no enforcement procedures or binding clauses. Its weakness became evident in the 1930s, when three of the nations that had signed the pact, Japan, Italy and Germany, all broke its terms without facing any consequences (see Chapter 9).

Discussion point

Was the Kellogg–Briand Pact idealistic or was it an accurate reflection of the feelings of the period? Why was there so much idealism in the 1920s?

Activities

1   Construct two spider diagrams. The first should show the reasons why there was support for disarmament and the second should show the reasons for its failure.

2   Copy and complete the chart below to show the successes and failures of the attempts to improve international co-operation in the 1920s.

Event	Year	Evidence of success	Evidence of failure	Overall judgement
Washington Naval Conference				
Geneva Protocol				
Kellogg–Briand Pact				

3   How successful were the agreements made in the 1920s at promoting international peace? Using the chart you drew up in the second activity, plan an answer to this question.

How successful was the League of Nations in resolving border disputes and other conflicts in the 1920s?

The Paris Peace Conferences created new states and redrew the borders between several others. These changes inevitably caused problems, as previously joined communities found themselves on different sides of the new borders. It was the League of Nations' responsibility to resolve arguments and conflicts that arose from the border disputes that resulted, of which there were several in the 1920s. In fact, some border disputes were addressed by the Conference of Ambassadors, which had been formed with the specific purpose of resolving conflicts arising from the peace treaties.

Vilna 1920

The first major dispute occurred over control of Vilna. Vilna had been the capital of Lithuania before the country was absorbed into the Russian Empire in the late 18th century, and by the terms of the peace treaties it was to be restored to this position. However, Poland objected, arguing that because more than 30% of the population of Vilna was Polish, the city should belong to Poland.

In 1920, during the Russo–Polish war, Polish troops occupied Vilna and refused to leave when the war ended. This was a direct challenge to the terms of the peace treaties, and Lithuania appealed to the League for help.

This was a test case for the League, as both Poland and Lithuania were members. There was a great deal of sympathy for the Polish cause because of the significant number of Poles living in the region, but it was clear that, having staged the invasion, Poland was the aggressor. The League ordered Poland to withdraw, but the Polish government refused. This placed the League in a very difficult position. According to its covenant, it could send in the military to force the Poles out, but this would mean committing British and French troops to action on the other side of Europe. France opposed military action, preferring to keep Poland on side as a possible ally against Germany and as a barrier to the spread of communism from Russia. Britain was unwilling to act alone.

The Conference of Ambassadors was brought in and, partly in response to pressure from the French, it awarded Vilna to Poland. The League approved the decision in 1923, although fighting continued occasionally in the region until 1927. Lithuania naturally resented the decision, which confirmed the fears of smaller nations that the main powers would take whatever action they liked to meet their own needs. It was not a good start for the League.

A map showing where the European border disputes and financial crises occurred in the 1920s

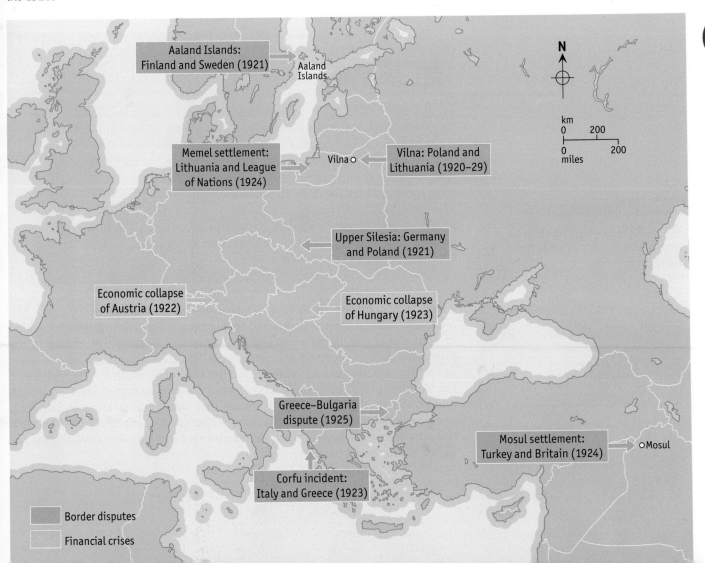

Upper Silesia 1921

Upper Silesia was a rich industrial area on the border between Germany and Poland. The large coal and iron deposits – as well as its mixed population – meant that both nations wanted control of it. The Treaty of Versailles stated that the future of Upper Silesia would be decided by a plebiscite (see page 15), but unrest broke out before the vote took place, and British and French troops were sent to maintain order. The referendum was held in March 1921; 780,000 people voted in favour of joining Germany and 480,000 of joining Poland. Further riots and confrontations followed.

In May 1921, the Poles seized control of the main industrial area in Upper Silesia. France refused to allow German troops to restore order and reclaim the region, as the French wanted Upper Silesia to be given to Poland to help boost its economy and strengthen the new country against Germany. By taking away rich industrial lands, the German state would be further weakened – a situation that the French actively supported. However, Britain wanted the area restored to Germany, in part because the plebiscite had returned that decision, but also because the industrial wealth generated by the region would help Germany pay its reparations.

The situation was made more complicated by the fact that the president of the Plebiscite Commission was French, and thus supported the Polish action. In contrast, the British prime minister, David Lloyd George, called for German forces to be allowed to restore order.

SOURCE E

Either the Allies ought to insist upon the Treaty being respected, or they ought to allow the Germans to do it. Not merely to disarm Germany, but to say that such troops as she has got are not to be permitted to take part in restoring order in what, until the decision comes, is their own province – that is not fair. Fair play is what England stands for, and I hope she will stand for it to the end.

David Lloyd George, in a speech following unrest in Upper Silesia, May 1921. Quoted in Williamson, D. 1994. War and Peace: International Relations 1914–45. London, UK. Hodder. p. 47.

Question

Why would David Lloyd George's speech in Source E have upset the French?

Allied troops moved in to restore order, which was achieved by July 1921. Meanwhile, the matter was referred to the League for a ruling, which decided to split the region between Poland and Germany. Despite the results of the plebiscite, Poland received a larger proportion, including much of the main industrial area. However, the League did insist on safeguards for the region and the German population. Rail links between the two countries were protected, and arrangements were made to ensure that water and power supplies from one side of the border reached the other. Although the League restored peace in this situation, once again France successfully achieved its demands against the rights of a defeated power.

The Aaland Islands 1921

Situated midway between Finland and Sweden, the Aaland Islands were a point of contention between these nations. Legally the islands belonged to Finland, but the majority of the population were Swedes who wanted to be ruled by Sweden. Both countries threatened military action to win control of the islands, but eventually they appealed to the League of Nations. The League investigated the situation and concluded that Finland should retain control of the islands. Although the Swedes did not like the decision, they accepted it and conflict was avoided. In this case, the countries involved in the dispute were willing to accept the League's authority.

The economic collapse of Austria and Hungary 1922–23

By 1922, the new states of Austria and Hungary were both facing bankruptcy. To relieve the financial difficulties, the League stepped in and arranged a series of international loans as well as sending commissioners to supervise economic activity. The League effectively took over the economic management of the two countries, and by the end of the decade there were signs of economic recovery in both Austria and Hungary. This process was repeated for Estonia in 1927, when the League negotiated a loan to help the struggling Baltic state. In all three instances of financial crises, the League was able to bring about economic stability – at least until the Great Depression.

Corfu 1923

The Corfu Incident was arguably the greatest challenge the League faced in the 1920s, largely because it involved Italy – a major power within the League – challenging its authority. The Conference of Ambassadors had been given the task of resolving the conflicting claims of Greece and Albania over the position of the boundary between their two countries. The Conference appointed an Italian general named Enrico Tellini to supervise the work of the International Boundary Commission. On 27 August 1923, Tellini's surveyors were ambushed on the Greek side of the border; some members of the group were injured and five were killed. Although the incident occurred close to the disputed border and could therefore have been carried out by either side, the Italians blamed the Greeks. On 29 August, Mussolini demanded that Greece pay compensation for the deaths and execute those who had carried out the crime. The Greeks refused, claiming they were not responsible for the incident. On 31 August, Mussolini attacked and then occupied the Greek island of Corfu. Greece appealed to the League of Nations for help.

As with the dispute over Vilna, both nations were members of the League, but this time the situation was more serious – Italy was a major power within the League but had acted in complete defiance of it. The League Council (see page 104) was in session and therefore able to act quickly. On 7 September, it ordered Italy to withdraw from Corfu and decided that although Greece should pay Italy compensation, this money would be held by the League until the murderers were found. Some members of the League sought a more forceful condemnation of Italy's actions, but the key powers in the League refused to do so. France was unwilling to risk its relationship with Italy, as it was involved in the Ruhr dispute (see page 141). Britain investigated both naval and economic sanctions against Italy, but decided that these would be too difficult to implement and might be dangerous to operate.

131

Mussolini initially accepted the League's decision, but he soon began to challenge it, arguing that because the officials were killed while working for the Conference of Ambassadors, the Conference should resolve the dispute. Once again, it was easier to influence the decisions of the Conference than the League. Greece was ordered to apologise for the deaths and to pay the compensation directly to Italy. Mussolini then withdrew from Corfu, claiming victory.

Although supporters of the League argued that without its intervention Mussolini would never have evacuated Corfu, others claimed that this was a further example of a major power successfully defying the League.

The Memel settlement 1924

The Memel settlement resolved an issue that had caused problems since the Paris Peace Conferences. At the peace talks, the Baltic city of Memel was awarded to Lithuania, providing the new state with a year-round ice-free port. However, the Conference of Ambassadors had later internationalised the port and its decision was enforced by French troops in the city. On 9 January 1923, Lithuania staged the Klaipeda Revolt (Klaipeda was another name for Memel), occupying the territory. Despite having troops in the area, France refused to become involved in the crisis, so there was nothing to prevent the Lithuanian seizure. Both the League and the Conference of Ambassadors allowed the occupation, and Memel became part of Lithuania. Force had once more triumphed – even if it did uphold the initial provisions of Versailles.

The Mosul settlement 1924

The oil-rich region of Mosul had been part of the old Turkish Empire, and after the new boundaries were drawn up it was situated close to the border between Turkey and the British mandate of Iraq. The Treaty of Lausanne stated that Mosul's future would be decided by direct talks between Turkey and Britain; however, these discussions broke down, and on 24 October 1924 Britain issued the Turks with an ultimatum – withdraw within 48 hours or face military action.

The League successfully intervened, recommending a line behind which Turkish troops would withdraw. A Commission of Enquiry was set up to consult the local population of **Kurds** about their future. Total independence for the Kurds was not an option – this would have been unacceptable to the Turks – but they expressed a desire to be ruled by Britain rather than Turkey. In response, the League recommended that Mosul become a mandate of Iraq and this was accepted by both sides. However, as Iraq was already a British mandate, in practice it meant that the area came under British control.

Kurds An ethnic (non-Arabic) group that was part of the Turkish Empire before the First World War, and which now lives in parts of eastern Turkey, northern Iraq, eastern Syria, Armenia and Azerbaijan. Initially, there was a proposition to create a separate state for the Kurds – Kurdistan – but objections from Turkey made this difficult to implement.

The Greece–Bulgaria dispute 1925

Only two years after the border dispute between Greece and Albania, the League was involved in another dispute concerning Greece – this time with Bulgaria. The Treaty of Neuilly (see page 58) had created numerous border tensions in the region, and these finally erupted in 1925. During a border skirmish, several Greek soldiers were killed; in response, Greece invaded Bulgaria. Bulgaria immediately appealed to the League of Nations and issued orders to its soldiers accordingly (see Source F).

The League ordered a ceasefire and instructed Greek troops to withdraw. In addition, the League ordered Greece to pay compensation to Bulgaria. The decision was accepted, but Greece did complain that there appeared to be two different rules in operation: one for the major powers such as Italy, and one for smaller states, such as Greece itself. However, the League had successfully stopped the violence from escalating.

A British cartoon from 1925 about the Greece–Bulgaria dispute; the characters are Tweedledee and Tweedledum from Alice's Adventures in Wonderland, who are always arguing

SOURCE F

Make only slight resistance. Protect the fugitives and panic-stricken population. Do not expose the troops to unnecessary losses in view of the fact that the incident has been laid before the Council of the League of Nations, which is expected to stop the invasion.

General order from the Bulgarian ministry of war to its army commanders, 22 October 1925.

Questions

Why do you think the Bulgarian government issued the message in Source F? How useful is the message as evidence about the attitudes of governments towards the League of Nations?

Questions

What impression of the League of Nations does this cartoon give? How useful is the cartoon in showing the effectiveness of the League of Nations in resolving disputes? Compare the message of the cartoon with that in Source G below. How similar are their views about the effectiveness of the League of Nations in resolving disputes?

SOURCE G

It had been shown that the criticisms which had been brought against the League of Nations to the effect that its machinery was cumbersome and that it found it difficult to take action in circumstances which required an urgent solution were unjustified. It has been proved that a nation which appealed to the League when it felt that its existence was threatened, could be sure that the Council would be at its post ready to undertake its work of conciliation.

Aristide Briand, speaking at a meeting of the Council of the League of Nations in October 1925 following the Greece–Bulgaria crisis. Quoted in Williamson, D. 1994. War and Peace: International Relations 1914–45. London, UK. Hodder. p. 74.

Conclusion

The League attempted to deal with a significant number of disputes during the 1920s, some with greater success than others. A careful consideration of its response to these disputes reveals some patterns. The League was far more successful when dealing with the smaller powers – it was able to resolve both the Aaland Islands dispute and the Greece–Bulgaria conflict without resorting to military intervention. This might be because smaller nations felt intimidated by the power of the League and wanted to avoid the threat of sanctions or the use of force against them.

However, when the League was faced with challenges that directly or indirectly involved major powers it was less able to implement its decisions. In some cases the League was overruled by the Conference of Ambassadors (which was dominated by the major powers) and made to feel that its role in resolving conflicts could be ignored. It was particularly noticeable that both France and Italy manipulated either the League or the Conference to obtain decisions that suited their interests, rather than resolving the issue in a fair and just way. Greece had every reason to suggest that there were two rules – one for the major powers and one for smaller states.

The League's failure to deal effectively with conflicts where the interests of major powers were at stake was a lesson that was not lost on other leading powers, and this became evident later on. The self-interest of nations was also a serious problem, demonstrated most clearly in the League's support of Poland in the conflict over Upper Silesia.

Activity

Copy and complete the following chart to assess how well the League managed the disputes it faced in the 1920s. Give each dispute a mark out of 5 depending on how well the League responded: the higher the mark the more successful the League.

Dispute	Evidence of success	Evidence of failure	Mark/5	Explanation
Vilna				
Upper Silesia				
Aaland Islands				
Economic collapse of Austria and Hungary				
Corfu				
Memel				
Mosul				
Greece–Bulgaria				

End of chapter activities

Summary

You should now be aware of the problems facing the League of Nations in trying to achieve two of its major aims: disarmament and settling border disputes. In both instances you have seen how self-interest often triumphed over the ideals of Wilson's Fourteen Points and the covenant of the League of Nations. In particular, you should understand the influence that the major powers had on decision-making and how their concerns often overrode those of other nations. This chapter has also explained how France's preoccupation with its own security influenced both the disarmament process and the resolution of border conflicts, making it much more difficult for the League to achieve its goals. During the 1920s, it became increasingly clear that the expectations and ideals that were present at the end of the First World War were gradually being replaced by pragmatism and reality. This became more marked during the 1930s, as nations faced the Great Depression. You should now be able to explain why the aspirations in the early years of the 1920s were not met, and why the success of the League was so limited.

Summary activity

Historians have offered the following explanations for why the League was unsuccessful in resolving so many international crises in the 1920s:

- The self-interest of members was more important than upholding the peace treaties or the aims of the League.
- The League of Nations was slow to act.
- The absence of the USA made the League powerless to enforce its decisions.
- Many nations still wanted to solve crises through alliances and old methods of diplomacy.
- The aims of the League were idealistic.

Work your way back through this chapter and find evidence that either supports or challenges each of the bullet points above. Summarise your findings in a chart similar to the one below.

Criticism	Evidence to support the claim	Evidence to challenge the claim
Self-interest of members was more important		
The League was slow to act		
The absence of the USA made the League powerless		
Many nations still used old methods of diplomacy		
League aims were idealistic		

Paper 1 exam practice

Question

Compare and contrast the views expressed in Sources A and B below about the success of the Washington Naval Conference in improving international stability.
[6 marks]

Skill

Cross-referencing

SOURCE B

A cartoon from the British newspaper the *Daily Star*, showing a French submarine blowing up the naval peace

Torpedoed.

SOURCE A

At the time the Washington conference was widely hailed as a significant step towards international stability. The prospect of a financially crippling naval arms race had been prevented, the first substantive arms control treaty had been agreed, the navies of the great powers were to be limited, a clash between the major powers for dominance in east Asia and the Pacific had been avoided, and the Anglo-Japanese alliance that had filled other states with such unease had been replaced by a broader agreement. It would prove to be only a short-term solution. Within ten years, the Washington system had collapsed, largely due to the renewed Japanese bid for hegemony.

Goldstein, E. 2002. The First World War Peace Settlements 1919–25. London, UK. Pearson. p. 79.

136

Before you start

Cross-referencing questions require you to compare **and** contrast the information/content/nature of **two** sources.

Before you attempt this question, refer to pages 212–13 for advice on how to tackle cross-referencing questions and a simplified markscheme.

Student answer

On the surface, Sources A and B appear to offer very different views about the impact of the Washington Naval Conference on international stability. Source A argues that the conference was 'a significant step towards international stability', whereas Source B suggests that any attempts to achieve stability were undermined by the French submarine policy. This latter point is reflected in the French submarine blowing up a ship, which represents 'Naval Peace' and is in the 'Washington Workshops'. However, the message of Source A is not as positive as it first appears, as it acknowledges that there were problems and that international stability was achieved only in the short term.

The two sources disagree on who was to blame. Source B shows by the actions of the French that it believes they were to blame, but Source A argues that the conference was undermined by a 'renewed Japanese bid for hegemony'. This suggests that the Japanese desire to dominate the Pacific caused a decline in international stability, and this was reflected in Japanese actions against Manchuria and China. However, Source A is more positive than Source B, suggesting that – at the time – the Washington Agreement created stability and that the fears caused by the old Anglo–Japanese alliance had been removed and replaced by a 'broader agreement'. Source B, on the other hand, shows only destruction because the French refused to accept the limitations.

Examiner comments

This is a very thorough answer that makes good use of the details of both sources but – more importantly in achieving the top level – it makes direct comparisons of points of similarity and difference. The student is also careful to link his or her observations back to the issue in the question, and does not simply make a general comparison. The opening takes a comparative view of the two sources and this forms the structure for the rest of the answer. Always read the whole source before making a decision about the view being offered – in Source A here, the apparent success suggested by most of the text is challenged in the final sentence. This answer then offers a subtle distinction between the sources about who was to blame. Once again, the student makes a direct comparison between the two sources and this is supported by precise reference to details within each of them. These differences are then explained by the clear use of contextual knowledge. The student also comments on the tone of the two sources, using details from both. This is a comprehensive and well-developed answer, and would be awarded full marks.

Paper 2 practice questions

1 Assess the seriousness of the border disputes that took place between 1920 and 1925.

2 Examine whether it was the self-interest of France, rather than the absence of the United States, that was responsible for the League's failings in the 1920s.

3 Analyse the extent to which the League of Nations overcame the difficulties it faced in the 1920s.

4 Compare the role of the Conference of Ambassadors and the League of Nations in resolving border disputes in the 1920s.

5 Assess the reasons why disarmament was so difficult to achieve in the 1920s.

6 Examine the view that the League of Nations was more successful in resolving social and economic problems than border disputes.

7 Assess the reasons why the optimism that surrounded the establishment of the League of Nations declined so quickly.

137

7 Germany and European diplomacy

Timeline

1918 Nov: Germany signs armistice; Kaiser Wilhelm II flees Germany

1919 Feb: Weimar Republic proclaimed

Jun: Treaty of Versailles signed

1921 Apr: Reparations Commission announces final figure of German reparations of 132 billion gold marks

1922 Treaty of Rapallo with Russia

Apr–Aug: series of international conferences fails to resolve problem of reparations and inter-Allied war debts

Dec: Germany defaults on reparations payments

1923 Jan: French and Belgian troops invade the Ruhr to force Germany to pay

Sep: Germany ends passive resistance in the Ruhr

1924 Dawes Plan presents new schedule for payment of reparations

1925 Locarno Pact between Germany, France and Belgium – guaranteed by Britain and Italy

Aug: last French soldiers leave the Ruhr

1926 Jan: evacuation of Cologne zone by Allied troops

Oct: Germany joins League of Nations; Treaty of Berlin signed with Russia reaffirms Rapallo for five years

1927 Jan: Allied Disarmament Commission withdrawn from Germany

1928 Aug: Britain, Belgium and France withdraw 10,000 troops from Rhineland garrison

Key questions

- How effectively was the German problem handled in the period 1919–23?
- How did Germany's diplomatic position improve after 1923?

Overview

- The peace treaties at the end of the First World War did not quieten many nations' fears about Germany's position within Europe. Germany was still strong enough to recover its place as the dominant power on the continent.
- The Treaty of Rapallo with Russia allowed Germany to rearm, and the union of these two 'outcast nations' caused concern amongst other powers.
- The invasion of the Ruhr by French and Belgian forces in 1923 was a turning point in international and Franco–German relations. Both sides realised that co-operation and reconciliation were the only way forward.
- The invasion of the Ruhr resulted in hyperinflation in Germany, causing serious economic problems from which the country only gradually recovered; in the long term the invasion undermined confidence in the Weimar Republic.
- The loans made through the Dawes and Young Plans meant that superficially the German economy recovered, but it relied on US loans and this became a problem after the Wall Street Crash in 1929.
- Germany's international status improved following the invasion of the Ruhr, and it was welcomed as an equal through signing the Locarno Pact and in its membership of the League of Nations.
- Gustav Stresemann's policy of co-operation appeared to reflect German willingness to co-operate in international affairs, but Stresemann did not give up trying to overturn some elements of the Treaty of Versailles.

A German woman uses paper money to fuel her stove during the period of hyperinflation in Germany

How effectively was the German problem handled in the period 1919–23?

The German problem

This chapter will focus on what the historian A. J. P. Taylor has called the 'German problem'. This existed before the First World War, but the peace treaties failed to solve it and the German problem remained, some argue, even after the country's defeat at the end of the Second World War.

militarism The belief that a nation should have strong military forces, which it can use not only to defend itself but also to pursue an aggressive policy.

SOURCE A

[The German problem was] not German aggressiveness or **militarism**, or the wickedness of her rulers. These, even if they existed, merely aggravated the problem; or perhaps actually made it less menacing by provoking moral resistance in other countries. The essential problem was political not moral. However pacific and democratic Germany might become, she remained by far the greatest Power on the continent of Europe; with the disappearance of Russia, more so than before. She was greatest in population – 65 million against 45 million in France, the only other substantial Power. Her preponderance was greater still in the economic resources of coal and steel which in modern times together made up power. At the moment in 1919, Germany was down and out. The immediate problem was German weakness; but given a few years of 'normal' life, it would again become the problem of German strength. More than this, the old balance of power, which formerly did something to restrain Germany, had broken down. Russia had withdrawn; Austria-Hungary had vanished. Only France and Italy remained, both inferior in man-power and still more in economic resources, both exhausted by the war. If events followed their course in the old 'free' way, nothing could prevent the Germans from overshadowing Europe.

Taylor, A. J. P. 1961. *The Origins of the Second World War*. London, UK. Hamish Hamilton. p. 24.

Taylor believed that despite the fact that the kaiser had fled and that the new Weimar Republic was on the verge of revolution, German recovery was inevitable and its future dominance of Europe was assured. This was a particular concern for France, which feared that Germany would seek revenge for defeat in the First World War.

Certainly the German people felt wronged by the terms of the Treaty of Versailles, and there was little support for the new democratic government. Most longed for a return to the authoritarian rule of the monarchy, and the glory associated with the policy of **Weltpolitik**. This included having a high-seas fleet that challenged British naval superiority as it had done before the war. This bitterness was strengthened by the exclusion of Germany from the League of Nations. The decisions made at Versailles regarding Europe's eastern frontiers (see Chapter 3) only added to anger among the German people, and fuelled nationalist sentiments.

Weltpolitik This literally means a 'world policy', as Germany looked to increase its influence and dominance across a global empire.

Despite its post-war problems, Germany was still in a strong position in Europe, surrounded by weak successor states that were unlikely to withstand any German claims. In the west, France was also in relative decline – both economically and demographically – and would find it hard to resist a revived Germany. Britain had more pressing concerns with its overseas empire, whilst the USA had embarked on a policy of isolationism in foreign affairs (see page 119). Under these circumstances, French security concerns were fully justified, and the problem of how to contain German nationalism remained. These were the challenges that faced the international community.

Activity

Construct a spider diagram to show what issues made up the 'German problem'.

The Treaty of Rapallo 1922

The handling of the 'German problem' at Versailles made Germany an outcast from Europe, isolated and with severely reduced power and influence. Throughout 1919–23, Germany attempted to overturn the limitations imposed on it during the peace conferences, and to force the Allied powers to modify or replace the Treaty of Versailles.

The peace treaties also made Russia an outcast, so it is not surprising given their diplomatic isolation that Germany and Russia formed an alliance for their mutual benefit. In doing so, Germany hoped to get round the military restrictions imposed at Versailles. Meanwhile, Russia was keen to ensure its own security; after the damage caused by the civil war it no longer wanted to spread communism worldwide, but to consolidate the revolution at home. Although both countries claimed that the 1922 Treaty of Rapallo was no more than a trade agreement, in fact it included clauses for military co-operation, as well as the building of weapons and the training of soldiers on Russian soil.

The signing of the treaty met with indignation in both Britain and France (the French were correctly convinced that the agreement contained secret military clauses). Unwilling to believe that it was the harsh restrictions imposed at Versailles that had forced Germany into an agreement with Russia, France was even more determined to take a hard line with Germany.

The invasion of the Ruhr

Causes of the invasion

The reason for the invasion of the Ruhr by French and Belgian troops in January 1923 appears on the surface to be straightforward: Germany had defaulted on its reparations payments. After the Treaty of Rapallo, France was determined to take a firm line with Germany, so the French invaded to force Germany to pay.

In reality, other factors also played a part. France had long-term ambitions to replace Germany as the main economic power in Europe. During the peace negotiations in 1919, the French hoped to make the Rhineland and the Ruhr into autonomous regions under French dominance. The director of economic relations in France planned a French-controlled tax and customs union in the Ruhr, and even intended to bring parts of German industry under French control and ownership. This suggests that the invasion might have been part of a wider objective.

However, it was probably the deteriorating relationship between France and Britain that forced the French government to act. Throughout the spring and summer of 1922, conferences between the two nations failed to solve the problem of the money owed by France to Britain from wartime borrowing. Britain made it clear that it considered a resolution to the question of wartime debts to be more important than the reparations issue. The French felt increasingly isolated, because they urgently needed reparations to cover the cost of their wartime debts.

Matters reached a climax in July 1922, when Germany requested a three-year **moratorium** on reparations payments. Britain was willing to consider this. However, the British then announced that, as the USA was demanding payment of wartime debts from them, Britain itself would need to receive the equivalent pay from former wartime allies. The French felt that Britain was demanding money from them, but was willing to make concessions to Germany.

moratorium The legal postponement of the payment of debts.

The economic situation in France heightened its difficulties – there were rising debts, inflation and a devalued currency. The French therefore had a very different view of their priorities than the British did. The French Finance Commission proposed that a seizure of the Ruhr region, with its valuable coal and coke resources (which accounted for a considerable amount of the reparations payments), would allow France to pay its debts. It would also give the country some control and influence over the 'commanding heights' (the major parts) of German industry.

In December 1922, Germany failed to meet its payment schedule. The following January, French and Belgian troops marched into the Ruhr to force Germany to pay, and to seize coal and timber as part of the payment process. Britain did not join the occupation of the Ruhr, believing that the only way to ensure lasting peace was for the Germans to accept the new situation in Europe rather than having it forced upon them. Britain also did not want to see a French-dominated Europe and knew that German economic recovery was in Britain's best interests.

Passive resistance

The German government claimed that the invasion of the Ruhr broke the terms of the Treaty of Versailles. Without an army, Germany was unable to resist militarily, but the government declared that employees, industry and commerce would obstruct the French and Belgian forces by all possible means; this was known as passive resistance.

Raymond Poincaré (1860–1934) Poincaré came from the province of Lorraine and this probably influenced his attitude towards Germany, as he could remember the German seizure of his native region following the Franco–Prussian War. As a result, he took a hard line towards Germany and was determined to ensure that it was punished. He was a member of the French Assembly from 1887 and served, at various times, as finance minister, foreign minister, prime minister and president.

SOURCE B

The blow which has been dealt us here is aimed at the greatest thing which we have saved from the war and the collapse, it is aimed at the unity of the Reich; this blow – we are convinced – will also be parried by the firm will and resolute loyalty of the Baden people. The days when one could separate north and south in Germany are gone for ever; every German has now the unshatterable consciousness that he is the son of a single people and the member of a single Reich; no foreign violence will ever separate what race, speech and culture have knit together in the course of an eventful history. Every German is aware to-day of the seriousness of the hour; every one of us knows that the future of the Reich, the very existence of the German Republic, is at stake. If in these fateful days we collect all our strength, we will repulse also all the attacks upon our national existence. By this resolute and determined resistance we hope and expect that, in spite of everything, we shall achieve a better future for our hardly proved people in the consciousness of our solidarity and our right, in the struggle for our freedom.

Friedrich Ebert, speaking during his visit to Karlsruhe immediately after the French invasion of the Ruhr. Quoted in Macartney, M. 1923. Five Years of European Chaos. London, UK. Chapman and Hall. pp. 157–58.

The French claimed that they were only there to take what was rightly theirs. **Raymond Poincaré**, the French prime minister, declared to the French Chamber of Deputies: 'We are fetching coal, that's all.' However, the reality was not so simple. The French believed that the leaders of the resistance were the same men who had pushed Germany into war in 1914 – and now was the chance to defeat them.

SOURCE C

Ruined, threatened and increasingly openly abused, the main victims, France and Belgium, had finally to find a way to avoid being cheated out of all the fruits of their sacrifice. France and Belgium demand their guarantees from the real holders of wealth in Germany, who are simultaneously the real power in the land: **Stinnes, Thyssen, Haniel, Krupps** etc. That is why we have entered the Ruhr district rather than some other piece of German territory.

A French explanation for the invasion, quoted in a local German newspaper.

Stinnes, Thyssen, Haniel, Krupps These were major industrialists in Germany who owned factories in the Ruhr. Krupp was the surname of the family that owned the factories, but the firm was known as Krupps.

Activity

Construct a spider diagram to show the reasons for the French and Belgian invasion of the Ruhr.

When France and Belgium launched the invasion on 11 January 1923, the German government had no plans for passive resistance. It simply stated that Germany would not transport any more coal to France or Belgium than it had before. The government was concerned that any resistance would anger the French and give them a reason to seize the area.

On 12 January, the French established Micum (*Mission Interalliée de Controle des Usines et des Mines*) to administer the area and its director opened negotiations with the mine owners. They agreed a deal, but this undermined German control over its own economic affairs and even threatened national sovereignty. It brought German companies into direct contact with the French and Belgian authorities while potentially freeing them from German control and regulations, allowing the companies to reach private agreements with Micum. The deal alarmed the German government. German leaders initially decided to stop reparations deliveries and then, on 13 January – as support grew for resistance to the French – announced a policy of passive resistance. Mine owners were warned by the German government that if they broke this order they could be punished by up to a year in prison.

In response to the refusal to deliver coal, the French arrested numerous industrialists and subjected them to **court martial**. Several of them were imprisoned, including Krupp. These men became national heroes – willing to make sacrifices for the German nation, instead of people who earlier had been negotiating with the French. This created a feeling of national solidarity.

court martial Trial by a military court, in which defendants are accused of breaking military law. The term is usually only applied to members of the armed forces, but in 1923 the Ruhr civilians were also tried by French military courts.

SOURCE D

The French rulers must be told that the Ruhr miners will not allow themselves to be played off against their employers or government under any circumstances. The miners regard themselves as German ethnic comrades and are afflicted by the profound humiliation visited on us. The miners in France are powerless as in no other land. The employers do not recognise the trade unions as equal partners. In contrast to that achieved by the German miners through their trade unions things appear wretched for the workers in France.

Extract from local newspapers from Cologne and Gelsenkirchen, published during the occupation of the Ruhr.

Questions

What reasons does the German newspaper in Source D give for a dislike of the French? The newspaper refers to the 'profound humiliation visited on us' – what does it mean by this statement? In what ways does the newspaper support the view that conditions for workers in Germany had improved since 1918?

143

SOURCE E

Thanks to the Revolution (1918) the trade unions had become negotiating partners with equal rights to the employers. However, France had expelled the trade union leaders from the Saar's mining industry and was impeding the emergence of French trade unions by every available means. If the French were really so pro-working class, then they should begin by treating the trade unions in their own country and in the occupied territories differently. Furthermore the German workers were provided for through social legislation covering sickness, accident and old age whilst, as far as he [the mine worker] knew, such provisions did not exist in France.

A mine worker, quoted in a German newspaper from the Ruhr region during the occupation.

Questions

How useful is Source E as evidence for the reaction of workers to the French occupation? What is the writer's view of the French attitude towards the trade unions? Compare the view of the trade unions given in this source with the view in Source D on page 143. How similar are they?

The response from the unions in Source E above suggests that the social reforms and gains made since 1918 under the new republic helped it win support. The workers were in no mood to compromise, and even refused to allow French soldiers to use the pit baths.

SOURCE F

It is the duty of our workforce to support this defensive struggle. We therefore demand that our management and our Works Council never consent under any circumstances to foreign troops bathing here.

Extract from a German newspaper from the Ruhr region during the occupation.

Question

How far does the attitude in Source F reflect the views offered in Sources D and E about attitudes to the French and passive resistance?

French soldiers ride into Essen, in the Ruhr, at the start of the occupation

The government supported the workers by paying their salaries and compensating the industrialists. However, this increased the pressure on the German economy. To finance the payments the government had to print more money, which caused hyperinflation. As there was so much money in circulation prices and wages rose, but the currency was worthless. The impact was more than just financial, though – as millions lost their savings, confidence in the government declined and opposition grew.

As the German economy collapsed, there was little choice but to end the passive resistance, and it was finally called off on 23 September 1923. During the period of occupation in the Ruhr, the French had expelled 28,659 railwaymen along with 76,290 members of their families. There were also a further 2564 arrests; 400 people were sentenced to a collective total of 400 years in prison and 20 years of hard labour. The resistance had also resulted in violence – eight railwaymen had been killed and 269 injured.

Results

The invasion initially united Germany behind its government like no other event, but the hyperinflation it caused also brought the republic close to collapse. The invasion proved that passive resistance alone was not enough to break the Treaty of Versailles and that other ways must be found. Although Germany was unable to force the French out of the Ruhr, the Germans won sympathy from other nations, including Britain. After the Ruhr occupation, even France realised that aggression would not solve the question of security and the 'German problem', and it began a more lenient policy towards Germany.

SOURCE G

The great disservice which France has done not only to herself but to all Europe has been the occupation with Belgium of the Ruhr. The threat of the occupation was a most valuable trump-card so long as it was unplayed; played, it has essentially weakened France's position and prestige and has had the very disconcerting effect of re-uniting Germany to a degree unknown since the first few weeks of the war.

Macartney, M. 1923. *Five Years of European Chaos*. London, UK. *Chapman and Hall*. pp. 11–13.

Questions

What is Maxwell Macartney's view of the impact of the invasion of the Ruhr in Source G? In light of your own knowledge and the rest of this section, how far do you agree with this historian's opinion?

The invasion only added to France's sense of isolation. It clearly demonstrated that France could not uphold the Treaty of Versailles alone. The cost of the occupation also damaged the French economy. France expected support within the Ruhr region from Rhineland separatists, who wanted independence from Germany and who might therefore promote unrest to put pressure on the government to allow their secession. France also hoped to win British support for the invasion, but this was not forthcoming. As a result, the French had little choice but to change direction and adopt a policy of conciliation and negotiation. Poincaré also lost popularity over the Ruhr invasion – he was attacked by those who wanted to continue the occupation and extend the amount of land under French control, but was also criticised by those who thought the invasion was a mistake. As a result of this, Poincaré was defeated in the French elections in 1924. This confirmed the fact that France had to co-operate with Germany to get reparations and to avoid international isolation.

Discussion point

In order to assess whether the invasion was a success from the French perspective we need to establish some criteria against which to judge success. What criteria would you use?

Activities

1   Copy and complete the following chart on gains and losses from the invasion of the Ruhr.

Germany		France	
Gains	Losses	Gains	Losses

2   Who do you think gained the most from the invasion of the Ruhr? Write a paragraph to explain your answer.

3   In this section and the next you are going to plan an answer to the question: 'How successful was Germany in improving its international position in the years from 1919 to 1930?' This section has covered the years up to the end of 1923. Draw up a plan for this period. You might want to consider the following issues:

*   overturning the Treaty of Versailles
*   reintegration into the international system
*   rearming
*   improving relations with France.

3   Organise a class debate over who gained the most from the Ruhr crisis: France or Germany. At the end of the debate, take a vote to decide.

4   You are the German foreign minister and have to make a speech to the Reichstag following the end of the Ruhr crisis. Outline the German position in international affairs and put forward suggestions as to how this could be improved.

How did Germany's diplomatic position improve after 1923?

The ending of passive resistance by the new German chancellor, **Gustav Stresemann**, did not resolve the problems in the Ruhr. Right-wing groups in Germany regarded it as a surrender to Allied forces. Riots broke out and Germany was placed under martial (military) rule. The invasion convinced both Britain and the USA that France could not be trusted to maintain peace, and that it was a danger to European stability. At the same time, France realised that any action against Germany needed Allied support. The invasion marked a turning point in post-war relations and attitudes towards the 'German problem'.

The Dawes Plan 1924

The Ruhr invasion highlighted the fact that the issue of reparations needed to be reviewed. This resulted in the Dawes Plan, drawn up by US banker Charles Dawes. The plan involved not just the issue of reparations, but also the withdrawal of French troops from the Ruhr. Although the Dawes Plan did not alter the final figure of reparations that Germany had to pay, it did draw up a new schedule for repayments so that the annual sum was reduced. It allowed Germany a two-year moratorium on payments and a US loan of 800 million marks to help it out of its current economic crisis.

Gustav Stresemann (1878–1929) Berlin-born Stresemann joined the right-wing National Liberal Party in 1902, and became a leader of the party's more moderate faction. He was elected to the German parliament in 1908. He became increasingly right-wing throughout the First World War and formed the German People's Party in 1918. Streseman had nationalist sympathies, but accepted the republic and became chancellor in 1923 at the height of the economic crisis. He resigned the same year, and worked as foreign minister until his death in 1929.

Discussion point

This section focuses on whether the policies towards Germany were effective in the period from 1923 to 1929. What criteria are you going to use to decide whether or not they were effective?

The plan was provisional and was to be renegotiated over the next ten years. Reparations repayments would start gradually and reach a peak after five years; they would be guaranteed by income from the German rail network and other key industries. A committee of foreign experts, based in Berlin, was assembled to ensure that the payments reached the former Allies in a way that did not damage the German economy. The Dawes Plan – including an undertaking that French troops would leave the Ruhr within 12 months – was formally agreed at a conference in London in August 1924.

SOURCE H

Germany's growing and industrious population; her great technical skill; the wealth of her material resources; the development of her agriculture on progressive lines; her eminence in industrial science; all these factors enable us to be hopeful with regard to her future production.

Germany is well equipped with resources; she possesses the means for exploiting them on a large scale, when the present credit shortage has been overcome, she will be able to resume a favoured position in the activity of a world where normal conditions of exchange are gradually being restored.

Without undue optimism, it may be anticipated that Germany's production will enable her to satisfy her own requirements and raise the amounts contemplated in this plan for reparation obligations.

Extract from the Committee of Experts Report. Quoted in Pollard, S. and Holmes, C. 1973. Documents of Economic History, Vol. III, The End of Old Europe 1914–1939. London, UK. Edward Arnold. pp. 294–95.

Some elements of the Dawes Plan caused resentment in Germany, particularly the placing of rail and industry under international control, as well as the failure to bring about an overall reduction in the total reparations bill. However, there was a growing understanding that such measures must be taken in order to force France from the Ruhr.

The French were concerned about how Germany would be made to pay if it defaulted again, particularly as the plan ensured that France would be unable to take matters into its own hands as it had before. If Germany failed to pay, Britain – as a member of the Reparations Commission – had a right to appeal to the International Court at The Hague, which would involve the USA in the matter.

As a result of such pressure to deal with the process through arbitration, Britain, the USA and Germany believed that France would be unable to invade, as it had done in 1923. The French therefore tried to make the agreement dependent upon concessions over inter-Allied wartime debts and a new security pact with Britain. These demands only achieved a promise from the British prime minister, **Ramsay MacDonald**, to 'explore' the issue of security once the Dawes Plan had been agreed. In the end the plan was forced through, as the US threatened to withdraw if France did not agree.

Questions

What view does Source H take about Germany's capacity to pay reparations? How do you think the French would feel about this summary of Germany's economic strength? How useful is the source as evidence for the strength of the German economy?

Ramsay MacDonald (1866–1937) MacDonald joined the Independent Labour Party in 1894 and became the first secretary of the Labour Party when it was established in 1900. He was elected to parliament in 1904 and was made leader of the party in 1911. MacDonald lost the position during the war, but returned as leader in 1923. He became prime minister of the first Labour government in 1924 and again in 1929. His second administration faced the problem of the impact of the Depression, which forced MacDonald's resignation as Labour prime minister in 1931. However, he was immediately reappointed as prime minister of a National Government, which resulted in his expulsion from the Labour Party.

147

> ## SOURCE 1
>
> What France obtained in return, however, was decisive. The German payments were henceforth guaranteed by pledges, established by the experts, recognised by all creditors and accepted by Germany. By this compromise France exchanged her freedom of action with regard to Germany and her illusions regarding the magnitude of what she could expect to receive, for the certainty of being paid to a certain extent.
>
> Néré, J. 1975. The Foreign Policy of France from 1914 to 1945. London, UK. Routledge and Kegan Paul. pp. 57–58.

The Dawes Plan had shown that even though the USA had not signed the Treaty of Versailles or joined the League of Nations, the country could not remain completely isolated, as it needed trade links with Europe to prosper. The Dawes Plan allowed US investment in Germany, although this came from individuals and banks rather than the US government. The flow of money into Germany created the illusion of prosperity, but economic recovery relied heavily on the US. If the USA stopped paying the loans, Germany would once again be unable to meet its reparations payments, which would mean that Britain and France would be unable to pay their own war debts.

The greatest concern for the French was, of course, that the Dawes Plan opened the way for German recovery and set it on the path of rejoining the international community. If the US withdrew from international affairs again, France would face a much stronger Germany from a position of isolation. This led the French to try and establish their security through the Geneva Protocol (see page 126) – another attempt that ultimately failed.

The Locarno Pact 1925

The invasion of the Ruhr and the crisis that followed demonstrated to all parties that the Treaty of Versailles could not be imposed by force. Co-operation was the only way to restore stability in Europe. After 1923, Germany was involved in a series of diplomatic meetings that culminated in the Locarno Pact. In summary, the pact reflected the realisation that a nation would only commit itself to peace if it was *willing* to accept the terms of the treaties rather than having them imposed without consultation or agreement. Some revisions to the Treaty of Versailles were therefore necessary to appease Germany. The major powers of Britain and France hoped that the process would allow Germany into the League of Nations, but also draw it away from Russia.

Cologne zone Cologne is a major German city on the Rhine. It lay within the zone allocated to France when the Rhineland and the Ruhr were divided into zones or regions for administrative purposes under the Treaty of Versailles.

The Locarno Pact took its name from the small Swiss resort where the conference was held in October 1925. The resulting pact was a series of treaties that involved France, Germany, Belgium, Britain and Italy. The agreement originated in a proposal by Gustav Stresemann (see page 146) to accept Germany's western frontiers, as agreed at Versailles, in return for the withdrawal of foreign troops from the Rhineland. This suggestion was driven in part by France's refusal to carry out the evacuation of the **Cologne zone** of the Rhineland, which had been scheduled for January 1925 by the Versailles agreement. France defended its decision by arguing that Germany had not honoured the military clauses of the Treaty of Versailles. To reassure the French of Germany's good intentions, Stresemann agreed to accept the permanent loss of Alsace-Lorraine, Eupen and Malmedy. In return, Germany hoped to gain further assurances that events like the Ruhr invasion would never happen again.

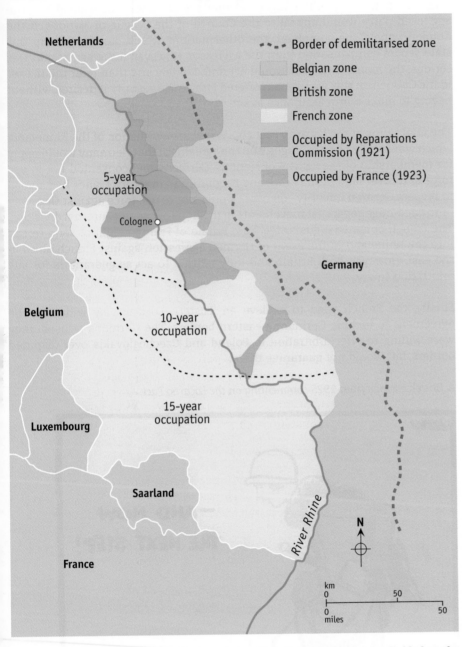

A map showing the zones of occupation into which the Rhineland was divided at the end of the First World War

The terms of the Locarno Pact effectively meant that France, Belgium and Germany accepted the frontiers between them that had been agreed at Versailles. No military action would be taken unless it was in self-defence. This finally gave France the security it had wanted for so long, and reassured Germany that there would be no repeat of the events of 1923.

Linked to this was a Treaty of Mutual Guarantee, by which Britain and Italy agreed to come to the aid of any country that was a victim of aggression in violation of the Locarno Pact. This treaty effectively committed Britain to the defence of France – something that all British governments since the First World War had refused to do. There were, however, clauses that limited British responsibility in this regard. In the case of minor border incidents, the aggrieved party would appeal to the Council of the League of Nations. If the Council upheld the complaint, the other nations would step in to help this state secure compensation from the aggressor. However, if the aggression was serious, the member nations would act immediately and then refer the matter to the Council. In this way, Britain offered France the security it desired without having to make a firm assurance to act.

The final terms of the Locarno Pact concerned the evacuation of the Rhineland, which would take place in stages, and the agreement that Germany would apply for membership of the League of Nations. Germany had consented not to use force to recover land from France and Belgium, and in return France had agreed to respect German integrity – in other words, not to use force against Germany or to encourage separatist movements in the hope of causing internal divisions. The French obtained a guarantee from Britain of France's right to send troops into the Rhineland in the event of German aggression against French allies in the east. However, both Britain and Italy refused to act as guarantors for any arbitration treaty.

Finally, the French tried to achieve an 'Eastern Locarno', by widening the agreement to include Germany's eastern borders. The Germans refused: they were willing to offer arbitration to Poland and Czechoslovakia over disputed borders, but would not guarantee them.

A British cartoon from 1925 commenting on the Locarno Pact

Activity

What is the message given in the cartoon about the Locarno Pact? Use details from the cartoon and your own knowledge to explain your answer.

French gains

The Locarno Pact was greeted with enthusiasm, particularly in France, which appeared to have gained its longed-for security and German goodwill. It might even be argued that Locarno was a masterstroke by the French. Compared to Germany, France was in decline and there was a limit to how long its dominance in Europe was likely to last. Locarno, therefore, provided France with the best possible solution, particularly as Britain and the US had been reluctant to offer aid. Perhaps surprisingly, there was also support for the pact from the French military, which had previously wanted a tough line to be taken against Germany. As Briand was also unconvinced about the Allies' willingness to supervise German disarmament and the British maintenance of the occupation of the Rhineland for 15 years, it was in France's interests to agree to an earlier evacuation, as it gained goodwill without losing anything. The agreement also brought France a political alliance with Britain. The French government faced some opposition in getting the pact approved, but ultimately it was able to show that the gains made outweighed the concessions given to Germany.

However, French gains were only short term. The treaty did not break Germany's links with Russia, and attempts to resolve disputes between Germany and Poland failed. More importantly, the French defensive military strategy, epitomised in the building of the **Maginot Line**, proved useless in the face of a German advance in 1940. In practice, French security would have been better served by upholding the terms of Versailles, which dealt with Germany's eastern *and* western borders; Locarno only guaranteed those in the west.

German gains

The Locarno Pact worked significantly in Germany's favour. During the negotiations, Stresemann had three clear aims. Firstly, he wanted to ensure the prompt evacuation of the Cologne zone (this was completed in January 1926). Secondly, he wanted to prevent an Anglo–French alliance, and in this too he was successful. Finally, he sought to undermine the Treaty of Versailles. This last aim was also achieved – although Germany had accepted its borders in the west, it had not accepted those in the east. In refusing to include its eastern borders in the agreement, Germany revealed that it was determined to change these borders. By signing the pact, it could be argued that Britain and France indicated their implicit agreement to some changes in the east. Therefore, although Germany showed a willingness to negotiate and adopt a peace policy, it did not accept the Treaty of Versailles in its entirety. At the same time, Britain – an ally of France in the First World War – adopted a neutral stance towards both France and Germany.

Nevertheless, the pact caused problems for Stresemann back in Germany. Many nationalists objected to the acceptance of any part of the Treaty of Versailles, and Stresemann struggled to win approval for Locarno from the Reichstag, which feared the pact might damage Germany's relationship with Russia. However, the level of concessions Germany had won eventually convinced the Reichstag to accept the agreement. The German signing of the Locarno Pact has raised questions about whether Stresemann was a 'good European' who wanted peace and stability, or whether he was just another German nationalist – not unlike Hitler – intent on restoring German power before embarking on a policy to recover land in the east.

Maginot Line This was a series of fortifications that the French built along the border with Germany after the First World War, in order to stop a future invasion. In 1940, the German army swept west and north through Denmark, Norway, the Netherlands, Belgium and finally France. The Maginot Line was ineffective in preventing this attack, and the Germans reached the Channel coast in just over a week.

SOURCE J

There are three great tasks that confront German foreign policy in the more immediate future. In the first place the solution of the Reparation question in a sense tolerable for Germany, and the assurance of peace, which is essential for the recovery of our strength … Secondly the protection of the Germans abroad, those 10 to 12 millions of our kindred who now live under a foreign yoke in foreign lands. The third great task is the readjustment of our Eastern frontiers: the recovery of Danzig, the Polish frontier, and a correction of the frontier of Upper Silesia.

Gustav Stresemann, in a letter to the former German crown prince, 7 September 1925. Quoted in Adamthwaite, A. 1980. The Lost Peace – International Relations in Europe 1918–1939. London, UK. Edward Arnold.

Questions

What does Source J tell us about Stresemann's foreign policy aims? How useful is the source as evidence of his aims?

Stanley Baldwin (1867–1947)

A Conservative, Stanley Baldwin first became prime minister in 1923 following Ramsay MacDonald's resignation due to ill-health. Baldwin called an election in 1924, at which the Conservatives failed to win a majority, and so Baldwin resigned. He returned to power in 1924 after the fall of the short-lived first Labour government, and remained prime minister until 1929. In the 1930s, Baldwin headed the National Government.

British gains

Britain was initially reluctant to respond positively to German proposals, but the need to find some form of security for France forced its hand. British defence spending had dropped and therefore any military commitment was even more difficult and unlikely. Public opinion was against an alliance, as the British people were afraid of being dragged into another war. However, the foreign secretary, Austen Chamberlain, believed that fear dominated Europe and wanted to offer France reassurance without driving Russia and Germany even closer together. With the support of the prime minister, **Stanley Baldwin**, the proposals were agreed by a reluctant cabinet.

Russia and its position in Europe

In many ways the Locarno Pact was a matter of grave concern for Russia. Germany appeared to have committed itself to the west, isolating Russia in the east. At the same time, the Dawes Plan had saved the capitalist economy in Germany and prevented the possibility of a communist revolution, further weakening Russia's position. However, Stresemann did not believe that improved relations with the west meant poorer relations with Russia, and he made this clear by signing the Treaty of Berlin (see page 153). Ultimately, Russia's position did not change as a result of Locarno, largely because remaining on friendly terms suited Germany's needs.

Conclusion

After the Locarno Pact, stability in Europe improved. Most people were pleased with the outcome of the Locarno talks, and Stresemann, Briand and Chamberlain shared the Nobel Peace Prize for their work in bringing it about. However, the success of the pact should not obscure the fundamental differences in aims between French and German foreign policy. France still wanted Germany restricted and Germany still wanted to overturn the Treaty of Versailles, at least in the east. As a result, it can be argued that in reality Locarno failed to solve the 'German problem' and define the role that Germany should play in Europe. For Germany, Locarno was the first step in gaining revisions to the terms of Versailles; for France, it was the first step towards German compliance with them.

Germany and the League of Nations 1926

The Locarno Pact required Germany to apply for and accept entry into the League of Nations, and this formally took place in October 1926. Germany was also given a permanent seat on the League's Council, setting aside earlier disagreements – at least superficially. Stresemann used the opportunity of joining the League to gain further concessions, so that in January 1927 the Allied Disarmament Commission withdrew and, by August 1928, 10,000 troops from the Rhine garrison had been evacuated – more than the agreements reached at Locarno. However, at the same time as entering the League and committing to its covenant, Germany signed the Treaty of Berlin with Russia. This reaffirmed the Treaty of Rapallo for a further five years and allowed Germany to continue rearming and training soldiers in Russia, despite the League's commitment to a reduction in armaments.

SOURCE K

Berlin, 2 October 1926 – Now that Locarno has been in force for nearly a year and that Germany is a member of the League of Nations, a definite period in history comes to a close. A fresh epoch for Europe commences, and the work here will assume a different and more normal character. The war spirit has been quelled, and the possibility of an era of peaceful development opens.

Edgar Vincent D'Abernon, the British ambassador to Berlin 1920–26. Quoted in Meyer, H. C. 1973. Germany – from Empire to Ruin, 1913–45. London, UK. Macmillan. pp. 144–46.

Questions

What is Edgar D'Abernon's view of German entry to the League of Nations? How useful is this source in understanding developments within Germany in the period from 1925 to 1926? How useful is the source in understanding British hopes about relations with Germany in the period?

153

The Young Plan 1930

In 1928, the German government launched a plan to persuade France and Britain to evacuate the remainder of the Rhineland earlier than had been agreed at Locarno, as well as to consider a revision of the reparations settlement. The Germans argued that the Dawes Plan had only ever been a temporary solution. The US was aware that once Germany had to pay the full annual reparations payments it would be unable to meet the interest on its US loans. For this reason, the US was willing to consider some revision to the amount of reparations that Germany had to pay. The French were also willing to consider an overall revised settlement and an end to the occupation of the Rhineland. However, they wanted it linked to the establishment of a new international body to ensure that the Rhineland remained demilitarised.

Throughout the winter of 1928–29, a committee guided by the US banker Owen Young considered the matter. Negotiations were not easy, as the Germans added new demands, including the return of the Polish Corridor (see page 52) and Upper Silesia (see page 87). However, recommendations were issued in June 1929. The Young Plan was, in many ways, a continuation of the Dawes Plan. Unlike the Dawes Plan, though, the terms included a reduction in the total amount of reparations to be paid, from 132 million gold marks to 40 million paid over a period of 59 years. The international controls over the German economy, which had caused such discontent in 1924, were to be dismantled and the Reparations Commission could no longer initiate sanctions.

The implementation of the Young Plan and the demilitarisation of the Rhineland were discussed at The Hague in August 1929. There were serious clashes between Britain and France over the share of reparations. As reparations payments were to be cut, Britain demanded some compensation from the US for the war-debt payments it had already made; in the end the British accepted only 75% of their original demands. The French initially refused to agree to a proposal for the complete evacuation of the Rhineland by 30 June 1930, but Stresemann would not sign the plan without full French co-operation. At the same time, Briand was forced to give up his hopes of establishing a commission to monitor the demilitarisation, as Britain argued that it would increase tensions.

The German government was forced to concede a referendum on the signing of the plan. It was pressured by the German Nationalist Party and the more extreme Nazi Party, which formed the Hartzburg Front in opposition to the Young Plan and argued that signing the agreement amounted to high treason. The government comfortably won the referendum, and the Young Plan was formally signed in January 1930. With the signing of the plan, and an agreement for the full evacuation of the Rhineland by June 1930, Germany effectively regained its power status in Europe.

The front page from a German communist newspaper, The Red Flag, *from March 1930; the headline reads 'In the chains of the Young Plan'*

Epilogue

By the end of the 1920s, it appeared as if Germany could be contained, and in 1929 Briand outlined a scheme for a form of European federation. This received a favourable reaction from Stresemann, who urged a customs union and a common currency. The European members of the League gave Briand the task of producing a clear programme, which was completed in May 1930. Superficially at least, European stability and harmony had been restored and Germany had accepted its place in the European system.

By the time the Young Plan was presented in 1930, however, the whole situation had changed. The world was engulfed by the Great Depression. Stresemann had died and Germany was moving towards political and economic crisis. In Britain, the new Labour government was struggling with a collapsing economy. Whether Stresemann was ever serious about a more federal Europe is open to debate. Historians such as Frank McDonough, for example, have argued that while he seemed a 'good European in public, in private he was a German nationalist who cherished the long-term objectives of recovering German territory in eastern Europe'. But even if Stresemann just saw it as just another opportunity to revise Versailles, the Young Plan was now an irrelevance. Other interests dominated international politics.

Activities

1 Consider each of the events in this section and decide how effectively the issue was resolved. Award each event a mark out of 5 depending upon the effectiveness of the solution – the higher the mark, the more effective the solution. Copy and complete the chart below to record your findings.

Event	Mark / 5	Explanation
Dawes Plan		
Locarno Pact		
Germany joins the League of Nations		
Young Plan		

2 What evidence is there to support the view that the period after the signing of the Locarno agreement deserves to be called the 'Locarno honeymoon'? Make a list of all the evidence to support the statement and the evidence that could be used to challenge it.

3 In the previous section you began to plan an essay on how successfully Germany improved its international position in the 1920s. You are now in a position to complete the plan using the same headings. Compare the position for each of the headings in 1923 and 1929. What do you notice?

4 Stresemann has often been seen as the great German statesman of the 1920s. He died in 1929. Write an obituary for Stresemann that summarises his achievements and failings, before reaching an overall judgement.

Fact

A Labour government came to power in Britain following the defeat of the Conservative Party in the 1929 election. Although Labour was the largest party, it did not have an overall majority, which meant that it could be defeated if the Conservative and Liberal parties combined. Labour difficulties were compounded by the onset of the Depression in 1929 and in 1931, divided over how to handle the economic crisis, Labour fell from power. Its leader, Ramsay Macdonald, stayed on to head the new coalition government.

Historical debate

The traditional view of Stresemann's foreign policy suggests that he was a moderate and conciliator whose main aim was reconciliation with France and the reintegration of Germany into European and world affairs, ending its isolation. However, revisionists, such as Frank McDonough, have argued that Stresemann followed a more double-edged policy – he appeared to be a peacemaker, but in fact was more of a German nationalist who wanted to recover German territory achieve German domination of Europe. In light of the information in this chapter, which view do you most agree with?

End of chapter activities

Summary

You should now have a full understanding of the 'German problem' and the attempts to solve it – or at least contain it – in the period after the signing of the Treaty of Versailles. You should be able to explain why attempts to enforce the treaty were not effective, why they created greater resentment within Germany, and why they did not bring its main proponent, France, any benefits.

Some historians have argued that the invasion of the Ruhr in 1923, and the Locarno Pact that arose from this event, were a turning point in international affairs – hence the use of the term 'the Locarno honeymoon' to describe the period that followed. However, the invasion also showed Germany that there were serious divisions between the former wartime allies that it was later able to exploit. You should be able to explain how and why, after 1923, there was a change in approach as attempts were made to bring Germany back into the European system through revisions to the Treaty of Versailles. You should be able to assess how successful this policy was, and how far France, Germany and Britain achieved their objectives. You should also be able to make a judgement on the reasons for Stresemann's conciliatory approach – whether it was motivated by a genuine desire for German reintegration in Europe, or by nationalist aims.

Summary activity

There were no major wars in the 1920s. This suggests that the League of Nations was a success, but is that a valid judgement? The following exercise is designed to help you reach your own conclusion about this.

Look at the list of statements below.

- German foreign policy still wanted to revise Versailles in the east.
- Nations were financially exhausted after the First World War.
- Germany had joined the League of Nations.
- The League had failed to solve border disputes where major powers were involved or had an interest.
- The USA was not a member of the League of Nations.
- The successor states in Eastern Europe were weak.
- Disarmament talks had not taken place and success in this area had been limited.
- The League had solved border disputes involving small nations.
- The Locarno and Kellogg–Briand pacts had given France the security it desired.
- The question of German reparations had been finally resolved.

Sort each of these statements into lists under two headings:

- What hopeful signs for peace in Europe were there in 1929?
- What signs of danger were there for Europe in 1929?

Having sorted the statements into two columns, use this chapter and Chapter 6 to find information to support each statement. You might find there is information that modifies your view, and that some of the statements could appear in both columns. Copy and complete the chart below to summarise your findings.

What hopeful signs for peace in Europe were there in 1929?	Evidence	What signs of danger were there for Europe in 1929?	Evidence

In light of the chart, which statement do you think is the most valid? Write a paragraph explaining why you have chosen one view and not the other.

Paper 1 exam practice

Question

Compare and contrast the views expressed in Sources A and B (on page 158) about the invasion of the Ruhr.
[6 marks]

Skill

Cross-referencing

Before you start

Cross-referencing questions require you to compare **and** contrast the information/content/nature of **two** sources.

Before you attempt this question, refer to pages 212–13 for advice on how to tackle cross-referencing questions and a simplified markscheme.

SOURCE A

A German poster produced in 1923; it states 'Hands off the Ruhr'

SOURCE B

Ruined, threatened and increasingly openly abused, the main victims, France and Belgium, had finally to find a way to avoid being cheated out of all the fruits of their sacrifice. France and Belgium demand their guarantees from the real holders of wealth in Germany, who are simultaneously the real power in the land: Stinnes, Thyssen, Haniel, Krupps etc. That is why we have entered the Ruhr district rather than some other piece of German territory.

A French explanation for the invasion, quoted in a local German newspaper, published in the Ruhr during the occupation.

Student answer

The two sources adopt very different views on the invasion of the Ruhr. This is largely due to the origin and purpose of the two sources. Source A portrays the French as aggressors who have invaded and destroyed the Ruhr industry, shown by depicting France as a monstrous woman crushing industry and taking what the French wanted. Source B is in partial agreement with the last point, stating that France and Belgium had invaded to 'avoid being cheated out of all the fruits of their sacrifice'; this is a reference to the reparations that had stopped reaching the two countries.

However, Source A suggests that the aim of the French was more than simply seizing goods; the French are portrayed as warlike and it implies that they wanted to destroy industry and possibly German power. This contrasts with Source B, which mentions only a desire to avoid being cheated out of reparations and implies the attack on the industrial region was because of the power held by the industrial magnates.

Source A portrays the French as aggressors: the woman is depicted with a demon-like face, wild hair and armed with a gun. This is in contrast to Source B, which suggests that France and Belgium were the victims, acting in defence against the real aggressors – the owners of German industry, such as Krupps. Source A is a call for the Germans to resist, hence the caption 'Hands off the Ruhr', whilst Source B attempts to justify the invasion. As Source A is a German poster from 1923, when the invasion took place, it is attempting to rally people behind the nation, showing how they have been treated badly, and that they are unable to defend themselves. The helmet on the ground represents military weakness. Although Source B is from a German paper, it is a French attempt to justify and win support for their actions.

Examiner comments

The student considers both sources and makes a comparison, largely of the differences in the messages of the two sources. The answer also gives a clear overview and shows that the main message of the two sources is completely different, suggesting why this is likely to be the case and raising the issue of their origin and purpose. The answer largely follows a point-by-point comparison, rather than a sequential treatment. The candidate is able to draw contrasts between the sources, particularly on how the French are portrayed. This argument is supported by precise details.

The student picks up on the one point of similarity, suggesting that the French wanted to obtain goods from the region; this could have been developed, as Source B says it was justified whereas Source A does not and suggests that Germany was defenceless. The answer states that the motives for the invasion were different, and again supports this with careful reference to both sources. The answer also explains the reasons for the differences, using the origin and purpose of the sources, and notes that the German newspaper report is outlining French attempts to justify their actions rather than representing German views. The answer is well focused on the key issue in the question – the views about the invasion. As a result, this answer would score the full 6 marks.

Paper 2 practice questions

1 How significant was the Locarno Pact?

2 How successful was the French government in achieving its aims towards Germany in the period from 1918 to 1930?

3 'The German problem was not solved in the period from 1919 to 1929.' How far do you agree with this assertion?

4 'It was the Germans, rather than the French, who gained the most from the agreements made in the period between 1919 and 1929.' To what extent do you agree with this statement?

5 How far was Germany satisfied by the revisions to the Treaty of Versailles in the period from 1919 to 1929?

6 How successful were the policies towards reparations?

7 'The French government's response to the German problem was ineffective.' How far do you agree?

8 The impact of the Great Depression

Key questions

- What was the social, economic and political impact of the Depression on the various states?
- What role did the League of Nations play in diplomacy from 1930 to 1932?

Overview

- The Great Depression that followed the 1929 Wall Street Crash in the USA had far-reaching social, economic and political consequences.
- The most severely affected nation was Germany, where unemployment levels reached 6 million and the democratic government fell. The Nazi Party took control and developed a dictatorship under Adolf Hitler.
- The USSR was not affected by the Depression and used this period to catch up with the Western powers in several areas. The impact in Italy and France was also less severe than elsewhere in Europe.
- The US response to the crisis was the New Deal, in which a wide range of social and economic measures were introduced to tackle the problems. However, the British government followed traditional policies and waited for the trade cycle to recover.
- The Japanese responded to the collapse of their trade and economic difficulties by adopting an aggressive policy in China, which culminated in full-scale war in 1937.
- The problems created by the Depression were a serious challenge for the League of Nations. However, it successfully resolved the Peru–Colombia dispute and expanded its membership in this period, most notably with the admission of the USSR.
- The challenges created by both the Great Depression and the rise of the Nazi Party contributed to the failure of the Disarmament Conference in 1933.

Timeline

1929 Oct: Wall Street Crash sends share prices tumbling

1930 assassination attempt on Japanese prime minister; London Conference and Treaty for the Limitation and Reduction of Naval Armament

1931 US president Herbert Hoover proposes one-year suspension of debt repayments

1932 Feb: Geneva Disarmament Conference begins

Sep: Colombia–Peru border clash begins

Oct: Lytton report on Manchuria published

1933 Jan: Hitler withdraws Germany from Disarmament Conference

Mar: Japan leaves League of Nations

Sep: Germany leaves League of Nations

1934 Sep: USSR joins League of Nations

1937 Dec: Italy leaves League of Nations

Unemployed men take part in a 'hunger march' in the UK at the height of the Great Depression in 1935

What was the social, economic and political impact of the Depression on the various states?

The impact of the Wall Street Crash was disastrous. It sent the world economy into collapse as bankruptcies in the USA hit other nations. It brought an abrupt end to the boom that had begun in the mid 1920s. Just as importantly, it had a profound impact on international relations, destroying the co-operation that had characterised the Locarno period.

The only nation not affected by the **Great Depression** that followed the crash was the USSR, as it did not trade with other states. Most countries suddenly found that they could not sell their goods overseas, as other nations could not afford them or chose to buy home-produced goods to aid their own failing economies. With a view to protecting their own industries, countries put tariffs or import duties on foreign goods. This made products expensive and unable to compete with goods produced at home. This policy of increased protection caused world trade to fall into rapid decline – dropping by an estimated 70% between 1929 and 1932. The fall in demand for goods resulted in factory closures and rising unemployment. People with no jobs could not afford to buy goods, causing a spiral of economic decline. Unemployment was five times higher in 1932 than it had been in 1929; in the US, 30% of the labour force was out of work.

Great Depression This is the term used to describe the collapse in world trade that followed the Wall Street Crash of October 1929. The collapse in trade had profound social, political and economic effects as nations looked to protect their own economies by imposing tariffs and trade barriers against foreign competition. Millions became unemployed, and this created large-scale social problems and widespread poverty.

162

A diagram showing the fall in trade and unemployment during the Great Depression

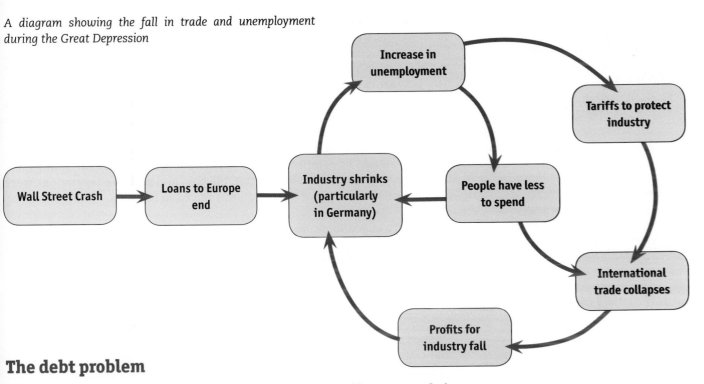

The debt problem

It was not just trade that was affected. Countries were unable to repay their debts – just at a time when the nations that had loaned the money needed the repayments to help their own economies. The USA began to demand a return of the loans it had made to European countries after the First World War. The close economic ties between the USA, Germany, Britain and France meant that the crash had a significant impact on those nations. The German recovery had been heavily dependent upon loans, largely from the US, but also from Britain and France. Now, Britain and France demanded that Germany repay them so that they could honour their own debts to the USA. This pushed the German economy into freefall.

SOURCE A

It was an international crisis. All over the world, prices were falling; this was leading to an increase in the burden of national debts, and to several cases of national default. World trade was declining, markets shrinking, interest from investments drying up, foreign exchange wobbling. Financial crashes became frequent – the Hatry case was followed by the crash of the British ship-owner, Lord Kylsant, and by the failure and suicide of the Swedish match-king, Kreuger. Early in 1931, one of the chief links in the European banking system snapped – the Austrian Kredit Anstalt. A loan from the Bank of England and a guarantee from the newly established Bank of International Settlements helped to keep Austria solvent, but business men lost confidence in Central Europe.

Graves, R. and Hodge, A. 1971. The Long Week-end: A Social History of Great Britain 1918–1939. London, UK. Penguin. p. 243.

163

economic nationalism This adapts the concept of nationalism – a devotion to one's country or a belief in its superiority – to an economic context. It meant protecting national industries from foreign competition by imposing tariffs and trade barriers.

autarky Economic self-sufficiency, by which nations aimed to produce all the goods they needed so they would not have to rely on imported materials.

Adolf Hitler (1889–1945)

Although an Austrian, Hitler fought in the German army in the First World War. He later took over the extreme nationalist right-wing German Workers' Party, and transformed it into the Nazi Party. Its increasingly violent attacks on left-wing groups were tolerated to begin with. However, when Hitler's attempted 'March on Berlin' in 1923 failed, he was imprisoned. While in prison, he wrote *Mein Kampf* ('My Struggle'), in which he set out his anti-democratic and nationalist views. On his release in December 1924, Hitler reorganised the Nazi Party. He decided to use the democratic process to achieve power, although violence was also used against opponents.

These demands created a climate in which the USA, Britain and France each believed that the other two were causing the financial crisis, which seriously limited attempts at co-operation just at a time when they were most needed. In 1931, the US president, Herbert Hoover, proposed a one-year suspension of debt payments. At first the French were reluctant, but they eventually agreed. In 1932, at a meeting in Lausanne, Britain and France agreed to accept German reparations payments in the form of government bonds, if the USA accepted a continued postponement of debt repayments. However, at the end of the year the US Congress refused this deal, and the Lausanne Agreement collapsed. Germany should have returned to the payments agreed under the Young Plan, but the new Nazi government rejected the plan and no more reparations were paid. Only $3 billion out of $10 billion was repaid to the USA.

This failure of economic co-operation symbolised the change in attitudes that followed the Wall Street Crash. Countries tried to solve their problems in new, radical ways. **Economic nationalism** was one of the most common responses, as states started to take steps to protect themselves and become self-sufficient, following a policy of **autarky**.

Economic nationalism was reflected in political relations, as many nations pursued more aggressive nationalist policies than they had before. The goodwill that characterised the 1920s was destroyed as leaders, most notably in Japan, Italy and Germany, tried to distract their populations from domestic problems by achieving foreign policy success. This response added to the growing tension – other countries felt threatened and began to take action to protect themselves. This had an impact on attempts at disarmament, as nations were less willing to disarm when others were building up their forces and threatening world peace.

Political repercussions of the Great Depression

The Depression also had far-reaching political consequences in the domestic sphere. As unemployment rose, many people started to turn away from traditional political parties and look to those that seemed to offer simple solutions to economic and social problems, such as introducing public work schemes or driving 'undesirables' from the workforce to allow others to take their place. The 1930s witnessed the rise of political extremism as more radical parties – often nationalist in outlook – gained support. The rise of the Nazi Party in Germany is the most obvious example of this, but right-wing groups also emerged to challenge the democratic process in countries such as Britain (the British Union of Fascists), Spain (Francisco Franco's Falange) and Romania.

Germany

The impact of the Depression in Germany was greater than in any other nation, and more than 6 million Germans were unemployed by 1932. Germany's economic recovery was dependent upon loans from the US, but these loans ceased when the Depression began. The coalition government of Chancellor Hermann Müller was unable to deal with the problem of rising unemployment and the coalition split over the issue of welfare and unemployment benefits, which it was struggling to pay. A series of elections followed, which resulted in the growth of support for extremist parties on both the left and right of the political spectrum, but most notably on the right for **Adolf Hitler**'s Nazi Party. The table on page 165 shows how support for the Nazis increased.

Year	Nazi seats in Reichstag	Percentage of vote
1928	12	2.6
1930	107	18.3
July 1932	230	37.3
November 1932	196	33.1
1933	288	43.9

The Nazi Party offered apparent solutions to the complex problems of unemployment and poverty, and support for the party grew rapidly. Although the Nazi Party never achieved a majority in the Reichstag, it was still the largest party. Despite the Nazis' electoral success, the German president, Paul von Hindenburg, disliked Hitler and was reluctant to appoint him chancellor. However, the failure of other politicians to secure a majority in the Reichstag made Hindenburg realise that this appointment was necessary. The decline in Nazi support in the second election of 1932 convinced both Hindenburg and the former chancellor, Franz von Papen, that Hitler could be controlled. He was invited to become chancellor in January 1933. In order to limit his power, only two other Nazis were permitted in the cabinet. However, events in the early months of 1933, including the Reichstag fire, allowed Hitler to gradually increase his power. By the time Hindenburg died in 1934, Hitler was able to combine the offices of chancellor and president to become führer.

Italy

Benito Mussolini came to power in 1922, before the Great Depression began. Italy was far from politically stable at the time, but Mussolini claimed to have found the solution through the establishment of a 'corporate state'. This was designed to resolve the clashes between socialism and capitalism. Mussolini believed that the corporate state would ensure that everyone worked for the benefit of the country, rather than for themselves. Each area of economic activity – such as coal mining or the steel industry – had a corporation of both workers and employers, who discussed all issues relating to that activity. A fascist representative was present to monitor the discussions and to ensure co-operation.

Gradually, this system was extended to the political sphere, as the old parliament was replaced by a new Chamber of Representatives. However, in practice the system favoured capitalists and big business, and did not resolve many of Italy's problems.

Italy did not escape the consequences of the Depression either. The country received a considerable amount of money from the USA after the war, but the payments were withdrawn when the Depression began. Italian farmers were hit by the collapse of grain prices, and industry and banks suffered from a drop in demand. As a result, government intervention increased, companies were reorganised, and price-fixing and wage cuts were introduced. Perhaps the most successful element of government policy was the introduction of public works.

Italy was not as badly affected by the Depression as other countries, and this helped Mussolini justify his claim that the corporate state was a success. More importantly, Italy escaped the political and social unrest that was widespread in other nations, and Mussolini was one of the few European leaders who did not lose power during the Depression.

Fact

After being appointed chancellor, Hitler was determined to secure a majority in order to begin creating his dictatorship. He called new elections for March 1933 but, just before the election, the German parliament building caught fire. The Nazis blamed the communists, and won emergency powers . The Communist Party was declared illegal, and Hitler then persuaded the Reichstag to pass the Enabling Act, which gave him the power to rule by decree for four years.

Soviet Union In 1924, Russia adopted a new constitution and became known as the Union of Soviet Socialist Republics (USSR), or the Soviet Union. However, it was often still referred to as Russia, the most powerful of its republics.

Joseph Stalin (1878–1953)

After Lenin's death in 1924 and the subsequent power struggle in Russia, Stalin emerged victorious and led the country until his death. A member of the Bolshevik Party from its early days, he was involved in the October 1917 seizure of power. He was party general-secretary from 1922 and used this to build up his position, appointing his supporters to key jobs. Stalin modernised the USSR and was able to defeat Nazi Germany during the Second World War. However, his period of rule is also associated with brutality as many people, including loyal party officials, were removed and killed in what became known as the Purges.

The Soviet Union

The **Soviet Union** was least affected by the Depression. A European outcast following the Russian Revolution, the USSR was not involved in world trade and therefore did not suffer the consequences of its collapse. The Depression gave the USSR the opportunity to catch up economically with the Western powers, and Soviet leader **Joseph Stalin** introduced a series of Five-Year Plans to develop heavy industry. Towards the end of the 1930s, these plans also concentrated on rearmament. In areas such as coal and steel production, levels of productivity rose dramatically and the USSR grew into a modern industrial nation.

There were also significant changes in agriculture. Instead of peasants owning their own small plots of land, these were joined together to form large farms known as collectives. This allowed increased mechanisation, as tractors and other machines produced by the Five-Year Plans could be used on these larger farms. However, the scheme faced a great deal of opposition, as peasants resented losing their land. Many chose to destroy their crops and livestock rather than hand them over to the state.

Politically, the 1930s saw Stalin increase his control over the Russian people. Potential opponents were rounded up and sent away to work camps – known collectively as the Gulag. Even loyal party officials were removed, and some were murdered. In this way, Stalin aimed to create a state that was completely loyal to himself.

Russian peasants working on a collective farm in the 1930s

Britain

Although the second Labour government fell from office in 1931 and unemployment reached 3 million at the height of the Depression in 1932, democracy was never seriously threatened in Britain, and political extremism gained little support. The Labour government that was in power when the Depression hit had to deal with the economic crisis but, lacking an overall majority in parliament, it was difficult for leaders to act. The cabinet split – in much the same way as several minority governments towards the end of Weimar Germany – over the issue of cutting welfare benefits. The resignation of prime minister Ramsay MacDonald might have caused a political crisis, but his immediate appointment as head of a new National Government averted this.

The new government did not adopt any radical economic policies, rejecting public work schemes as a solution to the crisis. The government was more concerned with ensuring that the budget was balanced, and this resulted in welfare cuts. Despite this, neither the communists nor the fascists in Britain gained much support, and it appears that the majority of the population adopted a resigned approach to the situation.

The export industries in Britain suffered most from the Depression, with iron and steel, cotton and shipbuilding all experiencing a decline. These traditional industries were largely located in the north and north-west of the country, and it was there that unemployment reached its highest, with Jarrow seeing an unemployment rate of 67%. However, for those in the south and east who had employment, this was actually a period of relative prosperity, as **real incomes** rose and they were able to buy new electrical goods, such as washing machines, or take advantage of low interest rates to buy a home or car. The social and economic impact of the Depression therefore varied according to the region in which people lived.

> **real incomes** Money incomes (or wages) refer only to the actual amount of money received. Real income takes into consideration increase in prices as well. For example, a money wage might increase by 10%, but if prices increase by 15% (as a result of inflation), then a person's *real* wage has *declined* overall.

167

France

Initially, France's greater self-sufficiency protected it from the worst effects of the Depression, although production did decline. As the 1930s progressed, however, France began to feel the impact of the economic crisis in the same way as other nations. In 1935, unemployment reached a peak of 425,000. This had an impact on government finances, as did the suspension and subsequent abandonment of German reparations payments, resulting in a 33% fall in government income. This made any attempt at economic and welfare reform impossible – the government was unable to increase expenditure and wages, or introduce shorter working hours, at such a time.

The economic problems in France also had political consequences. Political unrest was not uncommon – riots and strikes were a common response to the difficulties. Economic problems also contributed to a rise in extremism. There were six governments between June 1932 and February 1934, and 18 between 1930 and 1936. As a result, much of the population looked to bodies and organisations that would take direct action. This resulted in increased support for fascist or semi-fascist groups, who believed that the democracy of the **Third Republic** was weak. The republic survived, but the constant change of ministries made it very difficult for any government to pursue a clear policy. This weakness was significant in the government's failure to deal decisively with the increased foreign threat posed by Germany.

> **Third Republic** This refers to the constitution and system of government that was established in France in 1870, during the siege of Paris towards the end of the Franco-Prussian War of 1870–71. The First Republic was from 1792–1804, and the Second from 1848–52. Between these dates, France was ruled by kings or emperors.

Franklin D. Roosevelt (1882–1945) Despite being partially paralysed by polio, Democrat Roosevelt became a member of the US Senate in 1921 and won the 1932 presidential election. He is best known for the 'New Deal' he introduced in an attempt to lead the US out of the Depression. He went on to win the 1936, 1940 and 1944 elections. After his death, the US constitution was altered, limiting presidents to a maximum of two terms in office.

Historical debate

There has been disagreement among historians on the impact of the Depression, particularly in Britain and the USA. The traditional image as portrayed in pictures of the hunger marchers (see photo on page 162) or queues of unemployed looking for jobs in the US has been shown by historians such as Stephen Constantine and John Stevenson to ignore the considerable improvements in the standard of living experienced by those who remained in work during a period of rising real income. It is important, therefore, to remember that although the period was very bleak for those out of work, it was a time of contrasts – of 'economic gloom for some and prosperity for others'.

The USA

The Depression began in the USA with the collapse of the stock market in October 1929. This resulted in the decline of many industries, and by 1932 unemployment had reached 12 million. Nearly all areas of economic activity were affected: a quarter of all farmers had lost their land by 1932 and business failures reached 30,000 in the same year. This was a severe shock to the nation – only a few months before the crash, the president had announced that America was close to defeating poverty.

President Herbert Hoover initially argued that the Depression was simply part of the natural trade cycle, and that if the USA continued its policy of non-intervention the country would eventually emerge from the difficulties. By the early 1930s, however, few people believed this approach would work. The new president, **Franklin D. Roosevelt** (elected in 1932), took decisive action. He inherited a country in which there was widespread panic and a sense of hopelessness. Political extremism was limited, with perhaps the clearest sign of protest being the Bonus Marchers, a group of former soldiers who marched on Washington to demand that their wartime bonuses be paid to help them through the Depression. When their demand was refused, most simply returned home; those who continued to protest were dispersed by armed force, including tanks.

Roosevelt introduced several policies to tackle the high levels of unemployment and to restore confidence in the USA. These policies have become known as the 'New Deal'. Through this, Roosevelt hoped to correct the financial crisis, provide short-term relief for the unemployed, promote industrial recovery by increased government spending, and bring about greater co-operation between government, industry and unions. He introduced a whole series of measures in 1933, ranging from the Agricultural Adjustment Act to regulate farm production and restore prices, to the Public Works Administration, which created jobs through housing, energy supplies and conservation work. These policies had the desired effect of restoring confidence and preventing the rise of political extremism. Their success was reflected in Roosevelt's election victory in 1936, when he won over 60% of the popular vote. A Second New Deal was introduced throughout 1935–38, which brought further relief to the US public.

The real success of Roosevelt's policies has been the subject of some debate. In fact, unemployment levels began to rise again in 1938, with 19% of the workforce unemployed, compared with just over 14% the previous year. Some historians have therefore argued that it was only the onset of war and the need for rearmament that finally solved the problems in the USA.

Japan

There is little dispute that Japan suffered badly during the Depression. The most notable effect was in the highly lucrative silk industry. Silk was a luxury product and a great deal of the silk produced in Japan was exported to the USA. However, with rising unemployment in the US, the demand for luxury goods collapsed, and Japanese silk exports dropped by nearly 40% in 1929–30. Moreover, the price also fell by around 80% compared with the previous decade. This was not the only industry to suffer, though; about 50% of Japan's mining and heavy industry was forced to close down. The consequences were dramatic: both production and employment fell by 30% between 1929 and 1931.

Japan had few raw materials of its own, so it relied heavily on the import of these resources from Manchuria, and on production for an export market. As countries reduced their imports and put up protective tariffs, Japan was particularly badly hit. This was made worse by the rapidly growing Japanese population, which was rising at a rate of 1 million per year. Much of Japan is mountainous and there was very little fertile land, so it became increasingly difficult to feed the growing population. Poverty was widespread.

The Depression made it easier for military and patriotic groups to increase their power in Japan. This was evident as early as November 1930, when a member of a patriotic society attempted to assassinate the prime minister, Osachi Hamaguchi. The prestige of the army within Japanese society allowed it to pursue policies independent of the weak civilian government. Right-wing members of the army increasingly believed the country needed to follow a policy of autarky (see page 164) to guarantee the supply of raw materials and land for the growing population. Military influence made it difficult for the government to resist calls for expansion. Manchuria appeared to offer a solution to many of Japan's problems – it was rich in raw materials (especially coal and iron ore), was fertile enough to feed the Japanese population, and would offer a market for exports, stimulating the depressed Japanese economy.

SOURCE B

Behind Japan's urge to expansion are a number of impelling forces. There is the explosive pressure of rapidly increasing population in a land that is already overcrowded. There is the feeling of being unfairly treated in the world distribution of territory and raw materials. There is the exceptionally strong position of the fighting services vis-à-vis the civil authorities. There is the high flown sense of nationalism, which for many Japanese has all the force of religious conviction. There is the mythical idea of Japan's Pan-Asian mission, very popular with Japan's retired army officers and nationalist theoreticians, which envisages Japan as the leader of an Asia from which 'white imperialism' has been banished.

Chamberlin, W. H. 1941. Japan over Asia. London, UK. Little, Brown & Co. p. 8. Chamberlin was Tokyo correspondent for the Christian Science Monitor *and an author of books on interwar Japan.*

Question

Why was Japan so badly hit by the Depression?

Fact

In many countries, groups within the armed forces – particularly the officer corps and nationalist groups – were able to exert influence and act as pressure groups in the 1930s. Many of these groups claimed that the democratic government had failed to act in the best interests of the nation. They believed that these interests could be upheld by expansion. The public was often willing to listen to these arguments, as they believed governments to be corrupt, and trusted the armed forces.

169

Questions

What reasons does Chamberlin give for Japanese expansion? How useful is his explanation of the motives behind Japanese expansion?

Activities

1 Using the information in the section above, construct a mind map to summarise the impact of the Depression on international relations. Think in terms of social, economic and political consequences.

2 Research how the Depression affected different countries, such as Germany, Italy, Russia, the USA, Japan, Britain and France. Then summarise the social, economic and political consequences for each.

3 Following the research above, hold a class debate about which country was most affected by the Depression. Does it vary according to social, economic and political impact, or is it always the same country?

What role did the League of Nations play in diplomacy from 1930 to 1932?

The onset of the Great Depression made the work of the League of Nations much harder than it had previously been. The collapse in world trade meant that nations imposed tariffs on goods to protect their own industries. They also began to look for areas into which they could expand, to obtain both raw materials and new markets.

Meanwhile, the Depression increased political instability, which brought new leaders to power, many of whom believed that expansion was the best way to solve their nation's difficulties. As a result, the influence of the League declined and some nations started to leave the organisation or look for other ways to solve their problems.

The Colombia–Peru border dispute 1932–33

In September 1932, around 300 armed Peruvians seized the Amazon harbour town of Leticia. This was in protest against a 1922 treaty that had given the land to Colombia, and the imposition of tariffs on sugar from Peru. At first, the Colombian government took no notice of these actions. However, when Peruvian forces prevented two large ships reaching Leticia, the Colombians finally took action. The Colombian government announced plans to send a force of 1000 troops to the area. A fleet was also sent up the Amazon, although it did not arrive in Leticia until December. Meanwhile, Colombia assembled a temporary air force, equipping civilian planes as bombers and fighters.

Skirmishes between the two nations broke out in 1933. The Colombian navy carried out bombardments, but avoided targeting Leticia itself as it was on the border with Brazil. The Colombians did not want to give Peruvian forces a chance to flee into Brazil, as this might create an international conflict. When the Colombian army arrived, the Peruvian troops fled.

Meanwhile, the president of Peru was assassinated and his successor began negotiations with Colombia. A period of diplomatic argument followed, but the issue was taken to the League and was finally resolved in May 1933. The League assumed control of the region while negotiations between the two countries continued. In 1934, a resolution was passed by which the area was returned to Colombia and Peru issued a formal apology for its actions. Leticia was demilitarised to prevent further conflict.

The USSR and the League of Nations in the 1930s

Russia was excluded from initial membership of the League due to fears of communism and Russia's desire to spread revolution to other nations (see Chapter 5). However, by the 1930s the international situation had changed. The USSR was gravely concerned about the rise of fascism and militarism in Germany, Italy and Japan, prompting Stalin to adopt a very different attitude – at least in public – towards the League. Although he did not trust the Western democracies, he was desperate for an alliance with Britain and France as he tried to improve Soviet security. In 1934, the USSR was admitted to the League of Nations.

Colombians celebrate their victory over the Peruvians after the border conflict in 1933

Disarmament in the 1930s

Attempts at disarmament in the 1920s (discussed in Chapter 6) continued in the 1930s, but the impact of the Depression on international diplomacy in general made the work of the League on this, and on other issues, much more difficult. In particular, some countries badly affected by the Depression increasingly resorted to more aggressive foreign policies, and so were not prepared to consider limitations on their armed forces.

The London Conference and the Treaty for the Limitation and Reduction of Naval Armament 1930

The Washington Conference (see page 123) had started the process of naval disarmament; the London Conference of 1930 aimed to take it further. Initial attempts to extend the Washington Agreement to cruisers had been made at a Naval Conference between the US, Britain and Japan in Geneva in 1927. These had failed. However, the change in economic circumstances by 1930 meant that many nations were now eager to reduce spending – particularly on expensive fleets – or to reallocate limited resources to more pressing domestic needs, such as welfare. The London Conference therefore took place in a renewed atmosphere of co-operation.

The agreement that resulted from the London Conference (the Treaty for the Limitation and Reduction of Naval Armament), added more restrictions on submarines and smaller warships than the Washington Agreement. It altered the naval ratio between the US, Britain and Japan, but the Japanese benefited most as they were allowed to increase their numbers of submarines to match those of Britain and the USA. At Washington, nations had agreed not to fortify military bases within a certain distance of Japan, which made it difficult to ensure that Japan was fulfilling its obligations. The USA, Britain and France hoped that allowing Japan equal numbers of submarines would relieve the wider Japanese concerns about the fairness of the Washington Agreements.

However, the treaty did have its limitations. Most significantly, it did not reduce the likelihood of war. Nations were granted the right to extend their naval building programmes in the event of an attack by any country that had not signed the agreement. The treaty also did little to restrain Japan outside the territorial zones of influence that had been agreed at Washington. This would have required a co-ordinated Anglo–American action, and the declining relationship between these two countries made such action unlikely. This was seen in practice in 1931, when Japan invaded Manchuria without incurring any joint British–US response.

The Geneva Disarmament Conference 1932–34

Preparations for a general Disarmament Conference began in Geneva in 1926. The following year, the USSR joined the Preparatory Disarmament Commission's discussions. The Soviet foreign minister, Maxim Litvinov, proposed immediate and full disarmament. However, his suggestion was rejected as other nations feared that without defence, communism would spread. Few countries in Europe felt safe from either Germany or the USSR, and were reluctant to begin the disarmament process.

In the end, it took more than five years for the Preparatory Commission to complete an initial agreement that would form the basis of discussion by representatives at the conference that began in 1932. This long delay was an indication that any substantial progress was likely to be difficult – and would require goodwill and compromise from all parties.

The Geneva Conference aimed to take the disarmament process further than both the Washington Agreement and the 1930 Treaty for the Limitation and Reduction of Naval Armament, which had mostly considered naval matters. At Geneva, all aspects of weaponry came under discussion. The economic slump caused by the Great Depression meant that many nations were eager to see their defence spending cut so that their limited resources could be used for domestic projects to relieve social distress. However, the economic decline had also already caused some countries to attempt to solve their difficulties through acts of aggression, notably the Japanese invasion of Manchuria in 1931. It was thus unrealistic to expect states to disarm to the lowest point compatible with internal security.

Theory of knowledge

History and ethics

The British philosopher Bertrand Russell (1872–1970) said: 'I find myself incapable of believing that all that is wrong with wanton cruelty is that I don't like it.' The issue of disarmament raises questions about the morality of large-scale weapons. We have seen the dilemmas this presents in recent events in both Iraq and Iran. When attempting to write the history of a period, should historians simply offer explanations for developments – or should they also make value or moral judgements?

The Geneva Conference was attended by 61 nations, including both the USSR and the USA. The nature of the discussions quickly revealed how difficult it was to decide anything meaningful. The first problem was agreeing on the meaning of the word 'disarmament', as this defined what should be included in the process. Did it only include 'offensive' weapons or should it encompass 'defensive' weapons, too – and what constituted 'offensive' and 'defensive' weapons? The British wanted to broaden the disarmament process to include offensive weapons such as tanks, bombers, submarines, and poison gas and chemicals. Germany and the USSR refused to accept this resolution. Such negotiations only created friction between the nations.

Theoretical discussions on the classification of weapons were difficult, but talks on more practical issues were just as problematic. There were three main issues that surfaced during the conference. The first was about how to carry out any agreement reached. A mechanism needed to be in place to ensure that the terms were being implemented. This raised the equally difficult question of who would verify that the agreements were being honoured and what would happen to nations that did not comply. An international body could be formed to carry out checks, but some nations claimed this would be a challenge to their national sovereignty (the power of a state over its own affairs). Finally, there was concern about what would happen to a nation that had disarmed and was then attacked: who would help it?

These questions received a range of different responses, meaning that agreement was virtually impossible. All countries were aware of how difficult it was to enforce disarmament – a lesson learned from Germany's attempt to avoid the military restrictions in the Treaty of Versailles by allying with Russia. This, along with France's ever-present concern about German attack, was the greatest challenge delegates faced at Geneva. Germany was now a member of the League of Nations, yet it was not allowed the same weaponry as other League members. Germany thus argued that either other nations should disarm to Germany's level, or Germany should be allowed to rearm to the level of other nations. This demand particularly worried the French.

The French made a series of suggestions to resolve these issues. The first not only involved the creation of a League army, but also required each nation to allow its major offensive weapons to come under League control. Both these proposals were rejected, the latter because it was a direct threat to national sovereignty. France's second proposal, the Constructive Plan (November 1932), was in response to German demands for equality; this would have created a League force but also allowed national defensive militias, with the German militia as large as other nations'.

In January 1933, Hitler came to power in Germany – a fact that changed the situation and made any resolution harder to reach. The new German government stated that if equality could not be achieved through negotiation, then Germany would break the conditions of the Treaty of Versailles and build up its own arms. There was some sympathy for this view, particularly in Britain, but the French were horrified.

Historical debate

In explaining the failure of the Geneva Conference, historians such as Hans Mommsen have emphasised Germany's role, suggesting that it was never serious about disarming. Others, such as Graham Darby, have focused on the divisions between Britain and France as the main reason for failure. Certainly, Britain was much more sympathetic to the German position than France was. Britain's attitude is demonstrated by the Anglo–German Naval Agreement of 1935, which allowed the German navy to expand to 35% the size of the British. This agreement was made outside the League and without consultation with other nations, including France and Italy: a clear sign that self-interest came before the ideals of the League.

Britain proposed that France, Germany, Italy and Poland should be allowed armies of the same level (200,000 men), but this was rejected. The French then suggested a modified proposal. This involved an eight-year period, in the second half of which continental armies would conform to the figures put forward by Britain. Britain, France, Italy and the USA approved.

The Germans were trapped. Hitler could no longer claim that Germany was not being treated equally, but the agreement also limited the size of any German force and would prevent the provocative action Hitler had in mind to overturn the terms of the Treaty of Versailles. With no way of resolving the issue to his satisfaction, Hitler withdrew from the conference in October 1933 and soon afterwards renounced Germany's membership of the League. The conference continued for another year, but little was achieved. In the meantime, Germany began to rearm.

Questions

What reasons does Hitler give for withdrawing Germany from the Disarmament Conference? How useful is this speech as evidence for the failure of disarmament?

SOURCE C

For years Germany has been waiting in vain for the fulfilment of the promise of disarmament made to her by the others. It is the sincere desire of the national Government to be able to refrain from increasing our army and our weapons, insofar as the rest of the world is now also ready to fulfil its obligations in the matter of radical disarmament. For Germany desires nothing except an equal right to live and equal freedom.

We are unfortunately faced by the fact that the Geneva Conference, in spite of lengthy negotiations, has so far reached no practical result. The decision regarding securing a real measure of disarmament has been constantly delayed by the raising of questions of technical detail and by the introduction of problems that have nothing to do with disarmament. This procedure is useless. The illegal state of one-sided disarmament and the resulting insecurity of Germany cannot continue any longer. For fourteen years we have been disarmed, and for fourteen months we have been waiting for the results of the Disarmament Conference.

Extract from a speech by Adolf Hitler to the German Reichstag, March 1933.

VALENTINES FOR ALL.

A cartoon from the British magazine Punch, *February 1934, showing British foreign affairs minister Anthony Eden distributing Valentines at the Disarmament Conference*

Questions

What do you think is the message of this cartoon? Using the information in this section, how accurate is the view expressed in the cartoon?

SOURCE D

Question

How useful is the speech in Source D in explaining the reasons for the failure of disarmament talks?

I am very glad that the Disarmament Conference is passing out of life into history. It is the greatest mistake to mix up disarmament with peace. When you have peace you will have disarmament. But there has been during these recent years a steady deterioration in the relations between different countries, a steady growth of ill-will, and a steady, indeed a rapid increase in armaments that has gone on through all these years in spite of the endless flow of oratory, of perorations, of well-meaning sentiments, of banquets, which have marked this epoch. Europe will be secure when the nations no longer feel themselves in great danger, as many of them do now.

Extract from a speech made by Winston Churchill in July 1934, published in his book The Gathering Storm *in 1948.*

Activities

1 Divide into three groups, one each for Germany, France and Britain. Hold a debate in which each country defends its actions over disarmament in the 1930s. Which group provides the best defence of its actions?

2 Imagine you are a German journalist for a right-wing paper at the time of the failure of the Disarmament Conference. Write the front page for your paper, explaining the reasons for the failure of the conference.

3 How and why might what the journalist has written differ from Hitler's private reasons for the failure of the conference?

End of chapter activities

Summary

You should now have a clear understanding of the effect the Great Depression had on a range of countries. Some areas within countries, such as the south-east of England, escaped the worst ravages of the crisis, but for most it was a time of poverty and hardship. You should be aware not only that the Depression had an economic impact, but also that economic problems caused political upheaval and undermined the progress that had been made towards international co-operation. This chapter has shown that the improvement in relations with Germany was undermined by the rise to power of the Nazis, who were more concerned about overthrowing the Treaty of Versailles and restoring German pride than co-operating in disarmament talks.

Meanwhile, the economic problems in Japan further encouraged aggressive nationalism. You should realise that these issues were made worse by the Japanese desire to overturn what they saw as the unfairness of the Treaty of Versailles, and to solve their economic problems by the domination of the Pacific region. You should understand that the problems that eventually led to the complete breakdown of international order by the end of the decade were already present in the early years of the 1930s.

Summary activity

1 Draw a spider diagram to summarise the reasons for the failure of the Disarmament Conference. Then try to develop each of the points with supporting evidence.

2 Consider who was to blame for the failure of the Disarmament Conference. Copy and complete the following table to help you do this.

Country	Evidence it was to blame	Evidence it was not to blame	Judgement
Germany			
Britain			
France			
League of Nations			

3 Using the chart to help you, write a paragraph to summarise what you consider to be the most important reason for the failure of the Disarmament Conference.

Paper 1 exam practice

Question

With reference to their origin and purpose, assess the value and limitations of Sources A and B below for historians studying the Geneva Disarmament Conference between 1932 and 1934.
[6 marks]

Skill

Assessing the value and limitations (reliability/utility) of two sources

SOURCE A

For years Germany has been waiting in vain for the fulfilment of the promise of disarmament made to her by the others. It is the sincere desire of the national Government to be able to refrain from increasing our army and our weapons, insofar as the rest of the world is now also ready to fulfil its obligations in the matter of radical disarmament. For Germany desires nothing except an equal right to live and equal freedom. We are unfortunately faced by the fact that the Geneva Conference, in spite of lengthy negotiations, has so far reached no practical result. The decision regarding securing a real measure of disarmament has been constantly delayed by the raising of questions of technical detail and by the introduction of problems that have nothing to do with disarmament. This procedure is useless. The illegal state of one-sided disarmament and the resulting insecurity of Germany cannot continue any longer. For fourteen years we have been disarmed, and for fourteen months we have been waiting for the results of the Disarmament Conference.

Extract from a speech by Adolf Hitler to the German Reichstag, March 1933.

SOURCE B

I am very glad that the Disarmament Conference is passing out of life into history. It is the greatest mistake to mix up disarmament with peace. When you have peace you will have disarmament. But there has been during these recent years a steady deterioration in the relations between different countries, a steady growth of ill-will, and a steady, indeed a rapid increase in armaments that has gone on through all these years in spite of the endless flow of oratory, of perorations, of well-meaning sentiments, of banquets, which have marked this epoch. Europe will be secure when the nations no longer feel themselves in great danger, as many of them do now.

Extract from a speech made by Winston Churchill in July 1934. Published in his book The Gathering Storm in 1948.

Before you start

Value and limitations (utility/reliability) questions require you to assess **two** sources over a range of possible issues – and to comment on their value to historians studying a particular event or period of history. You need to consider both the **origin and purpose** and also the **value and limitations** of the sources. You should link these in your answer, showing how origin/purpose relate to value/limitations.

Before you attempt this question, refer to pages 213–14 for advice on how to tackle these questions and a simplified markscheme.

Student answer

Source A is a speech by the German leader to the German parliament, or Reichstag, in March 1933 – only two months after he had become chancellor, and at a time when he was threatening to withdraw Germany from the conference. Hitler had already started to rearm Germany secretly, in contravention of Versailles, and the purpose of the speech is to justify the reasons for withdrawing from the talks. Hitler did not want it to appear as if German withdrawal was due to rearmament, but rather the Allies' unwillingness to treat Germany as an equal. Hitler wanted to appear reasonable to both the German people and world opinion. The source is useful, as it is a clear example of how Hitler prepared the people for the withdrawal from the conference in October 1933. It is therefore helpful to the historian as a typical example of the propaganda used by the regime to appear reasonable. However, it does not consider the fact that Hitler had already started rearming. Nor does it represent the reality of events, as it ignores proposals made by both the French and British for German equality. It therefore needs to be treated with caution as a record of what actually happened.

Source B is from a speech by Churchill in 1934, soon after the failure of the conference, but published in a book produced after the Second World War. It explains Churchill's view that talks about disarmament were futile until nations felt secure. Churchill was a critic of the government in 1934 and wanted a firmer line about rearmament. The source is useful, as it gives a clear indication of Churchill's views and his attacks on the policies of the government. It also shows how he tried to win political support for a stronger line to be taken on rearmament. However, its publication in 1948 should also make us aware of its limitations. Churchill wanted to show, after the war, that his views had been right and would thus have been selective about what he used in his books. He wanted to show that the politicians of the 1930s were misguided in their policies, and so selects extracts from his own speeches that support his interpretation. Churchill was very critical of the politicians who dominated the early 1930s for their weak stance towards Hitler, and he believed that German aggression could have been stopped. Churchill here has the benefit of hindsight; he is trying to justify his position and this limits its usefulness.

Examiner comments

The response from the student is very full and all aspects of the question have been considered. The answer gives equal weight to the two sources and examines the origin and purpose of both, in order to see both the value and limitations. The student could have made greater use of the actual content of the sources to support the argument, particularly from Source A, where Hitler mentions 'nothing except an equal right to live and equal freedom' or 'It is the sincere desire of the national Government to be able to refrain from increasing our army', as neither of these points are true and they would illustrate clearly Hitler's purpose in making the speech. This is where carefully chosen examples from the source can help to reinforce a point. However, the candidate has referred to both origin/purpose and value/limitations, and would therefore be awarded full marks.

Paper 2 practice questions

1 Assess the impact of the Great Depression on any two countries from different regions that you have studied.

2 Compare the political and social impact of the Great Depression.

3 Assess the role of the Great Depression as a cause of the failure of the League of Nations.

4 Assess the reasons for the failure of disarmament in the period to 1933.

5 Discuss the view that the USA that suffered most from the Great Depression.

6 Analyse the reasons for the aggressive policies of Germany, Italy and Japan in the 1930s.

9 From co-operation to aggression 1931–36

Timeline

1896 Italian forces defeated by Abyssinia

1905 Japan wins Russo–Japanese war and takes control of Korean Peninsula and lease over South Manchurian railway

1919 Treaty of Versailles signed

1924 Abyssinia admitted to League of Nations

1928 Italy signs Treaty of Friendship with Abyssinia

1929 Oct: Wall Street Crash

1931 Sep: Mukden Incident; Japanese invade Manchuria

Dec: Commission of Enquiry set up

1932 Lausanne Agreement to resolve debt repayments; Italy draws up plans to invade Abyssinia

Feb: Japanese conquer south Manchuria and land forces in Shanghai

1933 Japanese forces occupy Jehol

1934 Dec: Italian and Abyssinian forces clash at border oasis of Wal-Wal

1935 Apr: Stresa Front; Mussolini believes this gives him the go-ahead to attack Abyssinia

Sep: League reports that border dispute at Wal-Wal is the fault of neither nation

Oct: Italy launches invasion; League imposes sanctions

Dec: Britain and France draw up Hoare–Laval Pact, but plan is quickly withdrawn

1936 May: Italian forces capture Addis Ababa

Jul: League ends sanctions against Italy

Key questions

- What was the impact of Japan's invasion of Manchuria?
- How did Italy respond to the rise of Nazi Germany?
- What was the impact of Italy's invasion of Abyssinia?
- What challenges to the Treaty of Versailles arose in 1936?

Overview

- The League of Nations faced two major challenges in the 1930s: Manchuria and Abyssinia.
- Japan experienced serious domestic problems and responded with aggressive tactics, including the invasion of Manchuria, which was prompted by an attack on the rail line at Mukden.
- The League had difficulty responding, as Japan's actions represented aggression by one League member against another.
- The self-interests of Britain and France further hindered the League's response to the crisis, but there were internal weaknesses that also prevented a successful resolution. The League's failure to respond quickly had a serious impact on international relations.
- At the start of the 1930s, Italy, France and Britain enjoyed cordial relations. These three countries acted to prevent the German seizure of Austria in 1934.
- However, Italy faced severe domestic problems, and responded to these by invading Abyssinia; again, this was an aggressive action by one League member against another.
- Once again, British and French self-interest, combined with other weaknesses within the League, damaged its capacity to resolve the crisis successfully. The major problem was Britain's and France's need to maintain Italy as an ally against Nazi Germany.
- In this case, the League responded quickly, but it failed to impose economic sanctions effectively. The impact of the League's failure was dramatic, and no future conflict involving European powers would be solved by the League. The outcome drove Italy into friendship with Germany and encouraged German aggression.
- The international situation declined further as Germany remilitarised the Rhineland, and Italy and Germany both aided nationalist forces in the Spanish Civil War. As a consequence, the Rome–Berlin Axis developed, forming the sides that would fight the Second World War.

What was the impact of Japan's invasion of Manchuria?

The Great Depression had a serious impact on the Japanese economy, and created the need to find raw materials and new markets. With Japan already in control of Korea, and wielding wide influence in Manchuria through its control of the South Manchurian railway, it is not surprising that expansion occurred in that area.

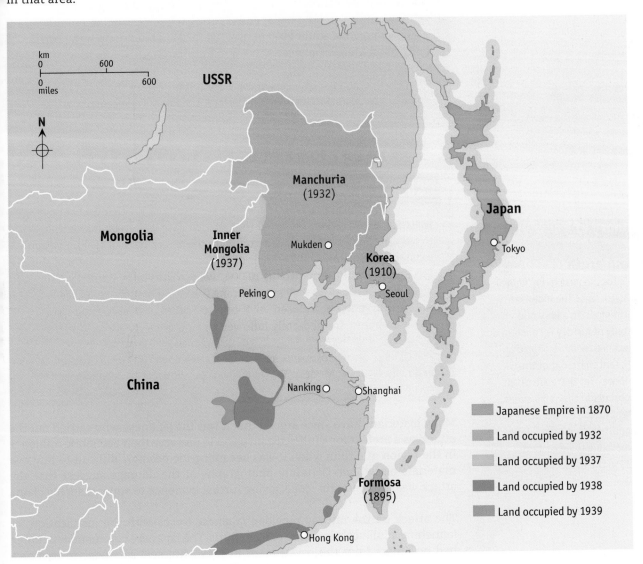

The Japanese Empire up to 1939, showing the dates when various territories in Asia were conquered

The Japanese invasion of Manchuria 1931

The trigger for the invasion of Manchuria was the Mukden Incident, which occurred on 18 September 1931. That night there was an explosion on the South Manchurian railway, which damaged the track just outside Mukden. The Japanese claimed that the explosion was the result of Chinese sabotage, and that Chinese soldiers then opened fire on the Japanese railway guards. The Chinese claimed that their soldiers were in their barracks and therefore could not have carried out the attacks.

SOURCE A

On arrival at the site of the explosion, the patrol was fired upon from the fields on the east side of the line. Lieutenant Kawamoto immediately ordered his men to deploy and to return the fire. The attacking body, estimated at five or six, then stopped firing and retreated northwards. The Japanese patrol at once started in pursuit and, having gone about 2000 metres, were again fired upon by a larger body, estimated at between three and four hundred.

The Japanese account of events given to the Lytton enquiry. Quoted in Lacey, G. and Kelly, N. 2001. Modern World History. London, UK. Heinemann. p. 77.

SOURCE B

Instructions had been received that special care was to be taken to avoid any clash with Japanese troops in the tense state of feeling which existed at the time. On the night of 18 September all the soldiers of the 7th Brigade, numbering about 10,000, were in the North Barracks. The west gate in the mud wall surrounding the camp, which gave access to the railway, had been closed. At 10pm the sound of a large explosion could be heard, immediately followed by rifle fire.

The Chinese version of events given to the Lytton enquiry. Quoted in Lacey, G. and Kelly, N. 2001. Modern World History. London, UK. Heinemann. p. 77.

Activity

Compare and contrast the views of Sources A and B about the explosion on the railway line at Mukden.

 Theory of knowledge

History and 'truth'

Is it possible for the past to be 'known' exactly by historians? The historian G. R. Elton claimed: 'In a very real sense the study of history is concerned with a subject matter more objective and independent than that of the natural sciences.' Yet there are often different accounts of the same event. To what extent do the events at Mukden support the opposing claim that it is impossible to be certain about events in the past?

Discussion point

Why do you think civilians were treated so brutally by the Japanese? What did Japan hope to achieve by this policy?

Many historians have since argued that it was the Japanese who carried out the attack, as a pretext for a full-scale invasion to preserve their economic influence in the region at a time when it was becoming increasingly difficult to buy raw materials elsewhere. Certainly photographs of the damage suggest that the attack was limited in its scope, giving further evidence to support such a claim.

The attack on the railway provided Japanese forces with the justification for launching a full-scale invasion of Manchuria. The Japanese commander in Korea had no orders from the government in Tokyo, but sent in troops to reinforce those already present to protect the railway line. He ordered them to destroy all remaining Chinese authority in the area.

The invasion was relatively straightforward for Japanese forces, and the outcome was never in doubt. In late September, the Japanese occupied the important towns of Mukden, Changchun and Kirin. Although the Japanese government initially expressed disapproval of the attack – having urged restraint in the area – military success aroused a sense of nationalism in the country and the government therefore had to accept it. The Japanese argued that these actions were vital to maintain their economic interests in the region, which the Chinese government had proven unable to protect. However, the attacks were brutal – large numbers of Chinese civilians lost their lives in indiscriminate killings, as Japan asserted its control. These stories never reached Japan, where returning soldiers were welcomed as heroes.

Japanese soldiers in Manchuria, 1932

By February 1932, the Japanese had conquered south Manchuria and landed 70,000 troops at Shanghai. This forced the Chinese to retreat and end their boycott of Japanese goods. The area was renamed Manchuko and the Japanese installed **Henry Pu-Yi**, the former Chinese emperor, as ruler. In reality, Pu-Yi was no more than a puppet for Japanese officials.

SOURCE C

Japan's great military adventure has, it seems, met with a full measure of success. She has seized, and to all intents and purposes secured, a protectorate over Manchuria, rounded off her conquests by the occupation of Jehol, defied the behests of the League of Nations, and … forced the Chinese to admit military defeat and to accept, at least tacitly and for the time being, the loss of Manchuria and the de facto position created by the Japanese army.

Sir Miles Lampson, British minister in China, writing in June 1933.

Manchuria and the League of Nations

China immediately appealed to the League of Nations for help. This was exactly the type of conflict for which the organisation had been established, and it should have been easy to resolve – one member of the League had attacked another and used superior military force to impose its will. There was little doubt that the Japanese were the aggressors and should be ordered to withdraw. However, the Japanese had spread confusion about the nature of the invasion, and claimed they were simply defending themselves. More importantly, Japan was a permanent member of the Council, and had the power to block any measures the League proposed to take.

<h3>Activity</h3>

Construct a spider diagram to show the reasons for the Japanese invasion of Manchuria. You will need to look back to the previous chapter for the long-term causes. Develop each point with a couple of facts to support the reason. Now try to rank the reasons in order of importance. Give reasons for your choices. Do any of the factors link together? Draw in the links on your spider diagram and explain the connections.

Henry Pu-Yi (1906–67)

Born into the Manchu clan and Qing dynasty, Pu-Yi became the last emperor of China, abdicating on 12 February 1912. In 1934, he was declared emperor of Manchuko by the Japanese. He served as a puppet ruler, controlled by Japan, throughout the Sino–Japanese War. He was captured by the Soviet army while fleeing to Japan, and was eventually returned to China but placed in a War Criminals Management Centre to be reformed. Pu-Yi was later released, after which he voiced his support for the communist regime. He worked in Beijing Botanical Gardens and finally in the literary department of the Chinese People's Political Consultative Conference until his death.

Questions

What is Lampson's view of the Japanese attack on Manchuria in Source C? How useful do you think this account is?

183

Gold Standard A monetary system by which the value of currency has a fixed value in gold. In 1931, the British government abandoned the 'standard' – turning away from a traditional policy believed to provide economic stability and security. However, this did allow the price of exports to fall.

At the same time, the dispute presented problems for Britain and France. Both countries were suffering from the impact of the Depression, and were more concerned with domestic problems than the crisis in Manchuria. Britain had recently been forced to abandon the **Gold Standard** and had faced a naval mutiny at Invergordon. Imposing economic sanctions against Japan would present further difficulties, as both Britain and France had trading interests in the Far East and did not want to antagonise the Japanese. Moreover, for sanctions to be effective they would need US support – and the US was also unwilling to take such steps at this time.

The League did, of course, have the option of threatening military force if the Japanese did not withdraw from Manchuria. This would need naval power from Britain, whose naval base in Singapore was still under construction. There were also fears of a Japanese attack on the British Empire in the Far East. The nearest naval power in the Pacific was the USA, which was not a member of the League.

SOURCE D

Although Japan has undoubtedly acted in a way contrary to the principles of the Covenant by taking the law in to their own hands, she has a real grievance against China. This is not a case in which the armed forces of one country have crossed the frontiers of another in circumstances in which they had no previous right to be on the other's soil. Japan owns the South Manchurian railway and has been entitled to have a body of Japanese guards upon the strip of land through which the railway runs. Japan's case is that she was compelled by the failure of China to provide reasonable protection for Japanese lives and property in Manchuria in the face of attacks of Chinese bandits, and of an attack upon the line itself, to move Japanese troops forward and to occupy points in Manchuria which are beyond the line of the railway.

Extract from a memorandum by British foreign secretary Sir John Simon to the British cabinet, 23 November 1931.

Some members of the League were sympathetic towards Japan's desire to restore order in Manchuria. Britain in particular – with economic interests in the region – had expressed concern over unrest there, as well as about the rise of Chinese nationalism. However, Manchuria was a long way from Europe, and neither Britain nor France was in a position to take effective action. The League was thus slow to respond, giving Japan the chance to secure its position.

The Lytton enquiry

The Japanese suggested that a Commission of Enquiry should be established to investigate the issue, and this was formed on 8 December 1931. The Commission was led by Lord Lytton who – along with representatives from France, Germany, Italy and the USA – went to Manchuria to gather information.

At the same time, the US secretary of state, Henry Stimson, informed signatories of the Washington Agreement (see page 123) that America would not recognise any territorial changes made by force because they went against the Kellogg–Briand Pact, which both the USA and Japan had signed (see page 127).

184

The Japanese government may have co-operated with the League, but the army did not. While Lytton and his group prepared their report, the Japanese advance continued. The army argued that this was necessary in order to protect both Japanese property and people in Manchuria.

The Commission spent several months gathering information, in order to produce a balanced report. This was eventually published in October 1932. It concluded that although Japan had special rights in the area, military action had not been taken in self-defence. The Commission blamed China for the deterioration in relations between the two countries, and acknowledged that internal Chinese instability affected Japanese economic concerns. However, the report firmly rejected the use of force to resolve the issue. It recommended that Japan withdraw its troops and recognise Chinese sovereignty over the region. The Commission also refused to recognise Manchuko as an independent state, and rejected Japanese claims that it was the result of a growing independence movement within the region. The final recommendations were that Manchuria should adopt self-government, under Chinese sovereignty, and that China and Japan should open negotiations to resolve their difficulties.

SOURCE E

An explosion undoubtedly occurred on or near the railroad between 10 and 10 30 pm, but the damage was not sufficient to justify military action. The military operations of the Japanese during this night cannot be regarded as legitimate self-defence … Without a declaration of war a large area of what was indisputably Chinese territory has been forcibly seized and occupied by the armed forces of Japan and has in consequence of this operation been separated from and declared independent of the rest of China.

Extract from Lord Lytton's report, published October 1932.

The report was approved by all members of the League – except Japan. Japan claimed that other countries in the League had used force against China in the past and had not been punished. This confirmed Japanese suspicions that they were being discriminated against. The leader of the Japanese delegation to the League, Matsuoka, commented: 'Read your History. We recovered Manchuria from Russia. We made it what it is today.' The Japanese refused to compromise, and withdrew from the League.

This was a major test for the League of Nations. How would it respond when a member rejected its decision, particularly when that member was a major power? The League refused to approve Japan's occupation, but it took no further action, and sanctions were not imposed.

SOURCE F

I think I am myself enough of a pacifist to take the view that however we handle the matter, I do not intend my own country to get into trouble about it. There is one great difference between 1914 and now and it is this: in no circumstances will this government authorise this country to be party to this struggle.

British foreign minister Sir John Simon, to the House of Commons, February 1933. Quoted in Boscoe, D. L. 2009. Five to Rule Them All: The UN Security Council and the Making of the Modern World. New York, USA. Oxford University Press. p. 11.

185

Activity

What is the message of this cartoon? What evidence is there in the cartoon to support your view? Look again at Sources E and F on page 185. Which does the cartoon most agree with in its view of the League? Explain your answer fully.

A British cartoon from 1933 showing a traditional interpretation of the League of Nations' management of the Manchuria crisis

The impact of the League's failure to act

During the 1930s, Japan sent increasing numbers of troops into Manchuria. The invasion may have encouraged further Japanese aggression on mainland China, as Japan was now in a favourable strategic position to widen its conquests (see map on page 181). Japanese and Chinese forces clashed in Shanghai in early 1932, and by 1933 Japanese forces occupied Jehol. A period of strained peace followed, but this was broken by a full-scale invasion in 1937. By the following year, Japan controlled many important Chinese cities. No action was taken against Japan until the outbreak of the Second World War – but by that time the League had ceased to exist in practice.

The invasion of Manchuria challenged the balance of power in the Pacific. Japan had broken the restraints imposed at Washington and preserved its access to valuable raw materials. According to Churchill, the consequences of the failure of the League to act went even further.

SOURCE G

In February, 1933, the League of Nations declared that the State of Manchuko could not be recognised. Although no sanctions were imposed upon Japan, nor any other action taken, Japan, on March 27, 1933, withdrew from the League of Nations. Germany and Japan had been on opposite sides in the war; they now looked towards each other in a different mood. The moral authority of the League was shown to be devoid of any physical support at a time when its activity and strength were most needed.

Churchill, W. 1948. The Gathering Storm. London, UK. Cassell and Co. p. 80.

Questions

What is Churchill's view about the consequences of the failure of the League over Manchuria? Why might Churchill have this view (look carefully at the date he was writing)?

The League's failure over Manchuria may also have encouraged other nations to solve their economic problems through acts of aggression. Some historians regard the Manchurian incident as the first link in a chain of events that led to the Second World War.

SOURCE H

The aggressor had defiantly retained his prize, and had departed from Geneva with little more than verbal censure as the price of his deed. In the smaller League states, even in France and Germany as well as Britain and the United States, there was disillusionment and dismay. Whatever the historian may observe at a distance, there is no doubt that in many minds at the time the episode did appear as a turning point; it also provided fresh evidence that the Covenant of the League was a seriously flawed document.

Thorne, C. 1972. The Limits of Foreign Policy: The West, the League and the Far Eastern Crisis of 1931–3. London, UK. Hamish Hamilton.

Activity

Compare and contrast Taylor's view in Source I about the impact of the Manchurian crisis on the League with that of Thorne in Source H.

Reasons for the League's failure

Although the invasion weakened the League and undermined the concept of collective security, not all historians agree that the Versailles system in Europe was doomed.

The League has been much criticised for its failure to act over the Manchurian crisis, but it must be remembered that taking action was problematic. The very nature of the League meant that the Mukden Incident had to be fully investigated and blame apportioned before any action could be taken, and this gave Japan time to firmly establish control.

SOURCE I

In 1933 peace was restored between China and Japan. In later years the Manchurian affair assumed a mythical importance. It was treated as a milestone on the road to war, the first decisive 'betrayal' of the League, especially by the British government. In reality, the League, under British leadership had done what the British thought it was designed to do: it had limited a conflict and brought it, however unsatisfactorily, to an end. Moreover, the Manchurian affair, far from weakening the coercive powers of the League, actually brought them into existence. It was thanks to this affair that the League – again on British prompting – set up machinery, hitherto lacking, to organise economic sanctions. This machinery, to everyone's misfortune, made possible the League action over Abyssinia in 1935.

Taylor, A. J. P. 1966. The Origins of the Second World War. New York, USA. Fawcett World Library. pp. 65–66.

The British and French governments knew they would struggle to justify to their electorate the decision to send troops to deal with an event so far away. No one considered events in Manchuria to be a threat to European collective security. The distance from Europe also meant that the invasion was not as damaging for the League's authority as a European conflict would have been. The two powers that were in the best position to take decisive action in the region – the USA and USSR – were not members of the League.

Discussion point

What can we learn from the conflict in Manchuria?

187

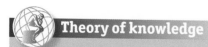

History, the present and the future

'Those who don't study the past are condemned to repeat it.' These words, by the philosopher George Santayana (1863–1952), suggest that it is possible – and even desirable – to decide our actions on what has happened in the past. What does a study of the failings of the League of Nations in Manchuria reveal about human nature? Do you think that the failure of the League of Nations to take action in places such as Manchuria has had an impact on the actions taken by the United Nations in the recent past? Can the past be used to justify present action?

Activities

1 Consider the following statements.

- The Japanese success in Manchuria changed the balance of power in the Pacific region.
- The Manchurian invasion was the first link in a chain of events that led to the Second World War.
- The Manchurian crisis did *not* signal the end of the League of Nations as an effective peacekeeping force.
- The Manchurian crisis proved that the self-interests of the 'great powers' were more important than collective security.

Which of the statements do you agree with? Why?

2 Write a press release on behalf of the League of Nations, explaining and defending its decisions over Manchuria. You should explain why the League's actions will not damage the future of the League as a peacekeeping body.

3 Copy and complete the following chart on the reasons for the League's failure to solve the Manchurian crisis. In what ways was each of the factors to blame for the failure to solve the crisis?

Factor	Role played in the failure
Structure of the League of Nations	
Japan	
China	
Britain	
France	
Impact of the Depression	

Now rank each of the factors according to how far they were responsible. Write a paragraph explaining which factor is most to blame and justifying your decision.

4 In the 1920s, the League of Nations had been successful in solving several border disputes. In 1931, it was unable to resolve the Manchurian crisis. Why do you think this was?

5 How brutal was the Japanese invasion of Manchuria? Research this incident, then build on this by looking at Japanese actions in other parts of China, for example the Rape of Nanking. From your research, collect a series of images of the impact of the Japanese invasion on Chinese civilians.

How did Italy respond to the rise of Nazi Germany?

While the Japanese were engaged in aggressive territorial expansion in Manchuria, tensions were building in Europe. Initially, Italy was very concerned by the rise of Nazi Germany, particularly its desire to unite all German-speaking peoples. This would mean overturning the clause in the Treaty of Versailles that forbade the union, or *Anschluss*, of Germany and Austria; the consequence of this would be a strong nation on Italy's borders. Mussolini was also concerned about whether his own expansionist programme in the Balkans would bring him into conflict with Germany. However, at first he tried to act as a mediator between Germany and Britain and France. Mussolini proposed a Four Power Pact in June 1933. By this, he hoped to promote Italy to a major role in European diplomacy – at the same time as allowing revisions to be made to the parts of the peace treaties that he did not like. Events soon changed Mussolini's position.

German attempts to seize Austria 1934

The reason for Mussolini's change of atttitude was the increased German threat to Austria. In August 1933, Mussolini met the Austrian chancellor, Engelbert Dollfuss, in order to discuss Italian military support in the event of a German attack. Mussolini took this further in March 1934, negotiating the Rome Protocols with Austria and Hungary. By the terms of the Protocols, the three countries agreed to consult one another over issues that concerned them all.

Hitler responded to these developments by visiting Mussolini in June 1934, in an attempt to improve relations. The success of this visit was soon put to the test. In July 1934, following the murder of Dollfuss during an attempted coup by Austrian Nazis, Hitler tried to take advantage of the unrest to bring about *Anschluss*. Mussolini acted decisively and Italian troops were sent to the Austrian border to indicate his opposition to a Nazi takeover. Hitler's attempt failed. Although it appeared that the Austrian Nazis had acted on their own initiative, Mussolini was well aware that Hitler was an Austrian by birth and wanted to incorporate his native country into the German Reich. Moreover, as Hitler now concentrated on rearmament, Mussolini was pushed into closer co-operation with Britain and France.

The Stresa Front

Initial talks between Italy and France resulted in the Rome Agreements in January 1935, in which the two countries reached an understanding on European security and Italian colonial issues. On 11–14 April 1935, the British prime minister Ramsay MacDonald and his foreign secretary, Sir John Simon, met with the French foreign minister Pierre Laval and Mussolini at Stresa, to discuss the questions of German rearmament and Austria. This meeting resulted in a strong condemnation of German actions, upheld the Locarno Pact agreements (see page 148), and confirmed Austrian independence.

The three countries then formed the Stresa Front, by which they agreed to oppose 'by all means, any unilateral repudiation of treaties, which may endanger the peace of Europe'. Mussolini thus appeared to have committed himself to supporting Britain and France. However, events later in the year demonstrated that he expected something in return for his support against Hitler. In particular, Mussolini believed that these talks and agreements – as well as his actions in preventing Hitler's annexation of Austria – would result in British and French approval of his planned invasion of Abyssinia.

What was the impact of Italy's invasion of Abyssinia?

The Italian state was relatively new, having been unified as recently as 1870. As a result, Italy had missed out on the 19th-century 'Scramble for Africa' (see page 89) and the development of an overseas empire.

Italian gains overseas had been quite modest, comprising Libya, Eritrea and Italian Somaliland. Italy considered this area of North and East Africa to be within its own sphere of influence, a claim that was recognised by both Britain and France in 1906. However, this process had still experienced setbacks. In 1896, Italian forces were defeated by the Ethiopians at the Battle of Adowa, and many Italians sought revenge not only for this humiliation, but also for their country's treatment at the peace conferences at the end of the First World War. This only added to Italy's desire to seize what was 'rightfully' its own, both on its borders in Europe, and also in Africa.

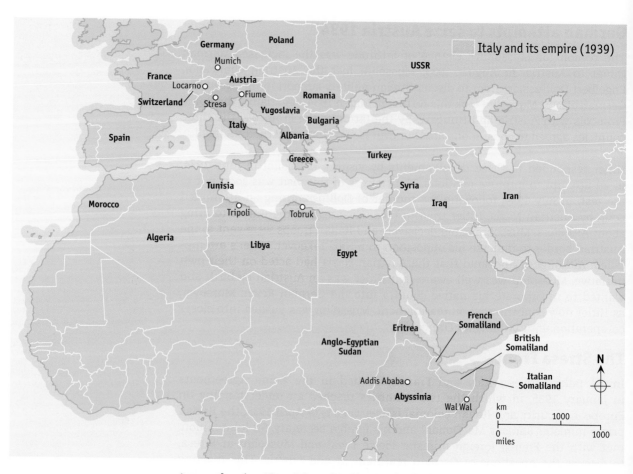

A map showing Abyssinia and Italian territories in Africa and Europe

Despite its imperial ambitions, Italy was relatively short of raw materials, crucially coal and iron. This limited economic progress, so the country was keen to acquire land that could provide the resources for further expansion. These issues had contributed to the rise of Mussolini's fascist government, with its nationalist ambitions.

Background to the invasion

The popular support for Gabriele D'Annunzio's seizure of Fiume in 1919 and its subsequent annexation in 1924 (see page 64) was not lost on Mussolini's government. Fascism encouraged 'war for war's sake' and the glory that accompanied military victory, and Mussolini was determined to seize any opportunity to develop Italy's overseas empire. He wanted to re-create the Roman Empire and turn the Mediterranean into an Italian lake, or *mare nostrum* ('our sea') to consolidate his own power.

However, the international situation had changed since the First World War. Woodrow Wilson's vision of a new moral order had made attempts at expansion more difficult. In addition, most of Africa had already been seized. Abyssinia was the only free African state that remained. It was an obvious place for Italian expansion because of its geographical location, between the Italian provinces of Eritrea and Somaliland. Although plans for an invasion had been discussed in 1925, since then Italy had built a closer relationship with Abyssinia, sponsoring its membership of the League of Nations in 1924 (against the wishes of both Britain and France, who believed that the country was not civilised).

In a further attempt to increase influence over Abyssinia, Italy had signed a Treaty of Friendship with the country in 1928. But progress was slow, and as the effects of the Depression took hold throughout Italy, Mussolini needed quicker results.

Reasons for invading in 1935

There is a great deal of disagreement among historians about why Italian policy towards Abyssinia became more aggressive and why an invasion was launched in 1935. Some possible factors are discussed below.

Aggrandisement and prestige

An annexation would allow Italy to unite the states of Eritrea, Somaliland and Abyssinia into an East African Empire. This would give Italy control over most of the Horn of Africa and provide Mussolini with the prestige he needed. It was particularly important for Mussolini to achieve success in his foreign policy, as the effects of the Depression within Italy were drawing attention to the evident failings of the corporate state (see page 165). Indeed, according to the historian Dennis Mack Smith, Mussolini's main concern was imperial expansion or aggrandisement, and he wanted to rival the Mediterranean influence of Britain and France. However, none of these factors fully explains the *timing* of Italy's invasion of Abyssinia.

The influence of key figures

Some people, including Mussoilini's biographer Renzo de Felice, have argued that the increasing aggressiveness of Mussolini's policy was due to the appointment of Dino Grandi as head of foreign affairs. A hardline fascist, Grandi urged a more active foreign policy. Other historians, such as Esmonde Robertson, have suggested that it was the death of Mussolini's younger brother Arnaldo in 1931 that allowed a more forceful approach, as Arnaldo had been a restraining influence on policy.

Plans for an invasion were drawn up in 1932, which might suggest that Mussolini's meeting with Pope Pius XI in February 1932 played a part in the Italian premier's decision. This meeting followed a rift between Mussolini and the papacy over the youth section of the Catholic Action group and the **Balilla**. At the meeting, the pope warned Mussolini of the growing influence of Protestants, Jews and communists. Some historians have therefore argued that Mussolini embarked on a policy of extending Italian and Catholic influence in order to restore relations with the papacy.

Fear of Germany

It can also be argued that changes in the international situation affected the timing of the invasion. Mussolini was concerned about Hitler's intentions. He feared a strong Germany on his borders and might have felt the need to act before Hitler became too powerful. This would explain Mussolini's policy in 1933 and 1934, and his pursuit of the Four Power Pact between Italy, Germany, France and Britain (see page 188), in which the four nations would co-operate to preserve peace for ten years. However, Hitler refused to sign the pact, and he also withdrew from the disarmament talks (see page 174).

Hitler's attempt to annex Austria in 1934 would certainly have worried Mussolini, hence his action to prevent the seizure. He may have felt that he needed to deal with the Abyssinia question before Hitler tried to take Austria again.

Question

Why do you think Mussolini had not invaded Abyssinia at an earlier date?

Fact

There was also an argument that Italy needed to expand to provide land to settle its surplus population, but this claim does not stand up to closer examination. By 1935, there were only 250 Italians settled in Somaliland and in 1937 just 1300 families in Libya.

Fact

Catholic Action was an international body of the Catholic Church. It had groups in many countries, including Italy. Each of these groups had various sub-sections – the most important of which were the youth sections. As Mussolini established his fascist dictatorship and abolished other potential opposition groups in Italy in the 1920s, Catholic Action was left as the only independent institution supporting Catholic interests. Its existence caused tension with the fascist government, which wanted full control over all aspects of life. Its membership of over 1 million made it difficult for Mussolini to suppress.

Balilla The fascist youth movement. This was established in 1926 and had various groups catering for different ages and sexes. The Balilla itself specifically covered boys aged 8–14 and was a valuable means of imposing fascist beliefs on children.

Mussolini's assessment of Britain's attitude

The Italian approach towards Abyssinia had already been made clear in a memorandum from the Italian chief of general staff in December 1934.

SOURCE J

The problem of Italian-Abyssinian relations has very recently shifted from a diplomatic plane to one which can be solved by force only … The object is nothing more or less than the complete destruction of the Abyssinian army and the total conquest of Abyssinia, in no other way can we build the Empire … The speedier our action the less likely the danger of diplomatic complications. In the Japanese fashion there will be no need whatever officially for a declaration of war and in any case we must always emphasise the purely defensive character of operations. No one in Europe would raise any difficulties provided the prosecution of operations resulted rapidly in an accomplished fact. It would suffice to declare to England and France that their interests would be recognised.

Memorandum from Marshal Badoglio, chief of general staff to Mussolini, December 1934. Quoted in Hite, J. and Hinton, C. 1998. Fascist Italy. London, UK. Hodder. p. 214.

Questions

Why does Badoglio believe that there will not be objections to an Italian invasion? How useful is Source J in explaining Italian actions against Abyssinia?

When a British Foreign Office assessment on Abyssinia was intercepted, which stated that Britain had no interests in the area, Mussolini calculated that Britain would not object to his planned invasion. Certainly, the British government did not feel able publicly to give Mussolini a free hand, as collective security was popular in Britain. Consequently, Britain avoided any mention of Abyssinia at the Stresa talks (see page 189). The French foreign minister, Pierre Laval, had already given Mussolini a verbal promise that Italy was free to take whatever action it felt necessary in Abyssinia, believing that by making concessions there Laval would win over Italy and prevent its rapprochement with Germany. It was not surprising, therefore, that Mussolini believed he was at liberty to act as he pleased.

Pretext for the invasion

An attack on Abyssinia was very appealing to Mussolini, as it was unlikely that a nation defended by tribesman with spears and outdated rifles would offer serious resistance to a modern army. This would ensure a quick and relatively cheap offensive, but would bring Mussolini the military glory he craved. It would also give Italian soldiers training and preparation for future conflict.

The pretext for the invasion was provided by a border incident at the disputed oasis of Wal-Wal in December 1934. The League responded by setting up a commission to investigate the case. Although Wal-Wal was 70 km (43 miles) inside Abyssinia, the League accepted that this was a disputed area and that no side was to blame. In the period after this clash, Mussolini built up his forces in both Eritrea and Somaliland in preparation for a full-scale attack. As tension mounted, Mussolini used the incident for propaganda gain.

SOURCE K

The Italian government have no intention of injuring in any way the prestige of the League of Nations or of lessening their own collaboration in the principle of collective security, since their action is directed against a State whose existence and activities have nothing to do with the principle of European collective security. To refuse to admit this standpoint of the Italian Government would be tantamount to a readiness to sacrifice deliberately the interests of a State such as Italy to the application of principles which in the case of Abyssinia cannot be applied. It would, moreover, be synonomous with granting impunity to the latter for her present action and making it possible for her to become an ever-growing danger in the future, merely for defending principles of which Abyssinia avails herself to her own exclusive advantage, but to which she is unable to make any contribution in the comity of the civilised nations of Europe.

Mussolini's communication to Sir Eric Drummond, Britain's ambassador to Italy, 31 July 1935. Quoted in Lowe, C. J. and Mazari, F. 1975. Italian Foreign Policy 1870–1940. *London, UK. Routledge and Kegan Paul. pp. 404–5.*

193

The League's response to the crisis

The probability of an attack presented the League of Nations with a difficult situation. Once again, the two nations involved were members of the League – and one of them was also a member of the Council. France had given Mussolini its support, but was afraid that the League might make a decision that would require direct French action in Africa. Britain wanted to avoid conflict, and hoped that the issue could be resolved by offering Italy territory elsewhere as compensation.

The British attitude was partly influenced by the general election that was due to take place in November 1935. Leaders knew that to win the election they had to tread carefully – the British public strongly supported the League. On 11 September, the British foreign secretary addressed the League of Nations to explain Britain's position on the matter of Abyssinia.

Question

Why do you think Hoare took such a strong line?

SOURCE L

I do not suppose that in the history of the Assembly there was ever a more difficult moment for a speech. When the world is stirred to excitement over the Abyssinian controversy, I will begin by re-affirming the support for the League by the government that I represent and the interest of the British people in collective security. On behalf of the government of the United Kingdom, I can say that they will be second to none in their intention to fulfil within the measure of their capacity, the obligations which the Covenant lays upon them. The League stands, and my country stands with it, for the collective maintenance of the Covenant, especially to all acts of unprovoked aggression.

Speech by Sir Samuel Hoare, British foreign secretary, to the League of Nations, 11 September 1935. Quoted in Bettey, J. H. 1967. English Historical Documents. *London, UK. Routledge and Kegan Paul.*

Two days later, the ruler of Abyssinia, Haile Selassie, made an impassioned plea to the democracies of the world.

SOURCE M

Five months before the pretext found in December in the Wal-Wal incident, Italy had begun the armament of her colonies, armament which since has been intensified and increased by the continuous sending of troops, mechanical equipment and ammunition during the entire duration of the work of the Council of the League of Nations and the work of the arbitration board.

Now that the pretext on which they planned to make war upon us has vanished, Italy, after having obtained from the powers their refusal to permit us to purchase armaments and ammunition which we do not manufacture and which are necessary to our defence, seeks to discredit the Ethiopian people and their government before world opinion.

They characterize us as a barbarous people whom it is necessary to civilize. The attitude of Italy will be judged by history.

We do not want war. Ethiopia puts her confidence in God. She wishes and hopes that an amicable and peaceful settlement, in accordance with right and justice, will intervene, and the officers of the Council of the League of Nations, in conformity with the pact, will compel all nations of the world, great and small, who hold peace as their ideal, to halt this crisis which threatens to stop all civilization.

Haile Selassie's appeal to the democracies, 13 September 1935. Quoted in Copeland, L. 1942. The World's Great Speeches. New York, USA. Garden City Publishers. pp. 450–51.

Questions

What is Haile Selassie's view of the League of Nations? What is his view of Italy?

Activity

Compare and contrast the hopes of Hoare and Selassie in Sources L (on page 193) and M about the functioning of the League in the Abyssinia crisis.

The invasion

Hoare's speech surprised Mussolini, but it did not prevent him from launching military action. On 3 October 1935, Italy invaded Abyssinia. The fascist leader claimed that it was Abyssinia's 'warlike, aggressive spirit that had imposed war upon Italy'. In contrast to the Manchurian affair, the League responded quickly. The Council met the very day the invasion began, and declared that Italy had broken Article 12 of the covenant, by which members agreed 'not to resort to war' within three months of a dispute being brought before the League. However, these words did nothing to deter Italy.

On 7 October the League declared Italy the aggressor, and there were signs that it would begin strong action to resolve the issue. This view seemed to be confirmed on 18 October, when the League voted to impose economic sanctions against Italy. A month later, 51 states agreed to ban the import of Italian goods and placed an embargo on arms sales and financial aid to Italy.

However, some goods, most notably steel and oil, could still be sold to Italy. The League delayed a decision on these items, fearing that the USA would not support the sanctions and that, in view of the Depression, members' economic interests would be damaged. Such concerns were reinforced in Britain when the cabinet was informed that 30,000 British miners would lose their jobs because of the ban on coal exports to Italy.

If full sanctions had been applied, Italy would probably have stopped the invasion – indeed, Mussolini admitted that it would have ended within a week. However, Britain and France were unwilling to provoke Mussolini more than necessary. Britain refused to close the Suez Canal (an action that would have severely limited Italian supplies reaching the invasion forces). The weakness of the British attitude was acknowledged by Philip Noel Baker, speaker at the last session of the League in April 1946, who commented: 'Yes, we know that World War began in Manchuria fifteen years ago. We know that four years later we could easily have stopped Mussolini if we had taken the sanctions against Mussolini that were obviously required, if we had closed the Suez Canal to the aggressor and stopped his oil.'

Nevertheless, it must be remembered that no sanctions had been imposed over Manchuria, and the League had been much slower to respond there. The action over Italy was the harshest the League had ever taken. By the end of the year, even tougher action was threatened – by this time, Britain had a naval force at Alexandria, while France, Yugoslavia, Greece and Turkey were all prepared to support British action against Italy. However, the British people kept their faith in the League and would not support action by an individual nation. There was also a strong feeling that sanctions were still the best form of persuasion.

Contrary plans

However, behind the scenes, the British and French governments were making plans that undermined the League. The foreign ministers of Britain and France, Samuel Hoare and Pierre Laval, met in December to work out how to bring the war to an end. Their plan split Abyssinia, with Italy gaining the fertile land in the north and south of the country. This would have reduced Abyssinia to about half its former size and left it with the mountainous central area and a corridor to the Red Sea, known as a 'corridor for camels'.

This strategy might have been acceptable to Italy, but it was leaked to the French press, causing a public outcry on such a scale that both Hoare and Laval were forced to resign. Even though the plan was not implemented, the damage was done. The two leading members of the League had been caught working beyond its bounds. It seemed as though Britain and France were willing to reward, rather than punish, Mussolini's aggression.

The British and French response left the League powerless. Its strongest members were unwilling to take further action, and Italy continued its conquest. The question of whether to stop selling oil was further delayed, even though a League committee concluded in February 1936 that if oil sales were halted, Italian supplies would be exhausted within two weeks. In a situation similar to that in Manchuria, these delays allowed Mussolini to seize large areas of Abyssinia. The USA was so disgusted by the League's weak response that it increased its supplies of oil to Italy.

Discussion point

The international community, through the League of Nations, declared the invasion unjust. How can the international community decide that an act is unjust? What elements do there need to be for action to be considered unjust?

Discussion point

How might Hoare or Laval have defended their actions in trying to solve the crisis outside the organisation of the League?

The Italian victory

The war in Abyssinia was brutal. The Abyssinian army was no match for modern machine guns, air power and the use of mustard gas. To Italians like Mussolini's son, Vittorio, it was 'a magnificent sport ... one group of horsemen gave me the impression of a budding rose unfolding as the bombs fell in their midst, and blew them up. It was exceptionally good fun.' The conflict resulted in the deaths of around 400,000 Abyssinians. In some villages, inhabitants were gassed and all men killed.

After early success, however, Italian progress slowed. This was partly due to poor communications, but also because of the low levels of training of the Italian troops. Any further attempts by the League to act were brought to an end in March 1936, when Hitler remilitarised the Rhineland (see page 200). His move was a direct threat to France, which now felt it needed to win Italy's support in the event that German aggression developed further. Italy was thus able to continue its conquest, and in May 1936 Italian troops entered the Abyssinian capital, Addis Ababa.

Abyssinian troops during the war against Italy, 1936

The Abyssinian emperor, Haile Selassie, was forced to flee. On 30 June 1936 he made a moving speech to the League of Nations.

SOURCE N

What have become of the promises made to me as long ago as October, 1935? I noted with grief, but without surprise that three Powers considered their undertakings under the Covenant as absolutely of no value. Their connections with Italy impelled them to refuse to take any measures whatsoever in order to stop Italian aggression.

The Ethiopian Government never expected other Governments to shed their soldiers' blood to defend the Covenant when their own immediately personal interests were not at stake. Ethiopian warriors asked only for means to defend themselves. On many occasions I have asked for financial assistance for the purchase of arms. That assistance has been constantly refused me. What, then, in practice, is the meaning of Article 16 of the Covenant and of collective security?

Finally a statement has just been made in their Parliaments by the Governments of certain Powers, amongst them the most influential members of the League of Nations, that since the aggressor has succeeded in occupying a large part of Ethiopian territory they propose not to continue the application of any economic and financial measures that may have been decided upon against the Italian Government.

I assert that the problem submitted to the Assembly today is a much wider one. It is not merely a question of the settlement of Italian aggression. It is collective security: it is the very existence of the League of Nations. It is the confidence that each State is to place in international treaties. It is the value of promises made to small States that their integrity and their independence shall be respected and ensured. It is the principle of the equality of States on the one hand, or otherwise the obligation laid upon small Powers to accept the bonds of vassalship. In a word, it is international morality that is at stake. Have the signatures appended to a Treaty value only in so far as the signatory Powers have a personal, direct and immediate interest involved?

Emperor Haile Selassie's address to the League of Nations, 30 June 1936.

197

Consequences of the invasion for the League and international relations

Historians agree that the Abyssinian crisis was a disaster for the League. Unlike the Manchurian crisis, the League had been able to impose economic sanctions if it had chosen, but failed to fully implement this opportunity. The major members of the League, Britain and France, formally supported the League, but weakened it by secret talks. The concept of collective security was undermined; smaller nations would look to other means to protect themselves in the future, whilst powerful states realised that the League could be ignored.

Discussion point

What could the League have done to prevent the Italian conquest? For each recommended action, what difficulty would it create?

If the League had been able to argue that Manchuria was too far away to take effective action, but that when there was a challenge nearer to home involving European powers it would respond with force, those words were now seen to be empty. The League's use of sanctions as a weapon had not made it more effective.

SOURCE O

Could the League survive the failure of sanctions to rescue Abyssinia? Could it ever impose sanctions again? Probably there had never been such a clear-cut case for sanctions. If the League had failed in this case there could probably be no confidence that it could succeed again in the future.

British foreign minister Anthony Eden describes his feelings about the Abyssinian crisis to the British cabinet in May 1936, just after the fall of Addis Ababa.

SOURCE P

The real death of the League was in December 1935, not in 1939 or 1945. One day it was a powerful body imposing sanctions, seemingly more effective than ever before; the next day it was an empty sham, everyone scuttling from it as quickly as possible.

Taylor, A. J. P. 1983. The Origins of the Second World War. London, UK. Hamish Hamilton. p. 96.

Questions

In what ways do Sources O and P agree? What does Taylor suggest was the reason for the failure of the League? Using the information in this chapter, how valid do you think his view is?

An Italian propaganda postcard about the Abyssinian situation, showing Mussolini shouting down the telephone to the British, 1936

Sanctions were the most powerful weapon that the League possessed, and many people believe that sanctions would have worked if the leading members had been willing to impose them fully. Britain and France had once again showed that they were more concerned with protecting their own interests than upholding the League's covenant.

Taylor, however, offers a different view on this, saying of the proposed Hoare–Laval Pact:

SOURCE Q

What killed the League was the publication of the Hoare-Laval plan. Yet this was a perfectly sensible plan, in line with the League's previous acts of conciliation from Corfu to Manchuria. It would have ended the war, satisfied Italy and left Abyssinia with a more workable, national territory. For the League action against Italy was not a commonsense extension of practical policies; it was a demonstration of principle pure and simple. No concrete 'interest' was at stake in Abyssinia – not even for Italy: Mussolini was concerned to show off Italy's strength, not to acquire the practical gains of Empire. The League powers were concerned to assert the Covenant, not to defend interests of their own.

Taylor, A. J. P. 1983. The Origins of the Second World War. London, UK. Hamish Hamilton. p. 96.

The Abyssinian crisis was a death blow to the League of Nations. Collective security had failed. Future aggression could no longer be prevented. After the invasion of Abyssinia, all European crises would be handled outside the League, reducing it to a powerless bystander.

SOURCE R

The crises of 1935–6 were fatal to the League, which was not taken seriously again. It was too late to save the League. Instead, it began the emotional preparation among the democracies for the Second World War.

Western, J. R. 1965. The End of European Primacy 1871–1945. London, UK. Blandford Press.

Question

Why does Taylor think that the Hoare–Laval Plan was the best solution for the Abyssinian crisis?

Historical debate

Historians are in general agreement that the League of Nations failed in the 1930s. However, their emphasis on the precise timing of the failure has been somewhat different. James Joll suggested that events in Manchuria had a profound impact on the attitudes of many, and that this was simply confirmed by events in Abyssinia. A. J. P. Taylor argued that the decline of the League was much more dramatic, going from a powerful body to an empty sham as a result of the Hoare–Laval Pact. Very few would agree with Taylor's view that it was a powerful body up to 1935, but historians such as Morris and Western agree that it was the Abyssinian crisis that marked the death of the League.

Activities

1 Look back to Chapter 3, to remind yourself of Italian gains at the Paris Peace Conferences. How valid was the claim that Italy had not been treated fairly and that a seizure of Abyssinia was justified?

2 Research what happened at Adowa in 1896 and why Italians viewed it as a humiliation.

3 Imagine you are the press officer for either Mussolini's government or for the former emperor Haile Selassie. Write a press release explaining the benefits or losses your country has made as a result of the conquest.

4 Copy and complete the chart below to provide a summary of the impact of the Manchurian and Abyssinian crises.

	Manchurian crisis	Abyssinian crisis
Impact on the League		
Impact on nation attacked		
Impact on Britain and France		
Impact on international relations		

Now write a concluding paragraph based on the chart above. Which crisis had the greater impact? Explain your answer.

What challenges to the Treaty of Versailles arose in 1936?

The actions of Britain and France had further implications for international relations. The two powers did not stop Italian aggression, but they destroyed any hope of a long-term reconciliation between the nations, driving Italy towards friendship with Germany. The hopes of the Stresa Front were replaced by the Rome–Berlin Axis.

The remilitarisation of the Rhineland

Most importantly, the weakness of the League encouraged Hitler. In March 1936, whilst the League was preoccupied with the problem of Abyssinia, the führer ordered German troops back in to the Rhineland – an act strictly forbidden by the Treaty of Versailles. Hitler argued that following the signing of a Mutual Assistance Pact between France and the USSR in 1935, Germany was under threat and should therefore be able to place troops on its own border. Despite this, he knew that the troop movement was a gamble and ordered his commanders to pull back if the French made moves against them.

In the event, neither France not Britain acted, sending Hitler a clear message that neither nation would take steps to prevent his territorial ambitions. The failure of the League to take any action against a clear breach of the Versailles Treaty also ended the hope of disarmament, as many nations began think that the only way to protect themselves now was to rearm.

Fact
The Mutual Assistance Pact was signed in May 1935, and stated that each country would give its support if the other country was the victim of unprovoked aggression, as judged by the League. Since 1934, France and the USSR had held various discussions to guarantee France's borders and the independence of Czechoslovakia. Britain disapproved of these aspects of French diplomacy.

The Spanish Civil War

By the end of 1936, Hitler had taken back the Saarland through a plebiscite and the Rhineland through military occupation. This increased his confidence. When civil war broke out between the republican government and right-wing nationalists in Spain, Hitler felt able to send aid to the right-wing rebels in their fight against the democratically elected Popular Front government. Once again, the League failed to act – even when German planes were used in bombing raids against Spanish cities (most famously Guernica). These raids encouraged further attempts to appease Hitler.

The Rome–Berlin Axis

The Italians also became involved in the Spanish Civil War in support of the nationalists. This drew Hitler and Mussolini even more closely into the friendship that had been developing since the Abyssinian crisis. As a result, in October 1936, Hitler and Mussolini signed the Rome–Berlin Axis, which bound them together in a military alliance.

SOURCE S

If new accounts by historians show that statesmen were able to use the League to ease tensions in the 1920s, no such case appears possible for the 1930s. Indeed, the League's processes may have played a role in that deterioration. Diplomacy requires leaders who can speak for their states; it requires secrecy; and it requires the ability to make credible threats. The Covenant's security arrangments met none of those criteria.

Pedersen, S. *Back to the League of Nations. Quoted in Walsh, B. 2009. Modern World History. London, UK. Hodder. p. 43.*

> **Fact**
> The term 'axis' referred to the idea that there was an imaginary axis, or line, connecting Rome and Berlin, around which European diplomacy revolved. In November 1936, Germany and Japan signed the Anti-Comintern (anti-communist) Pact; Italy added its signature to this in November 1937. This created the Rome–Berlin–Tokyo Axis that fought together in the Second World War. Their alliance was confirmed by the Pact of Steel between Germany and Italy in 1939, and the Tripartite Pact between the three countries in 1940.

201

Activities

1 'If Mussolini had known that he would lose the support of Britain and France he would not have invaded Abyssinia.' Do you agree with this assertion?

2 Write a response on behalf of the League of Nations to Haile Selassie's speech.

3 Copy and complete the chart below, showing the impact of the Abyssinian crisis on the countries/organisations listed.

Country/organisation	Impact
Italy	
Germany	
Britain	
France	
League of Nations	

End of chapter activities

Summary

You should now have an understanding of how the concept of collective security was undermined by the invasion of Manchuria in 1931 and by the Abyssinian crisis of 1935. Japan had shown that aggression went unpunished, and this provided Mussolini and Hitler with further incentive to pursue expansionist foreign policies to solve their domestic problems. You should also have an understanding of how these crises led to differences between Britain and France – undermining the League – and resulted in Germany and Italy moving closer together. From 1936, both countries increasingly adopted aggressive foreign policies: Germany re-entered the Rhineland in March 1936, in breach of the Versailles Treaty; while both Italy and Germany intervened in the Spanish Civil War. They then formed a military alliance in the form of the Rome–Berlin Axis in October 1936. Therefore, by the end of 1936, the two sides that would fight against each other in the Second World War had been created.

Summary activity

Construct a spider diagram to show the main international crises, and the causes and consequences of the League's failures, in the period 1931–36.

Paper 1 exam practice

Question

With reference to their origin and purpose, assess the value and limitations of Sources A and B for historians studying the Japanese invasion of Manchuria in 1931.
[6 marks]

Skill

Assessing the value and limitations (utility/reliability) of two sources

Before you start

Value and limitations (utility/reliability) questions require you to assess **two** sources over a range of possible issues – and to comment on their value to historians studying a particular event or period of history. You need to consider both the **origin and purpose** and also the **value and limitations** of the sources. You should link these in your answer, showing how origin/purpose relate to value/limitations.

Before you attempt this question, refer to pages 213–14 for advice on how to tackle these questions and a simplified markscheme.

SOURCE A

Instructions had been received that special care was to be taken to avoid any clash with Japanese troops in the tense state of feeling which existed at the time. On the night of 18 September all the soldiers of the 7th Brigade, numbering about 10,000, were in the North Barracks. The west gate in the mud wall surrounding the camp, which gave access to the railway, had been closed. At 10pm the sound of a large explosion could be heard, immediately followed by rifle fire.

The Chinese version of events given to the Lytton enquiry. Quoted in Lacey, G. and Kelly, N. 2001. Modern World History. London, UK. Heinemann. p. 77.

SOURCE B

Although Japan has undoubtedly acted in a way contrary to the principles of the Covenant by taking the law in to their own hands, she has a real grievance against China. This is not a case in which the armed forces of one country have crossed the frontiers of another in circumstances in which they had no previous right to be on the other's soil. Japan owns the South Manchurian railway and has been entitled to have a body of Japanese guards upon the strip of land through which the railway runs. Japan's case is that she was compelled by the failure of China to provide reasonable protection for Japanese lives and property in Manchuria in the face of attacks of Chinese bandits, and of an attack upon the line itself, to move Japanese troops forward and to occupy points in Manchuria which are beyond the line of the railway.

Extract from a memorandum by foreign secretary Sir John Simon to the British cabinet, 23 November 1931.

Student answer

Source A is a primary source, written by a Chinese commander who was present and would certainly be aware of the instructions that had been issued about avoiding antagonising the Japanese. He would also have knowledge of the movements of Chinese troops. However, it must be remembered that his purpose in reporting the events to the Lytton enquiry was to remove the blame for the incident from China and to undermine the Japanese justification for the invasion. He builds up a case to show that China could not be blamed for the explosion. Despite this being told to an official enquiry, it will limit the veracity of the source. However, it is still useful to the historian as it shows how the Chinese tried to remove blame.

Source B is also a primary source – a report from the British foreign secretary to the cabinet. His purpose will be to inform them about developments in Manchuria and allow them to make informed decisions about the British reaction. This might imply that Simon would produce a balanced report, but much would depend upon the accuracy of the information available. Simon also appears to be guiding the cabinet, as he seems to argue that the Japanese have some justification for their response. The source also suggests that at the time some were convinced that the Chinese had caused the explosion. It is useful to the historian in showing that already a major power was demonstrating some sympathy towards Japan, although this may limit the accuracy of the report.

Examiner comments

This is a very thorough answer that deals with most of the issues that are required – origin, purpose, value and limitations. It is better at dealing with some aspects than others, particularly in its coverage of Source B, where the analysis of the value and limitations of the source could be more fully developed. However, the student shows awareness of some of the strengths and weaknesses of both sources as evidence for the historian, and this would be credited. The answer is also well-balanced, with coverage split fairly equally between the two sources. The answer would therefore be awarded 5 out of 6 marks.

Activity

Look again at the question, the student answer above and the examiner comments. Now try to add to the answer so that it would achieve full marks.

Paper 2 practice questions

1 Assess the reasons why the League of Nations failed to resolve the Manchurian and Abyssinian crises.

2 Analyse the reasons for *either* Japan's invasion of Manchuria *or* the Italian invasion of Abyssinia.

3 Explain the consequences of the League of Nations' failure over the Abyssinian crisis.

4 Assess the reasons for the collapse of international order in the 1930s.

5 Explain the reasons for the changing relationship between Italy and Germany in the 1930s.

The final steps to war

This chapter is designed to provide an overview of how the developments that you have studied in this book finally resulted in the declaration of war in Europe in September 1939. It is important to understand that it was only in Europe that war broke out in 1939. People in China, and in Asia generally, could legitimately argue that the Second World War had already begun there, with the Japanese invasion of China in 1937 – or even in 1931, with the occupation of Manchuria.

Although events after 1936 are not part of the IB syllabus for Paper 1, it is helpful to have an understanding of how the situation developed up to the outbreak of war in Europe in 1939.

A German tank rolls through the streets of Czechoslovakia, March 1939

Hitler's strength

At the start of 1937, Hitler was supremely confident in his position. He had secured an alliance with Italy, and believed that neither Britain nor France would stop his expansionist policy. Many historians think it is unlikely that Hitler had a detailed plan for the events that led to the outbreak of war, and believe he did not envisage the 'total war' that followed his invasion of the USSR in 1941. However, there can be little doubt that Hitler sought war, even if it was only a series of short and localised conflicts in central, eastern and southern parts of Europe.

The Austrian *Anschluss*

Having secured his position at home and formed an alliance with Italy, Hitler turned his attention to his homeland of Austria. In 1934, Italy – in alliance with Britain and France – had prevented the German seizure of Austria, but the situation was now different. Hitler encouraged the Nazis in Austria to cause unrest, and then told the Austrian chancellor that this could only be repressed by a union of the two nations.

The Austrian chancellor asked Britain and France for help, but when they did not come to Austria's aid he called a referendum to discover what the Austrian people wanted. Fearing that the result would go against the *Anschluss*, Hitler sent troops into Austria in March 1938. He claimed that this move was to guarantee that the referendum was held in peaceful conditions; in fact it was to intimidate the population into voting in favour of union, which they duly did.

Meanwhile, in Britain and France, no action was taken. Many people felt that Germany and Austria had the right to be united, and that the principle of self-determination – which had been denied to these nations at the Paris Peace Conferences – was now being applied.

The Sudetenland

Hitler's next target was the Sudetenland. This area was occupied by 3 million German speakers, who had formerly been citizens of Austria-Hungary but who had been part of Czechoslovakia since 1919. The *Anschluss* with Austria deeply concerned the Czech president, Edvard Beneš, who feared that Hitler would next attempt to invade Czechoslovakia. Beneš turned to Britain and France for help. The French were bound to provide assistance by the treaties signed with the successor states in the 1920s. However, Britain made no guarantees of assistance, and France was reluctant to act alone.

In May 1938, Hitler stated that he intended to fight Czechoslovakia for control of the Sudetenland if necessary. Whether or not he genuinely meant to carry out this threat has been debated by historians, but it brought the issue to the centre of international affairs. The threat to Czechoslovakia encouraged the major powers to try and find a solution to Hitler's expansionist policies that would avoid war. Despite this, war appeared to be imminent, and throughout the summer of 1938 several countries began preparing for this eventuality.

A more serious crisis arose in September 1938, when the British prime minister, Neville Chamberlain, made three visits to Germany to meet with Hitler. The second meeting appeared at first to solve the crisis. Hitler's demands seemed moderate – he claimed to want only parts of the Sudetenland and then only if the inhabitants wanted to join Germany. This proposal was made to the Czechs, but Hitler then extended his demands to include the whole Sudetenland, claiming that Germans in the region were being mistreated. In an attempt to avoid war, Mussolini suggested a Four Power Conference between Britain, France, Germany and Italy to discuss the issue. At a conference in Munich on 29 September, the Allies gave in to Hitler's demands (a policy that became known as appeasement). The Czechs had been abandoned. They were told that they could fight, but they would not receive help from Britain and France.

Appeasement has been heavily criticised as immoral. However, there are some arguments to defend it. The economic depression had created other priorities in Britain and France, and neither country was in a military position to resist Hitler. It was therefore necessary to find a way to at least delay the outbreak of war. The Allies also feared that they would not be supported by either the USA or their own empires, and this seriously weakened their resolve. Most people were pleased by the agreement reached at Munich to prevent war. Nonetheless, the policy of appeasement only encouraged Hitler.

Although Hitler claimed that the Sudetenland was his last demand, his actions in March 1939 made it clear that he could not be trusted. German troops entered other areas of Czechoslovakia, in an act of open aggression that could not be justified. The Allies realised that Poland was almost certainly next on Hitler's list, and that they must take action to stop further German expansion. Britain and France warned the German leader that if he attacked Poland they would declare war.

The outbreak of war

Given their recent policy of appeasement towards him, Hitler probably regarded this as an empty threat. However, he took the precaution of strengthening his position in the east in August 1939 by signing a non-aggression pact with the Soviet Union. This shocked the Allies: Germany and the USSR were ideologically opposed, and Hitler had signed the Anti-Comintern Pact with Italy and Japan. The agreement also meant that Germany would not have to fight a war on two fronts (as it had in the First World War). Germany and the USSR also agreed to attack Poland together and divide the country between them. This pact allowed Hitler to launch his attack on Poland on 1 September 1939. On 3 September, Britain and France declared war on Germany.

Appeasement had failed. Britain and France were forced into war, and the era of international co-operation built up in the 1920s was clearly over. However, some historians have argued that the policy of appeasement also gave the Allies time to prepare for war, and that they were in a better position to fight in 1939 than they had been the previous year. If this is true, the Allies prevented Hitler from having his series of short wars, but instead forced him into the long-drawn-out conflict that ended with the collapse of the Nazi regime in 1945.

Fact
Appeasement was a policy intended to avoid another war, and is most associated with the British prime minister Neville Chamberlain. It was based on the belief that aspects of the Treaty of Versailles had been unfair to Germany. Consequently, there was a willingness to consider peaceful changes (revisions – hence the term 'revisionism' in this context) to Versailles and some of the other post-war peace treaties. Britain was more prepared than France to accept some changes; this caused tensions between the two countries, and increasingly undermined the effectiveness of the League of Nations.

History and historiography

Historiography and your exam

Some awareness and understanding of the historiography surrounding the topics you study will help you score highly in Papers 2 and 3. It is useful for Paper 1, too, as an understanding of the debate will aid the appreciation of the particular viewpoint of a source or historian. However, you will need to take care when considering some sources. Their authors may want to give the impression of being satisfied with developments and changes, whereas in reality they hoped the changes would go much further. This is particularly true of the comments made by many German, Italian and Japanese politicians in their dealings with other countries.

For this reason, you will find that there are several different explanations for the origins of the Second World War. Historians – like most other people – are rarely completely neutral when dealing with important or controversial issues. Thus, you need to be aware of the sympathies of historians and politicians writing about the events of the period. As you begin to read around the subject, you will come across 'orthodox', 'revisionist', 'post-revisionist' and even 'post post-revisionist' perspectives.

Although the main focus of this paper is on source analysis, you should be aware of some of the various historical debates that surround the topic – most notably the disagreement between historians over the reasons for the outbreak of the Second World War. There are two main controversies. One concerns the general reasons for the breakdown of international relations that culminated in the Second World War. The other is more focused on the extent to which Hitler actually intended the war that finally broke out in Europe in 1939.

The collapse of international co-operation

Historians such as A. J. P. Taylor see the Second World War as an almost inevitable consequence of the peace treaties, which failed to solve the problems that had caused the First World War – most notably the question of Germany's place in Europe. These historians argue that once Germany had recovered from the First World War, it was bound to seek to reverse the terms of the peace treaties and regain its dominant position in Europe. Even some contemporaries, such as the French general Ferdinand Foch, described the peace treaties as an 'armistice for 20 years'.

Such historians suggest that Germany would never have accepted the terms of the peace treaties, and that even in the 1920s its politicians were working to undermine these terms and reclaim Germany's 'rightful' place in Europe. They point to the reaction of the German people to the signing of the Treaty of Versailles and the scale of reparations. They argue that Hitler's expansionist policies were little more than a continuation of those followed by German statesmen in the 1920s. By this interpretation, the League of Nations and international agreements had little chance of success.

However, other historians argue that the peacemakers who drew up the treaties in 1919 did the best they could in very difficult circumstances, and should not be blamed for the outbreak of the Second World War. These historians suggest that there was an improvement in relations between Germany and France and a lessening of international tensions in the 1920s, as all nations recovered from the First World War. This interpretation suggests that modifications to the peace treaty had started to satisfy Germany, which had returned to the international stage through membership of the League and the signing of the Locarno and Kellogg–Briand pacts. The failure of the League was therefore not inevitable.

These historians also argue that it was the Great Depression that changed the international order. They believe that the economic decline allowed Italy to seek the territory it had been denied at the peace conferences, and brought to power aggressive regimes in Japan and Germany. This allowed Hitler to exploit the difficulties faced by other powers to embark on his policy of expansion.

Did Hitler intend the Second World War to break out?

The debate over how far Germany – and in particular Hitler – was to blame for the outbreak of war involves two main approaches. The traditional, or orthodox, view – put forward by historians such as Hugh Trevor-Roper – claims that Hitler systematically followed a foreign policy intended to result in wars of conquest. This opinion was challenged by the publication of A. J. P. Taylor's book *The Origins of the Second World War* in the 1960s. Taylor argued that the Allied powers should take as much responsibility as Germany for the outbreak of war, as they failed to solve the German problem in 1919 and then because of their policies throughout the 1920s and 1930s. Taylor also argued that Hitler was an opportunist, who took advantage of changing situations. This debate continues today, as revisionist historians such as John Charmley examine the role of appeasement in bringing about the Second World War.

A German soldier stands guard over a Stuka bomber, 1939

11 Exam practice

Introduction

You have now completed your study of the main aspects and events of international relations 1918–36. In the previous chapters, you have had practice at answering some of the types of source-based questions you will have to deal with in Paper 1. In this chapter, you will gain experience of tackling:

- the longer Paper 1 question, which requires you to use both sources and your own knowledge to write a mini-essay
- the essay questions you will meet in Paper 2.

Exam skills needed for IB History

This book is designed primarily to prepare both Standard- and Higher-level students for the Paper 1 *International Relations* topic (Prescribed Subject 1), by providing the necessary historical knowledge and understanding, as well as an awareness of the key historical debates. However, it will also help you prepare for Paper 2, by giving you the chance to practise writing essays. The skills you need for answering both Paper 1 and Paper 2 exam questions are explained in the following pages.

Paper 1 skills

This section of the book will give you the skills and understanding to tackle Paper 1 questions. These are based on the comprehension, critical analysis and evaluation of different types of historical sources as evidence, along with the use of appropriate historical contextual knowledge.

For example, you will need to test sources for value and limitations (i.e. their reliability and utility, especially in view of their origins and purpose) – an essential skill for historians. A range of sources has been provided, including extracts from official documents, tables of statistics, memoirs and speeches, as well as visual sources such as photographs and cartoons.

In order to analyse and evaluate sources as historical evidence, you will need to ask the following 'W' questions of historical sources:

- **Who** produced it? Were they in a position to know?
- **What** type of source is it? What is its nature – is it a primary or secondary source?
- **Where** and **when** was it produced? What was happening at the time?
- **Why** was it produced? Was its purpose to inform or to persuade? Is it an accurate attempt to record facts, or is it an example of propaganda?
- **Who** was the intended audience – decision-makers or the general public?

You should then consider how the answers to these 'W' questions affect the value of a source.

The example below shows you how to find the information related to the 'W' questions. You will need this information in order to evaluate sources for their value and limitations.

SOURCE A

We National Socialists must hold unflinchingly to our aim in foreign policy, namely to secure for the German people the land and soil to which they are entitled on this earth. State boundaries are made by man and changed by man. The fact that a nation has succeeded in acquiring an undue amount of soil does constitutes no higher obligation that it should be recognised eternally. At most it proves the strength of the conquerors and the weakness of the nations. And in this case, right lies in strength alone.

Adolf Hitler, in his book *Mein Kampf in* 1925, *outlining the chief aims of future German foreign policy for the* German people.

book WHAT? (type of source)
Adolf Hitler WHO? (produced it)
1925 WHEN? (date/time of production)
outlining the chief aims WHY?
(possible purpose)
German people WHO? (intended audience)

This approach will help you become familiar with interpreting, understanding, analysing and evaluating different types of historical sources. It will also aid you in synthesising critical analysis of sources with historical knowledge when constructing an explanation or analysis of some aspect or development of the past.

Remember – for Paper 1, as for Paper 2, you need to acquire, select and use relevant historical knowledge to explain causes and consequences, continuity and change. You also need to develop and show (where relevant) an awareness of historical debates and different interpretations.

Paper 1 contains four types of question:

1 Comprehension/understanding of a source (2 or 3 marks)

2 Cross-referencing/comparing or contrasting two sources (6 marks)

3 Assessing the value and limitations of two sources (6 marks)

4 Using and evaluating sources to reach a judgement (8 marks)

Comprehension/understanding of a source

Comprehension questions require you to understand a source and extract two or three relevant points that relate to the particular question.

Examiner's tips

Step 1 – Read the source and highlight/underline key points.

Step 2 – Write a concise answer. Just a couple of brief sentences are needed, giving the information necessary to show that you have understood the message of the source – but make sure you make three clear points for a 3-mark question and two clear points for a 2-mark question. If relevant, also try to make some brief overall comment about the source. Make it as easy as possible for the examiner to give you the marks by clearly distinguishing between the points.

Common mistakes

- Make sure you don't comment on the wrong source! Mistakes like this are made every year. Remember – every mark is important for your final grade.
- Don't just copy the source. Summarise the key points in your own words.

Simplified markscheme

For **each item of relevant/correct information** identified, award **1 mark** – up to a **maximum of 2 or 3 marks**.

Cross-referencing/comparing or contrasting two sources

Cross-referencing questions require you to compare **and** contrast the information/content/nature of **two** sources, relating to a particular issue.

Examiner's tips

For cross-referencing questions, you need to provide an integrated comparison, rather than dealing with each source separately.

Step 1 – Read the sources and highlight/underline key points.

Step 2 – Draw a rough chart or diagram to show the **similarities** and the **differences** between the two sources. That way, you should ensure you address both elements of the question.

Step 3 – Write your answer, ensuring that you provide an integrated comparison. For example, you should comment on how the two sources deal with one aspect, then compare and contrast the sources on another aspect. Avoid simply describing/paraphrasing each source in turn – you need to make **clear and explicit** comparisons and contrasts, using precise details from the sources.

Common mistakes

- Don't just comment on **one** of the sources! Such an oversight happens every year – and will lose you 4 of the 6 marks available.
- Make sure you comment on the sources identified in the question – don't select one (or two) incorrect sources!
- Make **explicit** comparisons – do not fall into the trap of writing about the two sources separately and leaving the similarities/differences implicit.

Timing
For a 3-mark question, you should not spend more than about seven minutes. For a 2-mark question, you should take no more than about five minutes. Don't spend too long on these questions or you will run out of time!

Examples of comprehension questions can be found at the end of Chapter 2 (see page 39) and Chapter 3 (see page 73).

Simplified markscheme

Band		Marks
1	**Both** sources **linked**, with **detailed references** to the two sources, identifying **both** similarities **and** differences.	6
2	**Both** sources **linked**, with **detailed references** to the two sources, identifying **either** similarities **or** differences.	4–5
3	Comments on both sources, **but** treating each one **separately**.	3
4	Discusses/comments on just **one** source.	0–2

> Examples of cross-referencing questions can be found at the end of Chapter 4 (see page 95), Chapter 6 (see page 136) and Chapter 7 (see page 157).

Assessing the value and limitations of two sources

Value and limitations (utility/reliability) questions require you to assess **two** sources over a range of possible issues/aspects – and to comment on their value to historians studying a particular event or period of history.

> **origins** The 'who, what, when and where?' questions
> **purpose** This means 'reasons, what the writer/creator was trying to achieve, who the intended audience was'.

Examiner's tips

The main areas you need to consider in relation to the sources and the information/view they provide are:

- **origin** and **purpose**
- value and limitations.

These areas need to be linked in your answer, showing how the value and limitations of each source to historians relates to the source's origin and purpose.

For example, a source might be useful because it is primary – the event depicted was witnessed by the person that produced the source. But was the person in a position to know? Is the view an untypical account of the event? What is its nature? Is it a private diary entry (therefore possibly more likely to be true), or is it a speech or piece of propaganda intended to persuade?

> Remember – a source doesn't have to be primary to be useful. Remember, too, that content isn't the only aspect to have possible value. The context, the person who produced it, and so on, can be important in offering an insight.

The value of a source may be limited by some aspects, but that doesn't mean it has no value at all. For example, it may be valuable as evidence of the types of propaganda put out at the time. Similarly, a secondary – or even a tertiary – source can have more value than some primary sources: for instance, because the author might be writing at a time when new evidence has become available.

For these questions it is best to deal with each source separately, as you are not being asked to decide which source is more important/useful.

Step 1 – Read the sources and highlight/underline key points.

Step 2 – For **each source**, draw a rough chart or spider diagram to show the origin/purpose of the source, and how it links to that source's value/limitations.

Step 3 – Write your answer, remembering to deal with **all** the aspects required: **origins, purpose, value and limitations**. To do this, you will need to make **explicit** links between a source's origins/purpose **and** its value/limitations to a historian.

213

Common mistakes

- Don't just comment on **one** of the two sources! As with cross-referencing questions, every year a few students make this mistake and lose up to 4 of the 6 marks available.
- Don't just comment on content and ignore the nature, origins and purpose of the sources.
- Don't say 'A source is/isn't useful because it's primary/secondary'.

Simplified markscheme

Band		Marks
1	**Both** sources assessed, with **explicit consideration** of **BOTH** origins and purpose **AND** value and limitations.	5–6
2	**Both** sources assessed, but without consideration of **BOTH** origins and purpose **AND** value and limitations. **OR Explicit consideration** of **BOTH** origins and purpose **AND** value and limitations – **BUT** only for **one** source.	3–4
3	**Limited** consideration/comments on origins and purpose **OR** value and limitations. Possibly only one/the wrong source(s) addressed.	0–2

> Examples of value and limitations questions can be found at the end of Chapter 5 (see page 114), Chapter 8 (see page 177) and Chapter 9 (see page 202).

Using and evaluating sources and knowledge to reach a judgement

The fourth type of Paper 1 is a judgement question. Judgement questions are a *synthesis of source evaluation and own knowledge.*

Examiner's tips

- This fourth type of Paper 1 question requires you to produce a mini-essay, with a clear/relevant argument, to address the question/statement given in the question. You should try to develop and present an argument and/or come to a balanced judgement by analysing and using the five sources and your own knowledge.

- Before you write your answer to this kind of question, you may find it useful to draw a rough chart to note what the sources show in relation to the question. This will also ensure you refer to all, or at least most, of the sources. Note, however, that some sources may hint at more than one factor/result. When using your own knowledge, make sure it is relevant to the question.

- Look carefully at the simplified markscheme below. This will help you focus on what you need to do to reach the top bands and so score the higher marks.

Common mistake

Don't just deal with sources **or** your own knowledge! Every year, some candidates (even good ones) do this, and so limit themselves to – at best – only 5 out of the 8 marks available.

Simplified markscheme

Band		Marks
1	**Developed and balanced** analysis and comments using **BOTH** sources **AND** own knowledge. References to sources are precise; sources and detailed own knowledge are used together; where relevant, a judgement is made.	8
2	**Developed** analysis/comments using **BOTH** sources **AND** some detailed own knowledge; some clear references to sources. But sources and own knowledge not always **combined**.	6–7
3	**Some developed** analysis/comments, using the sources **OR** some relevant own knowledge.	4–5
4	**Limited/general** comments using sources **OR** own knowledge.	0–3

Student answers

The student answers below have brief examiner's comments in the margins, as well as a longer overall comment at the end. Those parts of the answers that make use of the sources are highlighted in green. Those parts that deploy relevant own knowledge are highlighted in red. In this way, you should find it easier to follow why particular bands and marks were – or were not – awarded.

Question 1

Using Sources A, B, C, D and E **and** your own knowledge, analyse the extent to which Germany's international position improved in the period from 1923 to 1930.
[8 marks]

SOURCE A

It became clear that the occupation of the Ruhr constituted a turning point in the history of post-war Europe. It brought to a climax the Anglo-French conflict over the treatment of Germany and the application of the Treaty of Versailles; it signified the defeat of France and its slow subordination to British policy; it thereby pointed the way to the Treaty of Locarno and the resurgence of Germany. Lastly, the Ruhr occupation showed the inability of France, acting on its own, to produce any major changes in the territorial integrity of Germany.

Kochan, L. 1963. The Struggle for Germany 1914–1945. New York, USA. Harper & Row. p. 29.

SOURCE B

Germany's growing and industrious population; her great technical skill; the wealth of her material resources; the development of her agriculture on progressive lines; her eminence in industrial science; all these factors enable us to be hopeful with regard to her future production.

Germany is well equipped with resources; she possesses the means for exploiting them on a large scale, when the present credit shortage has been overcome, she will be able to resume a favoured position in the activity of a world where normal conditions of exchange are gradually being restored.

Without undue optimism, it may anticipated that Germany's production will enable her to satisfy her own requirements and raise the amounts contemplated in this plan [Dawes] for reparation obligations.

Extract from the Committee of Experts Report. Quoted in Pollard, S. and Holmes, C. 1973. Documents of Economic History, Vol. III, The End of Old Europe 1914–1939. *London, UK. Edward Arnold. pp. 294–95.*

SOURCE C

In my opinion there are three great tasks that confront German foreign policy in the immediate future. In the first place, the solution of the Reparations question in a sense tolerable for Germany, and the assurance of peace, which is an essential premise for the recovery of our strength. Secondly, the protection of Germans living abroad, those 10 to 12 million of our kindred who now live under a foreign yoke in foreign lands. The third great task is the readjustment of our eastern frontiers; the recovery of Danzig, the Polish Corridor, and a correction of the frontier in Upper Silesia.

Gustav Stresemann, in a letter to the former German crown prince, 7 September 1925. Quoted in Adamthwaite, A. 1980. The Lost Peace – International Relations in Europe 1918–1939. *London, UK. Edward Arnold.*

SOURCE D

Berlin, 2 October 1926 – Now that Locarno has been in force for nearly a year and that Germany is a member of the League of Nations, a definite period in history comes to a close. A fresh epoch for Europe commences, and the work here will assume a different and more normal character. The war spirit has been quelled, and the possibility of an era of peaceful development opens.

Edgar Vincent D'Abernon, the British ambassador to Berlin 1920–26. Quoted in Meyer, H. C. 1973. Germany – from Empire to Ruin, 1913–45. *London, UK. Macmillan. pp. 144–46.*

A British cartoon by David Low, published in 1925, showing the French, German and British foreign ministers; Aristide Briand is wearing a boxing glove

THE CLASP OF FRIENDSHIP (FRENCH VERSION).

Student answer

The sources offer two views as to how far Germany's international position improved in the years between the occupation of the Ruhr and the onset of the Great Depression. Sources A, B and D all suggest that Germany was able, or at least had the potential, to improve its position in international affairs and avoid being the outcast, which had been the situation since the signing of the Treaty of Versailles. However, Sources C and E suggest that there were still challenges for Germany. Source C sees the challenge coming from within Germany, where there was a desire for further advances, whereas Source E suggests that France, despite appearances, was determined that Germany should not be allowed a full recovery, but remain subordinate to the victorious powers.

Examiner's comment
This is a good, well-focused start, with a clear argument. All five sources are referred to, and an overview of their attitude towards the issue in the question is outlined, along with a little own knowledge.

Sources A and D clearly suggest that there had been an improvement in Germany's international position within Europe. Source A argues that the invasion of the Ruhr was the turning point in this improvement, as prior to that Germany had been an outcast, denied membership of the League and therefore allied to the other European outcast, Russia, through the Treaty of Rapallo. According to Source A, the invasion 'pointed the way to Locarno and the resurgence of Germany'. This view is supported by Source B, which argues that Germany had the economic potential to take advantage of its improved position, once the credit crisis had been overcome, which was achieved through the signing of the Dawes Plan. Once this happened Germany would, according to Source B, be able to trade and meet its reparation obligations, which it had not been able to do in the past, a problem that had caused the invasion of the Ruhr.

Source A also argues that as a result of the Ruhr invasion it was clear that France was unable to bring about any 'major change in the territorial integrity of Germany'. This also improved the German position and ensured that there would not be a subsequent invasion, as the source argues that French policy would now have to follow British wishes. This view of an improved position is given further credence by Source D, which was written after the signing of Locarno and German entry into the League of Nations in 1926. These two events both recognised an improvement in Germany's international position, as Germany was treated as an equal, unlike Versailles where the terms were simply dictated. The ambassador in Berlin also notes that a more 'normal' character had returned to his work there and that any 'war spirit' had been repressed, suggesting that Germany was happier with its position in international affairs.

Examiner's comment
The argument is maintained and Sources A, B and D are again clearly referred to and used, showing good understanding. There is also some own knowledge about international agreements, which is explicitly linked to Germany's improved international position.

However, Sources C and E suggest that the situation was not as straightforward, and that Germany still faced challenges and was not satisfied by the improvements that had taken place. Stresemann, who is usually credited with restoring Germany's international status, clearly expresses his view in Source C that there were still at least three issues that needed resolution in international affairs. He shows concern about 'assurance of peace' and these comments are supported by Source E, where Briand seems determined to deliver a knock-out blow to Germany, hence his wearing of the boxing glove. **Therefore, even events such as Locarno, which appear to have improved Germany's international position, did not fully achieve their goals.**

This view of a dissatisfied Germany is further developed by Stresemann. He states that the problem of Germans living outside Germany and the question of both Danzig and Upper Silesia need resolution if Germany is to consider its international position improved. Therefore, Source C suggests that even if there had been a partial improvement in Germany's position there was more to be done. Source E, however, suggests that although outwardly there appeared to be a resolution of conflicts between France and Germany, France was determined to keep Germany down.

Examiner's comment
As before, two more sources (C and E) are clearly used and linked. There is also some limited own knowledge. However, this needs to be fully developed, and more detailed and precise support given to explain and clarify the messages in the sources.

In conclusion, the sources suggest that there had been at least some improvement in Germany's international position. Although Germany wanted to take the improvements further and France wanted to limit German recovery, Sources A, B and D all suggest that Germany was now in a stronger and more secure position. Even Source C does not deny that the position had improved – Stresemann just wants even more.

Overall examiner's comments

This answer offers a clear argument and makes good use of the sources. However, although there is a mixture of some precise and general own knowledge, which is mainly integrated with comments on the sources, there are some omissions. The answer could have made greater use of Source B and how economic recovery would help Germany to regain its place on the international stage through trade. Own knowledge could also have been used more fully in the second half of the answer to support the view that improvements in Germany's international position were limited to some extent. The candidate could have given greater detail about Germany's desire to revise the terms of the Treaty of Versailles in the east, the opposition within Germany to some of the agreements, and the reliance for the improvement upon US loans, which made the German position precarious. The student could also have made some reference to the continuation of the agreement with Russia, which caused concern in the West, and also to French concerns about security. Hence, this answer fails to get into Band 1 – but this is a reasonably sound Band 2 answer and would probably score 6 marks out of the 8 available.

Activity

Look again at the all sources, the simplified markscheme, and the student answer above. Now try to write a few paragraphs to push the answer up into Band 1, and so obtain the full 8 marks. As well as using all/most of the sources, and some precise own knowledge, try to integrate the sources with your own knowledge rather than dealing with sources and own knowledge separately. And don't lose sight of the need to use the sources and your own knowledge to produce a sustained argument that explains how far Germany's international position had improved.

Question 2

Using Sources A, B, C, D and E **and** your own knowledge, assess to what extent reparations were the main reason why Germany disliked the Treaty of Versailles. [8 marks]

SOURCE A

The Allied and Associated Governments affirm and Germany accepts the responsibility of Germany and her allies for causing all the loss and damage to which the Allied and Associated Governments and their nationals have been subjected as a consequence of the war imposed upon them by the aggression of Germany and her allies.

Clause 231, The Treaty of Versailles.

SOURCE B

A British cartoon from 1919 entitled 'The Reckoning'; the caption read 'German: Monstrous, I call it. Why, it's fully a quarter of what *we* would have made *them* pay if *we*'d won.'

SOURCE C

A German cartoon from 1919 showing a German mother and her starving child; the caption read 'When we have paid one hundred billion marks then I can give you something to eat'

SOURCE D

The Allies could have done anything with the German people had they made the slightest move toward reconciliation. People were prepared to make reparations for the wrong done by their leaders. Over and over again I hear the same refrain, 'We shall hate our conquerors with a hatred that will only cease when the day of our revenge comes.'

Blücher, E. An English Wife in Berlin. 1920. London, UK. Constable and Co. pp. 302–4. Princess Evelyn Blücher was an Englishwoman who had married a member of the German royal family.

SOURCE E

The mistake the Allies made, and it did not become clear until much later, was that, as a result of the armistice terms, the great majority of Germans never experienced their country's defeat at first hand. Except in the Rhineland they did not see the occupying troops. The Allies did not march in triumph into Berlin, as the Germans had done in Paris in 1871. In 1918 German soldiers marched home in good order, with crowds cheering their way; in Berlin Friedrich Ebert, the new President, greeted them with 'no enemy has conquered you.'

Macmillan, M. 2001. Peacemakers: Six Months that Changed the World. London, UK. John Murray. p. 168.

Student answer

These sources give a mixed view of the extent to which reparations were the most important reason why Germany disliked the Treaty of Versailles. There are many reasons why Germany disliked the treaty and the sources do not consider all the possible reasons. They do consider the issue of reparations, war guilt and Germany's status as a great power, but fail to take into account some of the losses imposed on Germany, such as land and military losses.

Examiner's comment

This is a brief but good introduction, showing a clear understanding of the topic and the question. However, the candidate does not make any precise reference to the sources, and it might be advisable to group them in the opening according to whether they do or do not agree with the view proposed in the question.

Sources B and C appear to give the clearest indication that the issue of reparations was a major reason why Germany disliked the Treaty of Versailles. This is most strongly supported by Source C, as the caption claims 'When we have paid one hundred billion marks then I can give you something to eat.' The mother in the picture claims that she is unable to feed her child because of the scale of reparations payments. The thin and unclothed child is clear evidence of the impact of the reparations on ordinary Germans and why they would therefore hate the treaty.

A similar message appears to be put forward by Source B, which claims that the reparations are 'monstrous'. However, the rest of the caption goes on to explain that the level is far less than they would have imposed if they had won. Although it does not suggest that reparations were not an issue, it does indicate that Germans were hypocritical in complaining about the level of reparations as they would have demanded even more. Just as importantly, the two sources were published before the Allied Commission had fixed the final sum Germany had to pay, having decided that if an amount was agreed at Versailles, in the bitterness of the immediate post-war period, it would have been too high. As a result, the final sum was more moderate and was therefore more likely to have been payable. This suggests that the Germans simply did not want to pay reparations, rather than their protests being about the actual amount demanded.

Examiner's comment

There is good use of Sources B and C, and the use of some precise own knowledge, which is integrated in the answer. The answer also questions the usefulness of the sources by reference to their date of publication and is therefore able to suggest that if the Germans disliked reparations it was because of the principle, rather than the actual amount.

However, the view that reparations were a major concern is challenged by Source D. This source suggests that the Germans were willing to pay reparations and that it was the failure of the Allies to make the 'slightest move toward reconciliation' that was the main cause of German discontent. This implies that the problems were caused by the overall harsh nature of the terms, such as imposing them without consultation, making the treaty a diktat and excluding Germany from the League of Nations, thus turning it into an outcast and denying it the great power status to which it had been accustomed before the war and prompting Blücher to state that Germany will hate its 'conquerors'.

This image of conquerors is a very important reason why Germany hated the treaty, as many Germans did not believe they had been defeated. This is made clear in Source E. Macmillan argues that because of the armistice terms Germany was not a conquered country and this was made clear to most German people by the absence of Allied troops on German soil. This view is supported by the fact that Germany had won the war in the east and that when the armistice was signed Allied troops were still in France and Belgium. At the same time, the success of the 1918 offensives caused the German government to prepare its people for victory, making the idea of defeat and subsequent punishments unbelievable to many.

Examiner's comment
There is good understanding and clear use of Sources D and E, which are linked. There is also plenty of sound and relevant own knowledge, properly integrated with assessment of the sources.

223

The view of Source E about why the Germans hated the Treaty of Versailles is supported by Source A. This source – an extract from the 'War Guilt' clause of the Treaty of Versailles – would have been a huge shock to the Germans, particularly in light of the military situation during the spring of 1918. They would have resented the clause, as they did not believe that they were solely to blame for starting the war (they could argue that Russia was the first nation to mobilise), and also because the clause provided a legal justification for the raising of reparations. Although Source A claims that the Germans accepted it, in practice they had little choice as they were in no position to continue the war, due to political instability in the country – evident in 1919 through the Spartacist uprising.

Examiner's comment
Once again, there is a good synthesis of sources and some precise own knowledge, to produce a balanced assessment of the importance of reparations in causing hatred of the treaty.

The sources suggest that reparations were an issue, but not the major cause of anger. This is particularly clear in Source D, written by someone living in Germany. Sources D and E suggest that it was an overall feeling of being conquered that caused the greatest resentment. This is supported by Source A, which blames Germany for the war and suggests that it was completely defeated. This undermined the great power status that Germany had built up prior to the war, and many Germans did not understand why such harsh terms were imposed. They did not comprehend the scale of their defeat, as is made clear in Source E. Source B appears to exaggerate the importance of reparations as the main cause of discontent – a view supported by many historians, who have argued that Germany could afford to pay if there was the political will.

Overall examiner's comments

There is good and clear use of sources throughout, and constant integration of precise own knowledge to both explain and add to the sources. The overall result is a sound analytical explanation, focused clearly on the question. The candidate has done more than enough to get into Band 1 and earn the full 8 marks.

Activity

Look again at the all sources, the simplified markscheme, and the student answer above. Now try to write your own answer to this question. See if you can make different points with the sources, and use different/additional own knowledge, to produce an answer that offers an alternative view.

Question 3

Using Sources A, B, C, D and E **and** your own knowledge, assess the view that the Abyssinian crisis of 1935–36 was the most significant reason for the collapse of the League of Nations and of international order.
[8 marks]

SOURCE A

Yes we know that World War began in Manchuria fifteen years ago. We know that four years later we could have stopped Mussolini if we had taken the sanctions against Mussolini that were obviously required, if we had closed the Suez Canal to the aggressor and stopped his oil.

British statesman Philip Noel Baker, speaking at the last session of the League of Nations, April 1946.

SOURCE B

A 1933 cartoon by David Low showing the impact of the
Japanese invasion on the effectiveness of the League of Nations

THE DOORMAT.

SOURCE C

We must turn our eyes towards the lands of the east. When we speak of
new territory in Europe today; we must principally think of Russia and
the border states subject to her. Destiny itself seems to wish to point
out the way for us here. Colonisation of eastern frontiers is of extreme
importance. It will be the duty of Germany's foreign policy to provide
large spaces for the nourishment and settlement of the growing
population of Germany.

Adolf Hitler, in his book Mein Kampf, *1925.*

SOURCE D

The implications of the conquest of Abyssinia were not confined to
East Africa. Although victory cemented Mussolini's personal prestige
at home, Italy gained little or nothing from it in material terms. The
damage done, to the prestige of Britain, France and the League of
Nations was irreversible. The only winner in the whole sorry episode
was Adolf Hitler.

A modern historian comments on the impact of the conquest of Abyssinia.
Morris, T. A. 1995. European History 1848–1945. *London, UK. Collins. p. 315.*

SOURCE E

A British cartoon published in 1935; it shows Mussolini taking the lid off and a devil escaping

THE MAN WHO TOOK THE LID OFF.

Student answer

There were several reasons for the collapse of the League of Nations and of international order. These include the impact of the invasion of Abyssinia, the invasion of Manchuria by Japan in 1931, the rise to power and subsequent aggressive actions of Adolf Hitler, the absence of major powers – such as the USA – from the League of Nations, the terms of the treaties drawn up at the end of the First World War, and the rise of communism in Russia. The five sources mention some, but not all, of these.

Examiner's comment
This introduction shows a clear understanding of the topic, and a good grasp of the factors involved.

The most important reason for the collapse of the League of Nations and international order was the invasion of Abyssinia. This was more important than the invasion of Manchuria, as Manchuria itself was a long way from the major powers of Europe and did not involve them directly. They could therefore argue that it was difficult for them to take action in Manchuria, particularly as neither the USA nor Russia were members of the League.

The invasion of Manchuria also did not cause future acts of aggression, whereas the invasion of Abyssinia allowed Hitler to invade the Rhineland; the major powers were too busy trying to deal with the situation in Abyssinia to prevent him from remilitarising the Rhineland.

The invasion of Abyssinia also showed that the key members of the League, Britain and France, were willing to make agreements outside the League (including the Hoare–Laval Pact), and this seriously undermined the authority and credibility of the League. The League was also unwilling to use its full powers, such as economic sanctions against Mussolini, which led other nations to believe that action would not be taken against them. The failure to deal with the crisis in Abyssinia, despite appeals from Emperor Haile Selassie, worried smaller nations, who depended on the League's concept of collective security. As a result, many smaller states began to make alliances or rearm in an attempt to protect themselves.

Examiner's comment
There is good use of relevant own knowledge, which is mostly precise, and focused on the question. However, so far there has been no reference to, or use of, any of the sources.

227

Another important reason for the collapse of the international order was the rise to power of Adolf Hitler in Germany. Hitler's foreign policy aims of overturning the Treaty of Versailles, uniting all German-speaking people, destroying communism and gaining Lebensraum, or 'living space' in the east, were a direct challenge to international order and the League of Nations. Hitler's belief that Germany should seek expansion in the east (Source C) played a crucial role in bringing about the collapse of international order, as it led to his invasion of both Czechoslovakia and Poland, and ultimately the Soviet Union. It was these events that finally caused war to break out in Europe, and therefore Hitler's beliefs and actions were very important.

However, it should be remembered that in some ways it was only the League's failure to stop both Japan and Italy that encouraged Hitler (Source D). Hitler was very worried by the weakness of his forces when he entered the Rhineland in March 1936, and he would have been less likely to undertake this act of aggression if the major powers had not been distracted by the invasion of Abyssinia. Hitler realised that when the League failed to stop or take decisive action against Mussolini in Abyssinia, it was powerless to stop him, too. This encouraged him in other acts of aggression, such as the Anschluss with Austria and the threat of invasion of Czechoslovakia.

Examiner's comment
There is some more good use of relevant own knowledge, which is mostly precise and focused on the question. However, so far, only two sources have been (briefly) referred to, and neither of them has been used – there is no analysis of what they say or show.

Also important was the invasion of Manchuria (Source B). This played a crucial role – especially in undermining the League. Although the League had faced some challenges in the 1920s, with incidents such as Corfu, this was the first major challenge for the League as it involved a permanent member of the League's Council. The League's slowness to respond and ultimate failure to take definitive action clearly showed that it was unable to stand up to the major powers. The self-interests of Britain and France, particularly during a period of economic crisis, were more important than upholding the principles of the League. The unwillingness of the League to act made other nations, such as Italy and Germany, believe that the League was unlikely to act against a major power.

Examiner's comment

There is, unfortunately, the same approach as before – some good use of relevant own knowledge, which is mostly precise and focused on the question, but only the briefest mention of one source.

One of the reasons for the collapse of international order (often overlooked by historians) was the rise of communism. Many Western democracies were deeply concerned by the threat of communism and saw fascist powers as barriers to the spread of communism to the West. In this sense, they saw Hitler and Mussolini as useful weapons against communism. Some have even suggested that the West hoped for a war between communism and fascism, which would destroy both and allow the democracies of the West to emerge stronger. This view made even more sense given the economic crisis that gripped the West during the Great Depression, as nations such as Britain and France were not prepared for a war. This may also explain why they were unwilling to resort to force against either Japan or Italy.

Overall examiner's comments

There is good use of plenty of relevant own knowledge, which is mostly precise, and focused on the question. However, there are only a few – very brief – references to the sources, and **no use of sources**. Hence, as Paper 1 is mainly a source-based exam, this answer fails to get beyond Band 3.

Activity

Look again at the all sources, the simplified markscheme, and the student answer above. Now try to write a few paragraphs to push the answer up into Band 1, and so obtain the full 8 marks. As well as using all/most of the sources, and some precise own knowledge, try to integrate the sources with your own knowledge rather than dealing with sources and own knowledge separately.

Paper 2 exam practice

Paper 2 skills and questions

For Paper 2, you have to answer two essay questions from two of the five different topics offered. Very often, you will be asked to comment on two states from two different IB regions of the world. Although each question has a specific markscheme, you can refer to the general 'generic' markscheme (see page 230) to get a good general idea of what examiners are looking for in order to be able to put answers into the higher bands. You will need to acquire reasonably precise historical knowledge in order to address issues such as cause and effect, or change and continuity, and to learn how to explain historical developments in a clear, coherent, well-supported and relevant way. You will also need to understand, and be able to refer to, aspects relating to historical debates and interpretations.

Make sure you read the questions carefully, and select your questions wisely. It is important to produce a rough essay plan for each of your essays before you start to write an answer. You may find it helpful to plan both your essays **before** you begin to write. That way, you will soon know whether you have enough own knowledge to answer them adequately.

Remember to keep your answers relevant and focused on the question. For example, don't go outside the dates mentioned in the question, or answer on individuals/states different from the ones identified in the question. Don't just describe the events or developments – sometimes, students just focus on one key word or individual, and then write down everything they know about it. Instead, select your own knowledge carefully, and pin the relevant information to the key features raised by the question. Also, if the question asks for 'reasons' and 'results', or two different countries/leaders, make sure you deal with **all** the parts of the question. Otherwise, you will limit yourself to half marks at best.

Examiner's tips

For Paper 2 answers, examiners are looking for clear/precise analysis, a balanced argument linked to the question, and the use of good, precise and relevant own knowledge. In order to obtain the highest marks, you should be able to refer, where appropriate, to historical debate and/or different historical interpretations or historians' knowledge, making sure it is relevant to the question.

Common mistakes

- When answering Paper 2 questions, try to avoid simply describing what happened. A detailed narrative, with no explicit attempts to link the knowledge to the question, will get you only half marks at most.
- If the question asks you to select examples from **two** different regions, make sure you don't choose two states from the **same** region. Every year, some candidates do this, and so limit themselves to – at best – only 12 out of the 20 marks available.

Simplified markscheme

Band		Marks
1	Clear analysis/argument, with very specific and relevant own knowledge, consistently and explicitly linked to the question. A balanced answer, with references to historical debate/historians where appropriate.	17–20
2	Relevant analysis/argument, mainly clearly focused on the question, and with relevant supporting own knowledge. Factors identified and explained, but not all aspects of the question fully developed or addressed.	11–16
3	**EITHER** shows reasonable relevant own knowledge, identifying some factors, with limited focus/explanation – but **mainly narrative** in approach, with question only implicitly addressed **OR** coherent analysis/argument, but limited relevant/precise supporting own knowledge.	8–10
4	**Some limited/relevant** own knowledge, but **not linked effectively** to the question.	6–7
5	**Short/general** answer, with very **little accurate/relevant knowledge and limited understanding** of the question.	0–5

Student answers

Those parts of the student answer which follow will have brief examiner's comments in the margins, as well as a longer overall comment at the end. Those parts that are particularly strong and well-focused will be highlighted in red. Errors/confusions/loss of focus will be highlighted in blue. In this way, you should find it easier to follow why marks were – or were not – awarded.

Question

Assess the reasons why there were no major international conflicts in the 1920s.
[20 marks]

Skill

Analysis/argument/assessment

Examiner's tip

Look carefully at the wording of this question, which asks for a **range** of reasons to be considered in relation to the preservation of international order in the 1920s. Just focusing on one reason will not allow you to score the highest marks.

Student answer

The period from the end of the First World War up to the outbreak of the Great Depression in 1929 witnessed very little international conflict, although there were periods when relations between powers, particularly France and Germany, were strained. The conflicts that did break out were usually between small powers, such as Greece and Bulgaria, and did not escalate into major conflicts. The League of Nations was often able to solve minor disputes, as was the case with the dispute over the Aaland Islands.

Examiner's comment
This is a brief introduction, with a little supporting own knowledge, which is connected to the topic – though, as yet, nothing explicit has been said about reasons for the preservation of international order in the period. At best it could be argued that the candidate hints that the role of the League of Nations was important.

The First World War had resulted in the death of large numbers of people and had cost the major participants huge amounts of money. Most nations, particularly France, Britain and Germany, needed to rebuild their economies, which had been geared towards war production. They had also lost their markets, as nations outside Europe or those not involved in the war had taken advantage of the conflict to take over their trade. The war also had a huge impact on the general public, not just those who fought in it. There was a general feeling that it was 'the war to end all wars' and that such a conflict must not be allowed to happen again. Many people had lost someone and they did not want that loss to be in vain; those who had fought in the war and returned home related the horrors of trenches and the new tactics of warfare. There had also been a great deal of damage to much of the area where the conflict had taken place; towns such as Ypres had been virtually destroyed by the shelling. The same was true of farmland along the front lines, as repeated attacks had made the land useless for agriculture and farming.

Examiner's comment
There is some relevant own knowledge here about the reasons why there were no conflicts. However, the material is not specifically linked to the question and it is rather narrative-based. In addition, there is a section at the end of the paragraph that is not really relevant or necessary.

231

232

The peace treaties drawn up at the end of the First World War were designed to prevent future aggression. The treaties punished the defeated nations by taking away their land and overseas colonies, for example Germany lost East Prussia and Upper Silesia, as well as colonies in Africa, such as German South West Africa. The German military was reduced to 100,000 men, Germany was forced to pay reparations and declared guilty of starting the war. Its allies were treated in the same way. Austria and Hungary were divided and Austria was forbidden to unite with Germany, despite Wilson's promise of self-determination. Instead of the powerful Austro-Hungarian Empire in Central Europe, there arose a series of smaller and less powerful states such as Czechoslovakia.

International order was challenged with the Ruhr invasion of 1923, but this did not develop into a major conflict. Germany had not kept up with its reparations payments, so in early 1923 French and Belgian troops entered the Ruhr in order to take goods to make up for the reparations. The Germans responded with a policy of passive resistance, so the French brought in their own workers, but this was followed by violence and a number of workers and French soldiers were killed. The German government supported the striking workers and continued to pay them, but this resulted in hyperinflation. Meanwhile, the policy was unpopular in parts of France and in other nations, such as Britain and the USA, which did not believe that the invasion was the way to improve Franco–German relations. The issue was only resolved with the appointment of Gustav Stresemann as German chancellor. He called off passive resistance and brought in a new currency, which stabilised the German economy. Stresemann was helped in this process by the Dawes Plan, which rescheduled German reparations repayments and provided Germany with money to help rebuild its economy.

The policy of reintegrating Germany into the international order, from which it had been excluded at the end of the First World War, was taken further by the Locarno Pact of 1925, in which Germany freely accepted the borders between itself and France, by its joining the League of Nations in 1926 and by the Young Plan of 1929, which provided further loans and reduced reparation payments. As a result, Germany was returned to the world stage by 1929 and this helped to prevent conflict.

Examiner's comment

There is some relevant own knowledge here (but note the mistake over the loss of land – Germany lost West Prussia, not East, and this is crucial as it split Germany in two). However, most of the information on the loss of land and other punishments is not linked sufficiently to the question. This material could have been made relevant by pointing out that the treaties weakened Germany and therefore prevented it from overturning the terms. The answer could also have made relevant the emergence of the new states, as they needed time to develop and lacked economic stability – they were therefore unwilling to become involved in conflicts. The student has a good depth of knowledge about issues related to the topic but is unable to use this knowledge to answer the question set.

Examiner's comment

This answer has continued along the same lines – relevant own knowledge (some of it quite precise), but still essentially an account of what happened with just a brief attempt at the end of the paragraph to link the material to the question.

> The League of Nations had also been set up at the end of the war. This was part of US president Woodrow Wilson's plan to ensure peace. Peace was to be achieved through collective security, where member states would come to one another's aid if they were attacked. The League was dominated by Britain and France, as the USA did not join. It also dealt with social and economic issues; it promoted trade and resolved issues over refugees or health problems such as malaria. It also dealt with border disputes such as those over Upper Silesia, the Aaland Islands, Corfu and Greece–Bulgaria. This all helped to ensure that there was international peace.

Overall examiner comments

This answer makes no real attempt to explicitly address the reasons for the period of relative peace in the 1920s, although it does offer plenty of precise/accurate own knowledge. However, because the approach is almost entirely narrative, this supporting information has not been 'pinned' to the question. Consequently, the answer is not good enough to go higher than Band 3 – probably earning about 9 marks. To reach the higher bands, some **explicit focus on both reasons and results** is needed; frustratingly, much of the information needed to do this well is already in the answer, it is just not correctly applied. Also, for Band 1, it would be necessary to include some **mention of relevant specific historians/historical interpretations** – there are several to choose from on this topic.

Activity

Look again at the simplified markscheme on page 230, and the student answer above. Now try to write a few extra paragraphs to push the answer up into Band 1, and so obtain the full 20 marks. As well as making sure you explicitly address the question, try to integrate some references to relevant historians/historical interpretations.

Further information

Sources and quotations in this book have been taken from the following publications.

Adamthwaite, Anthony. 1977. *The Making of the Second World War*. London, UK. Allen and Unwin.

Adamthwaite, Anthony. 1980. *The Lost Peace – International Relations in Europe 1918–1939*. London, UK. Edward Arnold.

Andelman, David. A. 2008. *A Shattered Peace – Versailles 1919 and the Price We Pay Today*. London, UK. David Wiley.

Bassett, John Spencer. 1930. *The League of Nations – A Chapter in World Politics*. London, UK. Longmans, Green & Co.

Bettey, J. H. 1967. *English Historical Documents*. London, UK. Routledge and Kegan Paul.

Blücher, Evelyn. *An English Wife in Berlin*. 1920. Edinburgh, UK. Constable and Co.

Boscoe, David L. 2009. *Five to Rule Them All: The UN Security Council and the Making of the Modern World*. New York, USA. Oxford University Press. p. 11.

Chamberlin, William Henry. 1938. *Japan over Asia*. London, UK. Duckworth.

Churchill, Winston. 1948. *The Gathering Storm*. London, UK. Cassell & Co.

Copeland, Lewis. 1942. *The World's Great Speeches*. New York, USA. Garden City Publishers.

Elton, Geoffrey. 2001. *The Practice of History*. London, UK. Wiley Blackwell.

Eudin, Xenia. 1957. *Soviet Russia and the West 1920–1927, A Documentary Survey*. Stanford, USA. Stanford University Press.

Fry, Michael, Goldstein, Erik and Langhorne, Richard. 2002. *Guide to International Relations and Diplomacy*. London, UK. Continuum International Publishing.

Goldstein, Erik. 2002. *The First World War Peace Settlements 1919–25*. London, UK. Pearson.

Graves, Robert and Hodge, Alan. 1971. *The Long Week-end: A Social History of Great Britain 1918–1939*. London, UK. Penguin.

Henig, Ruth. 1984. *Versailles and After 1919–33*. London, UK. Methuen.

Hite, John and Hinton, Chris. 1998. *Fascist Italy*. London, UK. Hodder.

Kitchen, Martin. 2006. *Europe Between the Wars*. London, UK. Longman.

Kochan, Lionel. 1963. *The Struggle for Germany 1914–1945*. New York, USA. Harper & Row.

Lacey, Greg and Kelly, Nigel. 2001. *Modern World History*. London, UK. Heinemann.

Lagemaat, R. Van de. 2005. *Theory of Knowledge for the IB Diploma*. Cambridge, UK. Cambridge University Press.

Lansing, Robert. 1921. *The Peace Negotiations, A Personal Narrative*. London, UK. Constable and Co.

Lowe, C. J. and Mazari, F. 1975. *Italian Foreign Policy 1870–1940*. London, UK. Routledge and Kegan Paul.

Lynch, Michael. 1996. *China: From Empire to People's Republic 1990–49*. London, UK. Hodder.

Macartney, Maxwell. 1923. *Five Years of European Chaos*. London, UK. Chapman and Hall.

Macmillan, Margaret. 2001. *Peacemakers: Six Months that Changed the World*. London, UK. John Murray.

McDonough, Frank. 1997. *The Origins of the First and Second World Wars*. Cambridge, UK. Cambridge University Press.

Meyer, Henry Cord. 1973. *Germany – from Empire to Ruin, 1913–45*. London, UK. Macmillan.

Mimmack, Brian, Senes, Daniela and Price, Eunice. 2009. *History: A Comprehensive Guide to Paper 1 for the IB Diploma*. London, UK. Pearson.

Morris, T. A. 1995. *European History 1848–1945*. London, UK. Collins.

Mowatt, Charles Loch. 1972. *Britain Between the Wars 1918–1940*. London, UK. Methuen.

Néré, J. 1975. *The Foreign Policy of France from 1914 to 1945*. London, UK. Routledge and Kegan Paul.

Nicholson, Harold. 1933. *Peacemaking 1919*. Safety Harbor, USA. Simon Publications.

Peaple, Simon. 2002. *European Diplomacy 1870–1939*. London, UK. Heinemann.

Pollard, Sidney and Holmes, Colin. 1973. *Documents of Economic History, Vol. III, The End of Old Europe 1914–1939*. London, UK. Edward Arnold.

Schultz, Gerhard. 1972. *Revolutions and Peace Treaties 1917–1920*. London, UK. Methuen.

Siracusa, Joseph M. 2010. *Diplomacy*. Oxford, UK. Oxford University Press.

Taylor, A. J. P. 1983. *The Origins of the Second World War*. London, UK. Hamish Hamilton.

Thomson, Doug. 1991. *State Control in Fascist Italy, Culture and Conformity 1925–1943*. Manchester, UK. Manchester University Press.

Thorne, Christopher. 1972. *The Limits of Foreign Policy: The West, the League and the Far Eastern Crisis of 1931–3*. London, UK. Hamilton.

Walsh, Ben. 2009. *Modern World History*. London, UK. Hodder.

Western, John R. 1965. *The End of European Primacy 1871–1945*. London, UK. Blandford Press.

Williams, William Appleman. 1972. *The Tragedy of American Diplomacy*. London, UK. Norton.

Williamson, David. 1994. *War and Peace: International Relations 1914–45*. London, UK. Hodder.

Index

Acknowledgements

The volume editor and publishers acknowledge the following sources of copyright material and are grateful for the permissions granted. While every effort has been made, it has not always been possible to identify the sources of all the material used, or to trace all copyright holders. If any omissions are brought to our notice we will be happy to include the appropriate acknowledgement on reprinting.

Extracts on pages 39 (Source A), 60 (Source H), 62 (Source I), 175 (Source D), 177 (Source B) and 186 (Source G) reproduced with permission of Curtis Brown, London on behalf of the Estate of Sir Winston Churchill. © Winston S. Churchill.

Picture Credits

Cover The Granger Collection/Topfoto; p. 5 Popperfoto/Getty Images; p. 8 Library of Congress; p. 10 Getty Images; p. 11 Library of Congress; p. 12 Library of Congress; p. 13 (t) Getty Images; p. 13 (b) Library of Congress; p. 18 Photos 12/Alamy; p. 22 Library of Congress; p. 26 Punch Ltd/Topfoto; p. 30 Popperfoto/Getty Images; p. 35 Library of Congress; p. 36 (t) Press Association Images; p. 36 (b) Library of Congress; p. 42 Corbis; p. 43 Library of Congress; p. 47 Mary Evans Picture Library; p. 53 Library of Congress; p. 64 Getty Images; p. 68 Trinity Mirror/Mirrorpix/Alamy; p. 79 Library of Congress; p. 82 Underwood and Underwood/Corbis; p. 85 International Feature Service/Getty Images; p. 95 Roger Viollet/Topfoto; p. 104 Julien/UN Photo; p. 108 Library of Congress; p. 109 Library of Congress; p. 115 Getty Images; p. 118 Alinari Archives/Corbis; p. 120 Wikimedia; p. 122 Pictorial Press/Alamy; p. 125 Associated Newspapers Ltd/Solo Syndication; p. 126 Library of Congress; p. 127 Library of Congress; p. 133 Punch Ltd; p. 136 Associated Newspapers Ltd/Solo Syndication; p. 139 Getty Images; p. 142 Library of Congress; p. 144 Library of Congress; p. 146 Library of Congress; p. 147 Library of Congress; p. 150 Associated Newspapers Ltd/Solo Syndication; p. 152 Library of Congress; p. 154 Interfoto/Alamy; p. 158 Bettmann/Corbis; p. 162 Getty Images; p. 164 Library of Congress; p. 166 (l) Library of Congress; p. 166 (r) Library of Congress; p. 168 Library of Congress; p. 171 Bettmann/Corbis; p. 174 World History Archive/Alamy; p. 183 Library of Congress; p. 186 Associated Newspapers Ltd/Solo Syndication; p. 196 Popperfoto/Getty Images; p. 198 Getty Images; p. 205 Popperfoto/Getty Images; p. 209 Corbis; p. 217 Associated Newspapers Ltd/Solo Syndication; p. 220 Punch Ltd; p. 221 SZ Photo; p. 225 Associated Newspapers Ltd/Solo Syndication; p. 226 Associated Newspapers Ltd/Solo Syndication.

 Produced for Cambridge University Press by
White-Thomson Publishing
+44 (0)843 208 7460
www.wtpub.co.uk

Series editor: Allan Todd
Development editor: Margaret Haynes
Reviewer: Neil Tetley
Project editor: Sonya Newland
Designer: Clare Nicholas
Picture researcher: Sonya Newland
Illustrator: Stefan Chabluk